POSTCOLONIAL LOCATIONS

Postcolonial Locations seeks to clarify the meaning of 'the postcolonial' through close textual readings, and prioritises material and located readings over more abstract theoretical discussions; it seeks to re-orient the field by providing practical explorations of what the discipline is for. The book begins with an introduction to the key theoretical debates in the field – between the universal and the particular; the global and the local – but it then goes on to demonstrate, via a series of close textual readings, that these distinctions are not always useful and that we can achieve a more comprehensive and complete reading of the multiple times, places and texts in which colonial power is both exerted and fought.

An engaging and comprehensive guide to contemporary postcolonial studies, this book is essential reading for students as well as professors.

Robert Spencer is Senior Lecturer in Postcolonial Literature and Culture at the University of Manchester, UK.

Anastasia Valassopoulos is a Senior Lecturer in the English Department at the University of Manchester, UK.

POSTCOLONIAL LOCATIONS

New Issues and Directions in
Postcolonial Studies

*Robert Spencer and
Anastasia Valassopoulos*

LONDON AND NEW YORK

First published 2021
by Routledge
2 Park Square, Milton Park, Abingdon, Oxon OX14 4RN

and by Routledge
52 Vanderbilt Avenue, New York, NY 10017

Routledge is an imprint of the Taylor & Francis Group, an informa business

© 2021 Robert Spencer and Anastasia Valassopoulos

The right of Robert Spencer and Anastasia Valassopoulos to be identified as authors of this work has been asserted by them in accordance with sections 77 and 78 of the Copyright, Designs and Patents Act 1988.

All rights reserved. No part of this book may be reprinted or reproduced or utilised in any form or by any electronic, mechanical, or other means, now known or hereafter invented, including photocopying and recording, or in any information storage or retrieval system, without permission in writing from the publishers.

Trademark notice: Product or corporate names may be trademarks or registered trademarks, and are used only for identification and explanation without intent to infringe.

British Library Cataloguing-in-Publication Data
A catalogue record for this book is available from the British Library

Library of Congress Cataloging-in-Publication Data
A catalog record has been requested for this book

ISBN: 978-1-138-05118-8 (hbk)
ISBN: 978-1-138-05120-1 (pbk)
ISBN: 978-1-315-16837-1 (ebk)

Typeset in Sabon
by Newgen Publishing UK

THIS BOOK IS DEDICATED TO OUR PHD SUPERVISORS, PROFESSORS NEIL LAZARUS AND CAROLINE ROONEY.

CONTENTS

Acknowledgements		viii
	Introduction: the singular and the universal	1
1	Landscapes	16
2	Mobility	59
3	Reconciliatory practices	111
4	Memory and the past	148
	Conclusion	197
Index		221

ACKNOWLEDGEMENTS

We would like to thank Zoe Meyer from Routledge for her enthusiasm for this project and for her invaluable help in bringing it to fruition. Many thanks too to Zoe Miller for her meticulous help with the editing. Thanks a million to the undergraduate and postgraduate students at Manchester with whom, over the years, we have read most of the books and films discussed in these pages. They have immeasurably enhanced our understanding of these works and also demonstrated the instruction and the sheer pleasure to be had from close reading.

This book addresses several of the key questions in postcolonial writing and visual culture, including the land, mobility, the past and prospects of reconciliation, but also the supremely important and potentially existential question of climate change or global heating. As we wrote it, political movements across the globe were struggling for full decarbonisation. Some have sustained temporary setbacks but they all continue to fight. We'd like, therefore, to 'acknowledge' a powerful statement made in a slightly different context 30 years ago by John McGrath, the playwright whose brilliant dramatic history of Scotland *The Cheviot, the Stag, and the Black Black Oil* only just failed to make the final cut for inclusion in this book. *Postcolonial Locations* is dedicated to our PhD supervisors but also,

> for what it's worth, to The Resistance, to those who have had their lives distorted or destroyed so others could consume; to those who insist that co-operation rather than individual possessiveness is the better principle for the future happiness of humanity; may they survive, and that principle bring more joy to the lives of more people.[1]

Note

1 John McGrath, *The Bone Won't Break: On Theatre and Hope in Hard Times*, London: Methuen, 1990, p. x.

INTRODUCTION
The singular and the universal

The aim of this book is nothing less than to provide beginners to postcolonial studies as well as specialists with a practical explanation of what the discipline is for. *Postcolonial Locations* isn't yet another theoretical proposal: it is a practical demonstration. It seeks to clarify the meaning of 'the postcolonial', not through lengthy theoretical disquisition but through close readings. We look at a range of historical and geographical contexts in the pages that follow. We attend to various kinds of text and we endeavour to demonstrate the different methods required to read those texts. We begin by navigating perennial theoretical debates in the field about whether universality or particularity, the global or the specific, are the most important concepts to bear in mind when reading postcolonial texts. Indeed, our main purpose is to demonstrate, via a series of close readings, that this is a false choice: the four chapters read texts and contexts in a multiplicity of ways in order to elucidate the worldwide and ongoing experiences of colonialism and anti-colonialism.

By 'postcolonial' we mean the attempt to conceptualise a purportedly (though in truth only superficially, or incompletely) decolonised world. The postcolonial (alternatively, postcoloniality) is therefore understood here not just as an idea or even a discipline. More precisely then, 'postcolonial' names the concerted effort to grasp, at the level of ideas and through disciplined enquiry, a historical experience or even project: the multifaceted and so far unfinished efforts of peoples to free themselves from colonial rule. It goes without saying that that experience and that project are global and even universal, which is emphatically not the same thing as saying that they are everywhere the same. Indeed, we are convinced that the task of postcolonial criticism is to use its knowledge of texts and contexts in order to think through the diverse ways in which, historically and in the present, colonial power is exerted, negotiated, resisted and sometimes overthrown. Our aim, then, is certainly not to stress the local at the expense of the global. Nor, for that matter, will we express the global at the expense of the local. The aim, instead, is to use close readings and analyses in order to explore the variety of ways in which the global expresses or manifests itself at the level of different locations. Hence the book's title.

This is a book on postcolonialism and on what it can become as a discipline, one inspired by a conviction that the discipline is often too wedded to a small number of theoretical and analytical methods. Individual chapters read outwards from texts of various kinds, thus demonstrating the infinite ways in which a global process of power and counter-power is inflected and determined at specific locations in the world-system. Of course, postcolonial criticism has habitually been sceptical of universalising projects and systems of thought. Many in the discipline have sought recently, by contrast, to stress the universality of the experience of colonisation and of capitalism and to encourage attention to the forms and themes that postcolonial texts and contexts have in common, theorising that commonality under the rubric of world systems and world literatures. We will do neither. Our aim is to explore the connections between the global (which is singular) and the local (which is multiple), in the process fashioning something of a politics of location that does two things: recognising that the local cannot be understood until it is connected to the global and recognising at the same time the multifarious ways in which the global articulates itself at the level of the local.

One of the ironies of postcolonial criticism is that, despite its suspicion of the global and the universal, it has not always paid very close attention to the particularities of specific locations in its readings. That is what we wish to do. The discipline has relied in the past on a particular set of theoretical concepts, regional specialisations and generic preferences that fail to do justice to the multiple articulations of postcolonial culture. Naturally, we don't pretend to be able to do all of this ourselves. Indeed, we are convinced that no scholar or pair or group of scholars could possibly command all the linguistic, disciplinary and other resources required to explicate the total breadth and extent of postcolonial culture. The finite span of human life would of itself preclude such a quixotic venture! But by showing readers some of the many ways of reading postcolonial texts, we are laying down a challenge to students and critics: to give both globality and locality their dues. *Postcolonial Locations* formulates a collective endeavour for the discipline; our mission, should we choose to accept it, is to develop and enlarge our resources as critics in order to attend instructively to the multiple times, places and texts in which colonial power is both exerted and fought. Nobody should be able to get away with readings that are so fixated with the local that they lose sight of the larger contexts (disciplinary, political, economic, etc.) in which the local is invariably implicated. Nor should those who take it upon themselves to explicate the global neglect the specific local ways in which the global is always disclosed and takes effect. Location, in our argument, therefore denotes particular places as well as particular texts: both locations in the more material sense of spaces, positions, landscapes, geographies and archaeologies, as well as locations in the sense of memories, myths, ideologies, traditions and, of course, texts (not just novels but also poems, plays, films, cultural and aesthetic products of all kinds). The colonial, then (and by implication also the anti-colonial), as something embedded within and throughout the diverse articulations of postcolonial culture – that is the research agenda that *Postcolonial Locations* sets out.

Postcolonial studies has been used over the years to advance a number of different theoretical and political perspectives. We don't necessarily endorse any of these. But nor do we want to advocate a kind of apolitical eclecticism whereby anything goes in postcolonial studies and multiplicity is an end in itself. The discipline stands or falls on its ability to read texts and contexts in ways that clarify the project of colonialism and the counter-project of anti-colonialism. That, in a nutshell, is this book's purpose. We are convinced, in other words, that reading is a directly political activity and that reading well is a political achievement. Thus, J.M. Coetzee, when a member of the audience asked him at a launch reading for *Disgrace* in 1999 whether he found it 'strange' 'that we should be here tonight discussing literature while bombs are falling in Kosovo?' replied, '"Frankly, no."'[1]

We hope that this study will appeal to specialists, since it revisits familiar concepts and current debates but also tries to move beyond them by articulating an agenda for future work. For the same reason, it will serve as an introduction to the field's theoretical concerns for beginners, laying out the existing terrain of postcolonial studies but also exploring future directions. *Postcolonial Locations* will give both undergraduate and postgraduate students an indication of how postcolonial criticism might be undertaken with various methods and in relation to various kinds of text.

Now might be the best moment to declare that this study is in large part the product of thirteen years of collaborative work in the Department of English Literature, American Studies and Creative Writing at the University of Manchester in the UK. Robert has taught there since 2006, Anastasia slightly longer. During that time we have taught together on various Master's level courses such as Issues and Directions in Postcolonial Studies and Postcolonial Literatures, Genres and Theories. Postcolonial Fiction and Film, Postcolonial Literature and Theory, and Writing, Identity and Nation are among the courses we have taught at undergraduate level. It is a gratifying but also quite sobering experience reckoning up the sheer number and range of texts that we have read with students over the years. Many of those texts are discussed in subsequent chapters so it's important to acknowledge our enormous debt of gratitude to the hundreds of students whose careful readings and varied interpretations have honed both our own understanding of individual texts and our appreciation of the rigours and pleasures of close reading. They have vindicated T.S. Eliot's statement about 'true judgement' being a 'common pursuit'.[2] Two heads are better than one and several hundred heads are better still! We have taught a lot and also learned a great deal. This study is the product of those experiences in the classroom.

INTRODUCTION

Discussing these texts alongside students with a range of backgrounds and views, attending patiently and forensically to texts' details and nuances of technique, form and language, identifying and testing the theoretical and political concepts required to understand those texts, thinking *through* texts, in short, and not just thinking about them is the approach or reading practice that *Postcolonial Locations* wants to demonstrate. We believe that is the way to do postcolonial criticism.

One might equally say, of course, that this is just how to do criticism per se. We think it is. So, while we're on the subject of teaching, let us observe that one of the most interesting and in some ways challenging developments of recent years has been the welcome advent of a student-led movement to 'decolonise the curriculum' in British universities. Since 2015, the National Union of Students has been running two campaigns asking to #LiberateMyDegree and 'Why is My Curriculum White?'[3] Having taught courses that were literally and directly *about* decolonisation, covering the colonial and postcolonial Caribbean, the Maghreb, West Africa, Southern Africa and especially South Africa, Palestine, the legacies of partition in South Asia etc., this is not a movement that has exerted particular pressures on our syllabuses, though it's clearly one that interests and even inspires many of our more radical students. One of the ideas that these courses have encouraged students to think through, incidentally, is the possibility that decolonisation has been a much more fraught and difficult, not to mention far-reaching, project than many students seem to realise. We see it as a political and social as well as economic, rather than solely cultural or ethical undertaking, on a global scale. A truly 'decolonial' syllabus would therefore not, in our view, be one on which some courses are labelled 'BME modules' because they cater to the 'wellbeing' of BME students with texts by BME writers while other courses are labelled, presumably, non-BME modules on the frankly wrong-headed and patronising grounds that texts by non-BME writers cannot speak meaningfully to BME students (and vice versa). The decolonised syllabus will endeavour to make available to all students a full range of different forms of cultural expression from diverse historical and geographical locations that will radically improve their 'wellbeing' by making them think intensely about themselves and their place in the world. So, the decolonised syllabus is not a matter of enabling students to place modules that are superficially more conducive to their 'wellbeing' in their online baskets when selecting their modules each semester. In fact, it will hopefully be a part of a more substantive agenda for decolonising the university, which will involve tackling everything from the effort to transform students into heavily indebted consumers, the top-down corporatisation and managerialisation of universities, investments in fossil fuel corporations, the transformation of universities into securitisation vehicles (issuing bonds and borrowing against future tuition revenue), unequal access for working-class and especially BME students, and so on.

INTRODUCTION

Decolonisation, in other words, is part of a much larger political project that includes, most urgently, the liberation of territories and polities, and ultimately the overturning of the world's grotesquely imbalanced social and economic structures; decolonisation 'sets out to change the order of the world', in Frantz Fanon's magnificently bold summation, and 'is, obviously, a programme of complete disorder'.[4] Decolonisation necessitates the critique of discourses and ideologies as well as the transformation of financial, political and of course educational institutions. Higher education, after all, as Gurminder K. Bhambra, Dalia Gebrial and Kerem Nişancıoğlu have argued, is 'a key site through which colonialism – and colonial knowledge in particular – is produced, consecrated, institutionalised and naturalised'.[5] It is also a site in which, we are anxious to add, colonial knowledge is already widely contested (this being postcolonial studies' very raison d'être) in a way that we too would like to see consolidated at all universities and in all subjects and disciplines.

We have heard calls from students for more representative and far-reaching syllabuses. On courses that address, say, nationality and identity in British and Irish writing and especially on introductory undergraduate courses on Modernism that focus on a more traditionally conceived canon of British and Irish (as well as Anglo-American) modernisms (Joyce, Woolf, Lawrence, Eliot, etc.) and even on postgraduate courses on global modernisms that begin with the likes of Conrad and Lawrence before moving on to Zora Neale Hurston, Tayeb Salih, Claude McKay and Jean Rhys, one now hears tricky, but in a way also invigorating, challenges about the paleness and staleness, as well as the predominant maleness of some of the syllabus. There is a pressure, in short, a constructive and on the whole extremely salutary pressure, to justify the teaching of certain texts. That's all to the good, in our view, since the construction of syllabuses and the formation of canons is an everlasting task. These questions make us all think about what we mean by aesthetic value and focus on the political assumptions that usually undergird critical judgements. So they are always productive subjects for discussion in the classroom.

For what it's worth, our own contribution to these debates is a simple reminder (later, a practical demonstration) that the question of how we read texts is every bit as important as the question of which texts we read. In other words, we can decolonise *how* we teach in addition to decolonising *what* we teach. Indeed, the constructive influence of postcolonial studies on the wider discipline of literary studies as a whole can be seen most clearly here, in the increased sensitivity to the presence of the global and the colonial (and of resistances to colonialism) in the reading methods of critics working with texts that were already considered canonical before the advent of postcolonial studies as a discipline and with texts that were not composed by postcolonial writers. Modernist studies, for example, first became the study of modernisms and then of global or peripheral or planetary modernisms, in the process giving due weight not only to what Fredric Jameson has demonstrated to be the decisive impact of imperialism on the forms and themes of European modernism but also to the pioneering (as opposed to belated or derivative) modernisms of a Claude McKay or a Tayeb Salih or a Lu Xun.[6] Decolonising our courses is a process that is very far advanced in most British university departments of literature and has been underway for a good while. Let's not forget that the call for decolonised curricula that got right-wing newspapers so hot under the collar a couple of years ago was directed at the highly untypical and in fact conservative syllabus at Cambridge. The point is that decolonisation also means decolonising our reading practices, and if a dwindling, if vocal, band of cultural reactionaries objects to new global and postcolonial readings of Shakespeare or Dickens or Austen or Charlotte Brontë or Dante or Chaucer ad infinitum then no matter, for that ship has already sailed.

So a decolonised curriculum consists, most obviously, of courses about race and race theory, about imperialism and its legacies, about the literature of decolonisation in the decades after the Second World War in addition to courses about postcolonial writing more broadly that are as representative as any selection of texts can be of the range of writers, genres, forms, themes and locations in Anglophone and translated literatures. When we were undergraduates twenty odd years ago it was still possible to study a course on the American novel that covered Hawthorne, Melville, Dreiser, Faulkner, Fitzgerald, Steinbeck and Hemingway, with Toni Morrison's *Beloved* tacked on in Week 12. That is simply not permissible any longer, not as *The Daily Telegraph*'s leader writers think because 'political correctness' has led to a lowering of critical standards but because, by any reasonably objective standards of aesthetic merit, a representative list of great American novelists includes, for example, many more female and African-American novelists. It goes without saying that *Moby Dick* will still be on there but that novel's far-reaching meditations on whiteness, slavery, imperialism and manifest destiny ought to be addressed in discussions. Importantly, therefore, our ideal decolonised curriculum will also include courses that do not focus exclusively on the history of race, racism and decolonisation as well as courses that do not contain many, or even any, BME writers. A course on medieval writing, for example, which is not only unlikely to include texts by BME writers but which addresses texts like *Beowulf* or *Sir Gawain and the Green Knight* whose authors may in fact be unknown, is nonetheless virtually guaranteed these days to encourage students to wrestle with texts that are mediated by adaptation and translation and that require students to reflect on gender, power and sex, on warfare and conquest, on conflicts and communications between cultures in the Anglo-Saxon and later medieval periods, on the reciprocal relationship between genre and form on the one hand and cultural and historical contexts on the other, on the political and other implications of periodising categories like the 'medieval', on the

INTRODUCTION

sensitivity and self-awareness demanded by the scholarly engagement with a historically distant culture, and so on. Such courses exist; they speak powerfully to all students; they do not need to be decolonised.

The point we are trying to make can be more concisely summarised by recalling a disarming question that Robert was asked in a seminar on Joyce's *Ulysses*: Is Bloom woke? The short answer to this question is 'No'! The longer answer, which we pondered and reached as a group, involves thinking about why it's the wrong question or at least an extraneous or insufficient one. The novel's main protagonist, admittedly, thinks some decidedly unkind and even obnoxious, not to say misogynistic, things about Gerty MacDowell, the young woman whom he masturbates over on the beach in 'Nausicaa'. More moralistic students tend to lose sympathy with him at that point, though his desire to eye up the 'moving hams'[7] of women passing in the street and his Orientalist daydreams plus his occasional casually racist language have, understandably, already convinced them that the Richard Ellmann-style humanist reading of Bloom as the Christ-like hero of this Dublin epic does not quite stand up to scrutiny.[8] Yet Bloom is also, students tend to recognise, a principled opponent of nationalism and imperialism and of anti-Semitic hatred and violence. He is thoughtful, generous and compassionate, not to mention '[o]ne of those mixed middlings' (*U*, 439) according to the jingoistic old soaks in Barney Kiernan's bar in 'Cyclops', a 'finished example of the new womanly man' (*U*, 614) even, a promising though perhaps hardly 'finished' representative of some sort of androgynous transcendence of received gender definitions and identities. He is also a literary character, which means that it is a kind of category error and ultimately a redundant critical exercise to discuss whether we like him and approve of him or not.

Bloom's admittedly limited (because historically situated) capacity to transcend or reinvent orthodox definitions of national, ethnic, racial and gender identity cannot be understood in isolation from the whole novel's inevitably limited capacity to reinvent everything from ideologies and identities, character, subjectivity and narrative methods to the novel form and even language itself. Awarding marks for writers or characters who look or behave like us will not get us very far in our attempts to grapple critically with works of literature from other periods, not least because our own outlooks are, like Bloom's, situated and limited in various ways. We trust that our own historical and cultural vantage points will give us certain insights into such texts. But let's also be prepared for the fact, which is not always congenial to those naturally Whiggish students who see themselves as the end point of a smooth course of moral and political progress and who therefore view the literature of the past with what the historian E.P. Thompson once called 'the enormous condescension of posterity'[9], that these texts will teach us about our own shortcomings and blindnesses. Bloom is not woke, not fully anyway! Nor is *Ulysses* or any other text. And nor are we. Let us read and study texts that, for a variety of reasons, stretch and bother us, baffle and even offend us, as opposed to texts that flatter our complacencies. A decolonised curriculum consists not of the right kind of text or author but of texts of all kinds that, when they are read carefully and rigorously, speak eloquently about their *and our* locations in time and space. Indeed, it is precisely because the characters and worlds dramatised for us in literary texts usually do *not* resemble us and *cannot* simply be measured up with some familiar moral or political yardstick that they can so profoundly destabilise our expectations and preconceptions. This is a call for diversity or, to use this book's idiom, for multiple locations in curriculum building.

Without further ado, then, we want to think about the perennial conceptual or philosophical distinction in postcolonial scholarship between the singular and the universal. These are terms for postcolonial scholars' competing and even, for some, incompatible focuses on specificity (or locality) and the global. The Warwick Research Collective (WReC) has recently argued that all modern literature is the literature of the modern capitalist world-system, all texts being shaped, albeit in different ways and to varying extents (but nonetheless unavoidably and at the most minute level of their forms and not just of their contents), by the universal experience of capitalism's spread and entrenchment across the globe. World capitalism is a totality, WReC argue, with consistent features (class and state power, the extortion of surplus value, the commodification of labour and its products, colonial exploitation, and so on) but it is a totality that is immensely differentiated and unequal, variable and irregular as well as essentially incomplete. To describe capitalist modernity as a system, therefore, is certainly not to say that everywhere it assumes exactly the same shape. Indeed, it gives rise to complicated combinations and juxtapositions of a variety of different social and economic formations and modes of organisation in addition to forms of development, mal-, under- and even de-development. Leon Trotsky's theory or figure, on which WReC's conceptualisation of the world-system is based, describes capitalist 'development' as simultaneously combined *and* uneven, homogenising *and* differentiating. It is a process that conjoins classes and regions with the social relations and economic forms peculiar to commodity production, wage labour and capital accumulation but it renders them radically unequal. Similarly, the tendentially universal world-system of capitalism leeches off both pre-capitalist economic forms, such as subsistence agriculture, as well as pre- or non-capitalist forms of social reproduction and religious and cultural belief systems. Capitalism also, more auspiciously, helps inadvertently to engender the motivations, the social and political solidarities, the ideologies of liberation and the cooperative and labour-saving technologies of an incipiently post-capitalist mode of production.

In short, therefore, capitalism's expansion is far more uneven and contradictory than the bald term 'development' might lead us to expect. Capitalist social relations, WReC insist, are unevenly inflicted and, in any case, the ways in which these relations are lived is 'different in every given instance for the simple reason that no two social instances are the same'.[10] This multifariousness means that any theory of world literature needs to appreciate the different ways in which the tremendously complex system of world capitalism is registered by texts. It has to grapple, in other words, with the peculiar ways in which capitalist modernity is mediated and expressed at the level of aesthetic form.

Vivek Chibber, too, has sought to pitch a universalist cat among the postcolonial pigeons by arguing in his *Postcolonial Theory and the Specter of Capital* that postcolonial theorists' critique of Eurocentrism and their consequent focus on local knowledges and experiences have not adequately reckoned with the sheer universalising force of capital. Neither Chibber nor WReC think that the world-system brought into being by capitalism's remorseless expansion is everywhere the same. Rather it is one but unequal, universal but inescapably uneven. For Chibber, the expansion and consolidation of capitalism does not homogenise the globe; still less does it universalise 'Western' values or social forms. Capitalism universalises market dependence,[11] as Chibber puts it, or the commodification of labour and its products, 'albeit at different tempos and unevenly' and, by so doing, it also generates 'the *universal interest* of the subaltern classes to defend their well-being against capital's domination, inasmuch as the need for physical well-being is not merely specific to a particular culture or region'.[12] But capitalism does not universalise experiences, interests, cultures, wealth, political institutions, forms of aesthetic and cultural expression, and so on. These twin universalisms, of capital and of labour effectively, have only become more pertinent, Chibber points out, in the wake of the financial crash of 2008 and the consequent crisis across the globe of discredited political hegemonies, inequalities, unemployment, indebtedness, stagnating or falling wages and living standards and ecological catastrophe. 'For the first time since the 1980s', Chibber observes, '*everyone* is talking about capitalism – not alterity, or hybridity, or the fragment, but the ubiquitous, grinding, crushing force of capital.'[13] This fact does not obviate but positively accentuates the need to illuminate the workings and prospects of this remorselessly global system through critical engagements with its different articulations and locations.

Interestingly, Chibber's thesis has been subjected to some pretty searching criticisms by Neil Lazarus, one of the leading lights of the Warwick Research Collective. Notwithstanding his credible claim that Chibber's account of postcolonial studies, like most Marxist accounts of the discipline, fails to make use of Trotsky's helpful conceptualisation of the world-system as combined *and* uneven, Lazarus's critique strikes us as a case of looking a gift horse in the mouth.[14] Chibber does in fact refer repeatedly to capitalism's 'uneven' universalisation. More importantly, the Marxist Chibber and his Marxist critics agree on the essential point, which is that capitalism is a universal because imperialist system but one that does not manifest itself

INTRODUCTION

in the same way at all points in that tendentially global order. This system is therefore experienced and aesthetically represented in an immense variety of different ways and forms. Whether or not postcolonial studies' frequent emphasis on the fundamental cultural and historical *difference* between West and East or between Global North and Global South makes postcolonial studies a form of 'Eurocentrism', as Chibber thinks, or a 'conjuncturally distinct version of 'Third Worldism', as Lazarus believes, is an interesting but very much ancillary point, in our view.[15] The same goes for the question of whether this polemical account of a discipline so besotted with cultural difference that it has failed to spot the enduring and probably intensifying structuring power of capitalism in the contemporary world-system points a finger at the discipline as a whole, as both seem to suggest, or just at certain tendencies within it. To stress difference at the expense of durably oppressive systems, which Chibber and Lazarus think is the cardinal or even original sin of postcolonial criticism, may be a result of a kind of Eurocentrism (a postmodern belief in the incommensurability of cultures reminiscent of Orientalist clichés about the mysterious or exotic 'otherness' of 'the East'[16]) or of a Third Worldism retooled for the era of neoliberalism (a militant rejection of everything that apparently originates in 'the West', including the critique of capitalism). What matters is that both Chibber and Lazarus have put their finger not on a problem that all critics and students of postcolonial literatures are guilty of but a problem that at least they must all think through: How, in our readings, can we combine an awareness of the uneven and unequal world-*system* with an appreciation of the heterogeneous ways in which that system is lived and resisted and also aesthetically registered and expressed? In other words, it is texts of various kinds that tell us most informatively about the tremendously diverse ways in which the admittedly universal system of capitalist imperialism is experienced, contested, modified and even transformed. Chibber does not broach this question of how the universal intersects with the singular, though all the texts discussed in *Postcolonial Locations* do, which is why, as Timothy Brennan has suggested, 'the literary remains the blind spot of [his] otherwise admirable polemic'.[17]

We do not think that scholars have to choose between the singular and the universal. We take it as read that capital has structured – and *still* structures – the globe through practices that are, broadly speaking, imperialist. But we maintain that it does so in ways that actively produce unevenness, inequality, a multiplicity of different contexts, perspectives and experiences. Our task in *Postcolonial Locations* is not to announce yet again that this multiplicity exists and to set it as a research agenda for other scholars. Rather, we wish to pursue those multiple perspectives and experiences, to try and capture them through close readings with the aid of the full methodological and critical repertoire of postcolonial scholarship.

The first chapter, Landscapes, will build on contemporary interest in what has been called the 'spatial turn'. The purpose here, however, is not

INTRODUCTION

to impose a theoretically current concept in order to build bridges between disciplines. Rather, in the postcolonial context, we rely on this framework in order to draw attention to the very materiality of land: its usage, its ownership and its abuse. We argue that the ways in which land is understood, negotiated and articulated all contribute to the experience of space. This experience carries with it the very texture of difference. To begin to appreciate others is to be able to come close to experiencing the air that the other breathes and the soil on which he or she walks. Although these possibilities have been imaginatively reconstructed for us in a wide range of postcolonial fiction, it has not always been politically judicious to pay close attention as to do so would have been to forego more urgent questions of human rights, gender equality, labour requirements and economic stability. Nevertheless, we believe that without this focus on geographical surroundings and their impact on narrative, we risk homogenising the postcolonial experience and sacrificing specificity. To this end, this chapter looks closely at texts that fold within themselves a deep preoccupation with their surroundings, fully understanding the risks and also the opportunities that reside there. Films such as Charles Chauvel's *Jedda*, Ray Lawrence's *Jindabyne*, Nicholas Roeg's *Walkabout*, Peter Weir's *Picnic at Hanging Rock* and novels such as David Dabydeen's *Disappearance*, Nadine Gordimer's *The Conservationist*, Kate Grenville's *The Secret River* and Alexis Wright's *Carpentaria* open up possibilities for geocritical engagement, revealing how landscapes can be both familiar and alienating at once and, more importantly, how navigating the spatial terrain requires the sharing and the giving up of knowledge. These, in turn, play into colonial forms of power and postcolonial attempts at liberation.

The second chapter looks at Mobility. When we speak of space and location, we are often instinctively speaking of freedom of movement or mobility. Often though, in the contexts within which we work, movement can sometimes be forced, unwished for, unexpected. Rarely is it without complication. Movement therefore, whether hurried or slow, desired or forced, is embarked upon with excitement and trepidation, fear and anticipation. It almost always, however, requires leaving one space for another – a space that is almost certainly unknown. What is left behind in this act of mobility cannot always be measured – its texture is difficult to quantify. Often it is a feeling, an affect, but one that comes to being out of material experiences: of touch, of smell, of sight. These spaces left behind are important to locate and to articulate but they contribute to a form of resistance, to a form of safekeeping for the place that was. The movement between spaces is also crucial as it contains its own artefacts and its own needs and rhythms. Films such as Elia Suleiman's *Divine Intervention*, Ismael Ferroukhi's *Le Grande Voyage* and texts such as Nadine Gordimer's *The Pickup* and Joe Sacco's *Palestine* expand our understanding of mobility and, in so doing, engender an appreciation for the political possibilities contained within spatial knowledges.

INTRODUCTION

The chapter also takes a detailed look at Mohsin Hamid's novel *Exit West* in order to think through the multiple political possibilities brought into view by the global mobility of refugees and other migrants. In ingenious ways through its structure, syntax, language and central metaphors, Hamid's novel urges on its readers an extremely consequential political choice. We face, Hamid suggests, a crossroads and his novel is a road sign pointing one way towards societies transformed into more provisional and egalitarian as well as hospitable post-national and post-imperialist communities while in the other direction, indicating a sinister revival of twentieth-century totalitarianism in the shape of violent exclusions and border walls.

In Chapter 3, Reconciliatory Practices, we look at how such practices have sought inspiration from local geography in order to ensure that attempts at lasting collaboration are drawn from within. Reconciliation is understood in this chapter as both a structural and political process but also as an attempt to voice, in narratives of all kinds, a desire for connection. These attempts are not always successful and we are mindful of historical contexts in which a national conversation on colonialism has not been fully aired or debated. Practices of reconciliation ordinarily look to remove shame, address perceived past injustices and encourage a conciliatory approach to the future. We have found, however, that oftentimes the very terms of reconciliatory attempts ignore or pay scant attention to the specificity of perceived wrongs that coalesce around the ownership (legal or informal) and use of land and the extent to which this specificity binds communities to place. Narratives such as Alan Duff's *Once Were Warriors* (and Lee Tamahori's subsequent film), J.M. Coetzee's *Disgrace*, Achmat Dangor's *Bitter Fruit* and Romesh Gunesekera's *The Match* illustrate ways in which locality, and the knowledge – or lack of knowledge – of one's surroundings fully informs the extent to which compromise is permissible. This idea of reconciliation has for too long in literary studies operated as an unquestioned but favourable outcome for the postcolonial process. This chapter looks closely at the requirements for such outcomes, pointing out the frequent complexities and limitations of knowledge itself.

The final chapter is Memory and the Past. The prospects and challenges of liberation are obviously central to many postcolonial texts. What this chapter seeks to do is think through the ways in which these imaginings of the future are bound up with and, in fact, are inseparable from, different imaginings of the past. Histories of dispossession and of struggle, at a variety of levels from the individual to the national and even the global, are variously stressed, repressed, censored and contested in texts. How do these imaginings and reimaginings of the past inform strategies and prospects of liberation in the present and future? How is the past memorialised, registered, shaped in and by narratives and images – in short, constructed and made use of in the course of ongoing efforts to reckon with colonialism's legacies and continuities and to forge strategies and visions of liberation? Novels

INTRODUCTION

such as Assia Djebar's *Fantasia* and Nikita Lalwani's *Gifted* and films such as *Rolf de Heer and Peter Djigirr's Ten Canoes*, *David Lean's Lawrence of Arabia* and *Richard Attenborough's Gandhi*, in addition to the poetry of Pablo Neruda, Eavan Boland and Derek Walcott, are all compulsively preoccupied with various pasts to the precise extent that they are involved in fashioning and contesting various kinds of future.

Notes

1 Andre Brink, *A Fork in the Road: A Memoir*, London: Vintage, 2010, p. 378.
2 T.S. Eliot, 'The Function of Criticism', *Selected Prose*, ed. Frank Kermode, London: Faber & Faber, 1975, pp. 68–76, p. 69.
3 Noha Abou El Magd, 'Why is My Curriculum White? – Decolonising the Academy'.
4 Frantz Fanon, *The Wretched of the Earth*, trans. Constance Farrington, Harmondsworth: Penguin, 1990 [1961], p. 27.
5 Gurminder K. Bhambra, Dalia Gebrial and Kerem Nişancıoğlu, 'Introduction: Decolonising the University?' *Decolonising the University*, ed. Bhambra, Gebrial and Nişancıoğlu, London: Pluto Press, 2018, pp. 1–15, p. 5.
6 As well as leaving traces on the content of 'metropolitan literary works,' Jameson claims, 'imperialism also makes its mark on the inner forms and structures of that new mutation in literary and artistic language to which the term modernism is loosely applied.' Fredric Jameson, 'Modernism and Imperialism', in Fredric Jameson, Terry Eagleton and Edward W. Said, *Nationalism, Colonialism, and Literature*, Minneapolis, MN: University of Minnesota Press, 1990, pp. 43–66, p. 44. The best anthology that we know of work on global modernisms is *The Oxford Handbook of Global Modernisms*, Oxford: Oxford University Press, 2012. But we have reservations about the eclecticism of some recent work in this vein. Susan Stanford Friedman, for example, wants to detach the terms 'modernity' and 'modernism' from the world-historical processes of capitalism's expansion and consolidation over the last two centuries. The advantage of this critical move, as Friedman presents it, is that it alerts us to the sheer variety of non-European modernisms over a much longer timeframe. Unmoored in this way, however, there is a danger that modernity and modernism become indiscriminate concepts. Periods are modern and texts are modernist, according to Stanford Friedman, not in relation to the complex and contradictory process of capitalist modernisation but in relation to, well, the periods and texts that went before them. Everything is modern or modernist, therefore, at least until something else comes along to make it 'traditional', and so the terms cease to mean anything. A glazed earthenware bowl made in Basra during the Abbasid Caliphate in the ninth century CE is no more nor less modernist than Aimé Césaire's long surrealist anticolonial poem *Cahier d'un retour au pays natal* from Martinique in the 1930s. Susan Stanford Friedman, *Planetary Modernisms: Provocations on Modernity Across Time*, New York: Columbia University Press, 2015. The approach of the Warwick Research Collective strikes us as much more productive, since it stipulates that while capitalist modernity may be a singular and global process it is also immensely contradictory, differentiated and uneven. Therefore, the forms of

cultural expression to which the global (emphatically not exclusively European or Euro-American) process of capitalist modernity gives rise (its modernisms, if you will) are themselves extremely linguistically, thematically and formally diverse.

> We need to do away once and for all with the still-dominant understandings of modernism that situate it both in terms of writerly technique (self-conscious, anti- or at least post-realist, etc.) and as a Western European phenomenon, whose claims to being *the* literature of modernity are underscored precisely by this geo-political provenance.
> (Warwick Research Collective, *Combined and Uneven Development: Towards a New Theory of World-Literature*, Liverpool: Liverpool University Press, 2015, p. 19, emphasis in original)

7 James Joyce, *Ulysses*, Annotated Student Edition, Harmondsworth: Penguin, 2011 [1922], p. 71. Subsequent references are given in brackets in the main text after *U*.
8 Ellmann's classic biography of Joyce declares the theme of *Ulysses* to be simply: 'Casual kindness overcomes unconscionable power.' 'The divine part of Bloom is simply his humanity – his assumption of a bond between himself and other created beings.' Richard Ellmann, *James Joyce*, New and Revised Edition, Oxford: Oxford University Press, 1982, pp. 279 and 362.
9 E.P. Thompson, *The Making of the English Working Class*, Harmondsworth: Penguin, 1968, p. 12.
10 WReC, *Combined and Uneven Development*, p. 12.
11 Vivek Chibber, *Postcolonial Theory and the Specter of Capital*, London: Verso, 2013, p. 100.
12 Ibid., p. 203.
13 Ibid., p. 294, emphasis in original.
14 Another critique of Chibber's book, from the standpoint of the Warwick Research Collective, is Benita Parry's 'The Constraints of Chibber's Criticism', *Historical Materialism*, 25:1 (2017), 185–206.
15 Neil Lazarus, 'Vivek Chibber and the Spectre of Postcolonial Theory', *Race and Class*, 57:3 (2016), 88–106, 89. The 'conjuncture' that Lazarus has in mind is that of global neoliberalism after the 1970s, the period during which the power of capital was restored in the first world, the nominally socialist second world was vanquished, and the social and economic achievements and ambitions of the so-called third world were rolled back by structural adjustment, indebtedness and imperialist war. This was also the period during which the field of postcolonial studies and its prevailing methods and priorities were established. The sometimes implicit and sometimes explicit belief that an identifiably modern order of imperialism and state and class power has been transcended by a new epoch that is in some ill-defined way now 'post-modern' and 'post-colonial' has resulted in the field's frequent hostility to Marxism, according to Lazarus, as well as its consequent neglect of the continuing exigencies of political and economic struggle, its sense that nations and states are dying out, and its hostility to the socialist or 'liberationist' goals of the era of decolonisation after the Second World War. It has also led to a denial of the structuring centrality of capitalism in favour of a frankly idealist and 'Third Worldist' belief that imperialism is the product of the political and cultural dominance of an imprecisely conceptualised 'West' or

'Global North'. See Lazarus, *The Political Unconscious*, Cambridge: Cambridge University Press, 2011, pp. 21–88.
16 Vivek Chibber, 'Confronting Postcolonial Theory: A Response to Critics', in Rosie Warren (ed), *The Debate on 'Postcolonial Theory and the Specter of Capital'*, London: Verso, 2016, pp. 169–179, p. 171.
17 Timothy Brennan, 'Subaltern Stakes', *New Left Review II*, 89 (2014), 67–87, 74.

Bibliography

Bhambra, G.K., Gebrial, D. and Nişancıoğlu, K., 'Introduction: Decolonising the University?', in Gurminder Bhambra, Dalia Gebrial and Kerem Nişancıoğlu (eds), *Decolonising the University*, London: Pluto Press, 2018, pp. 1–15.
Brennan, T. 'Subaltern Stakes', *New Left Review II*, 89 (2014), 67–87.
Brink, A., *A Fork in the Road: A Memoir*, London: Vintage, 2010.
Chibber, V., *Postcolonial Theory and the Specter of Capital*, London: Verso, 2013.
Chibber, V., 'Confronting Postcolonial Theory: A Response to Critics', in Rosie Warren (ed), *The Debate on 'Postcolonial Theory and the Specter of Capital'*, London: Verso, 2016, pp. 169–179.
Eliot, T.S., 'The Function of Criticism', *Selected Prose*, ed. Frank Kermode, London: Faber & Faber, 1975.
Ellmann, R., *James Joyce*, New and Revised Edition, Oxford: Oxford University Press, 1982.
Fanon, F., *The Wretched of the Earth*, trans. Constance Farrington, Harmondsworth: Penguin, 1990 [1961].
Friedman, S.S., *Planetary Modernisms: Provocations on Modernity Across Time*, New York: Columbia University Press, 2015.
Jameson, F., 'Modernism and Imperialism', in Fredric Jameson, Terry Eagleton and Edward W. Said (eds), *Nationalism, Colonialism, and Literature*, Minneapolis, MN: University of Minnesota Press, 1990, pp. 43–66.
Joyce, J., *Ulysses*, Annotated Student Edition, Harmondsworth: Penguin, 2011 [1922].
Lazarus, N., *The Political Unconscious*, Cambridge: Cambridge University Press, 2011.
Lazarus, N., 'Vivek Chibber and the Spectre of Postcolonial Theory', *Race and Class*, 57:3 (2016), 88–106.
Parry, B., 'The Constraints of Chibber's Criticism', *Historical Materialism*, 25:1 (2017), 185–206.
Thompson, E.P., *The Making of the English Working Class*, Harmondsworth: Penguin, 1968.
Warwick Research Collective, *Combined and Uneven Development: Towards a New Theory of World-Literature*, Liverpool: Liverpool University Press, 2015.
Wollaeger, M. and Eatough, M., *The Oxford Handbook of Global Modernisms*, Oxford: Oxford University Press, 2012.

Websites

Noha Abou El Magd, 'Why is my curriculum white? – Decolonising the Academy'. Available at: www.nusconnect.org.uk/campaigns/liberatemydegree.

1

LANDSCAPES

This chapter attends to contemporary theoretical interest in what has been dubbed the 'spatial turn'. In the postcolonial context, we rely on this framework in order to draw attention to the very materiality of land: its usage, its ownership and its abuse, and also to the experience of landscape. We argue that the ways in which land is understood, negotiated and articulated all contribute to the experience of space. This experience carries with it the very texture of difference. To begin to appreciate the other is to be able to come close to experiencing the air that the other breathes and the soil on which he walks. Although these possibilities have been imaginatively reconstructed for us in a wide range of postcolonial fiction, it has not always been politically judicious to pay close attention as to do so would have been to forego more urgent questions of human rights, gender equality, labour requirements and economic stability. Nevertheless, we believe that without this focus on geographical surroundings and its impact on narrative, we risk homogenising the postcolonial experience and sacrificing specificity. To this end, this chapter looks closely at texts that fold within them a deep preoccupation for their surroundings, fully understanding the risks and also the opportunities that reside there. Films such as Ray Lawrence's *Jindabyne*, Nicholas Roeg's *Walkabout* and Peter Weir's *Picnic at Hanging Rock*, and novels such as Nadine Gordimer's *The Conservationist*, David Dabydeen's *Disappearance*, Kate Grenville's *The Secret River* and Alexis Wright's *Carpentaria*, open up possibilities for geo-critical engagement, revealing how landscapes can be both familiar and alienating at once and, more importantly, how navigating the spatial terrain requires the sharing *and* the giving up of knowledge. These in turn play into colonial forms of power and postcolonial attempts at liberation.

Initially when considering what work needed to be undertaken here, it seemed that it was enough to look at the subject of land and space and to consider the representation of the environment in postcolonial literature and film. In most cases, this consisted, and rightly so if seen from a historically and politically engaged critical standpoint, of pointing out the extent to which we had previously perhaps paid less attention to the environment in favour of the unequal contact zone of the coloniser and the colonised. As Helen Tiffin and Graham Huggan point out in *Postcolonial Ecocriticism*,[1] notwithstanding some strategic overlaps, 'ecocriticism has tended as a whole to prioritise extra-human concerns over the interests of disadvantaged human groups, while postcolonialism has been routinely, and at times unthinkingly, anthropocentric'.[2] Where in postcolonialism the emphasis, typically, was on locating unequal distribution of power and unearthing the extent to which writers and filmmakers could conceptualise this in such a way as to make it palpable, this was often then followed up by further emphasis on measuring the extent to which creative and cultural responses were working hard to redistribute this power. The aims of this were to generate much more effective and complex representations of, first, the experience of the colonised and the context of postcoloniality and then, of course, to further integrate the now changed experiences of all those involved in the long history of imperialism.

This largely constituted what Afzal-Khan and Seshdari-Crooks termed 'The Preoccupation of Postcolonial Studies'.[3] This preoccupation was largely justified and will continue to be justified so long as there are socio-political imbalances and inequalities around the globe. These have now come to be figured alongside environmental changes that are no longer background material to the seemingly immediate danger to humanity.[4] Postcolonial studies has, in its own resolute way, contributed to the discursive lens required to see the changes in our surroundings, not as additional or marginal to those changes experienced at the economic or judicial level, but as constituting our very experience of that change. In many ways, as Eyal Weizman has noted in relation to Dipesh Chakrabarty's work,[5] changes in the environment 'from the point of view of the history of colonialism [can no] longer simply [be seen] as a collateral effect of modernity, but rather as its very target and aim'.[6] The problem has often been, however, that it has taken us a while to move our attention away from identifying and arguing *for* the collateral damage: in most instances, this identification has been slow and it is still ongoing. One cannot, however, overstate the difficulty in even arguing for this collateral damage in the face of sometimes brutal human damage that always seemed to come first. For example, it is impossible to exaggerate the extent to which we needed to prioritise the 'human' experience in postcolonial studies in order to be able to move the debate along. Specifically, there was so much work to do providing the geographical, historical, political and ideological context for the 'other' and this attempt was not always immediately attentive to the ways in which the environment intimately coexisted and even perhaps laid the groundwork for the context. For sure there have been changes lately to the ways in which postcolonial studies is taught, where the priority has been the intersection of the economy with ecology, and this has been important and constructive. To emphasise the mutuality of these is to point to the various ways in which ecocriticism could have always been a feature of postcolonial studies. The question now is how might we now go about attending to it from the beginning? 'One thing seems certain', state Huggan and Tiffin: 'if the wrongs of colonialism – its legacies of continuing human inequalities, for instance – are to be addressed, still less redressed, then the very category of the human, in relation to animals and the environment, must also be brought under scrutiny'.[7] This is compelling as what we aim to show here is how this relation can take hold before it is even scrutinised. As urgent as scrutiny is, the very modes through which we might see or recognise the non-human precedes this more critical position.

One short example might be Witi Ihimaera's *The Whale Rider*.[8] Here, the instinct in teaching was always to make much of the ways in which Ihimaera constructed another world for any reader by alternating realist and non-realist writing. This could be and was read as forcing an alternative cosmology without exoticisation – structurally a very difficult thing to achieve. Giving the whales a voice was a writerly move that, however, leant itself to various forms of critique – is this metaphor, is this symbolism, is it giving a voice to the unsaid? On the other hand, to attempt to say that it did not require explanation was met with suspicion – how could this be a valid reading when there was so much urgent work to be done on sustainability and biodiversity? This could be seen as another move altogether – to make political use of this worthy symbol now seemed appropriate. The whales are honoured and their voice stood as a harsh critique of human intervention and destruction. *This* reading made for a powerful sense of having achieved something; the complexity was brought into service and blame was apportioned. Does this reading allow us to learn anything about the whale? Does our need to appropriate its value and ensure it performs a function bring us any closer to a strong sense of another place or another thing? Our sense has always been that one of the great conundrums of postcolonial studies is the need and compulsion to bring closer what we sometimes wish would remain far away. Of course the great paradox of this perspective is that the socio-historical impulse that generated the longevity of imperialism was the act of *bringing close*. Texts that attempted to evoke this duality had to find ways to allow for it to flourish. When the convict Thornhill looks up at the stars in Grenville's *The Secret River*[9] he does not recognise the sky in New South Wales – he is disoriented as the stars he sees in the Sydney skies have replaced his celestial centre in London. This disorientation seems to then play out in the rejection of, or adaptation to, this new configuration. In turn, much of the dynamic and tension in postcolonial critique seems to stem from wanting to reveal rejection and point to salutary means of adaptation – to show how things could be otherwise. This compulsion sometimes takes us away from the discomfort of not knowing, a space that we argue is, however, worth inhabiting.

The brief examples above are poignant because they reveal opportunities to retrain curiosity around instances of alterity in the context of an encounter between a man and the sky or between an animal and its waters. Erin James[10] talks of how we might attend to 'opening up channels of communication concerning different environmental experiences across space, time and culture'.[11] In the readings offered in this chapter, characters are immersed in environments that they do not fully understand. When they do attempt to engage with them, their context is overwhelmingly one guided by ideas provided through socio-historical paradigms (in particular when these paradigms are used to understand geology). Land is old, ancient, fertile, or barren, open and infinite. Land and the natural environment contain either the possibility of change through manipulation or retain the impossibility of change and are thus framed as adversarial. Audiences – readers and viewers – however, need not align themselves with these readings as though they are inevitable. In other words, an active and conscious resistance to rehabilitate the environment might allow for an experience of environmental difference. This is the challenge. The concept of econarratology might help us on our way. James, in relation to postcolonial narratives, advocates 'reading strategies [that] highlight such moments of cultural dissonance' and prioritises 'the potential of narratives and their world-creating power to increase understanding among readers of *different environmental imaginations*'.[12] This might be a productive way of alighting to the depictions of the environment while keeping in mind the observation that 'creative representations of the physical world can encode local particularities and nuance'.[13] In other words, seemingly familiar features of place can produce wholly indecipherable signs depending on the viewer. By environment here we do not intend to provide eco-critical readings of place but rather to prioritise how place and space, as populated by landscape, have the potential to form an understanding of environment. In each reading here it is possible to extend the debate to include reflections on issues such as the sustainability of ecosystems and the acceptance of the need for diversity in the natural environment. However, in the context of postcoloniality, how this alterity is revealed to us in representation is also of value as it creates a space itself through which we can begin to experience the place of the other, the 'My Place' of Sally Morgan.[14]

The portrayal of landscape and land is crucial to our understanding of the condition of postcoloniality, not only in order for us to better understand its misuse and to rehearse established ideas on the material gains of land confiscation and exploitation, but also in order to investigate how the relationship to the land has the ability to either alter or ingrain perceptions and experiences of place and by extension, belonging. We are interested in the consequences and reverberations of alterations to the landscape and indeed, to the imagined dialogues and contexts that writers and filmmakers have produced in order to investigate this land. Films such as Charles Chauvel's 1955 *Jedda*,[15] one of the first Australian films to feature professional indigenous Aboriginal actors (though the film's trailer works hard to weaken this claim, seeking instead to emphasise the actors' seamless alignment with the natural world, thereby performing authenticity), sought to interrogate certain ideas around the connection between indigeneity and land. In an attempt to reveal the ways in which indigenous communities manoeuvred themselves in accordance with inherited understandings of the historical and cultural value of the land, the film clumsily, though interestingly, could not help but show the indigenous characters to be somewhat under the 'spell' of the land.

Here, certain well-established colonial fascinations around the connection between indigeneity, primitivism and unreconstructed associations with 'earth' in practice meant that it was difficult to make room for a more reasoned and historicised indigenous approach to the value of knowing and understanding terrain and geological complexity. In the film, an orphaned Aboriginal baby Jedda is taken up by a white farmer and his wife and raised on their cattle station. Aboriginal workers are shown to labour on the farm and are understood to straddle the two seemingly incompatible cultures until the arrival of Marbuck, a character presented to us as a 'true' Aboriginal – lawless and primal. As problematic as this is, Jedda's seemingly instinctive desire for Marbuck results in what looks to be an abduction, with Marbuck taking Jedda down the river and into uncharted territory – the *terra nullius* of colonial fantasy. Though in the contemporary political moment it is impossible to view this film without thinking about the implication of land rights and the historical mistreatment and abuse of indigenous Aboriginals, it is also the case that the film acts as a firm portrait on the ways in which the use, and passing through, of certain landscapes has the power to alter behaviour and shape encounters. *Jedda* is quite a fascinating film and even more so when its popularity among indigenous Aboriginals is understood and appreciated.[16] In a strictly politicised postcolonial paradigm, it would not be possible to allow for the film to teach us anything and yet teach us it does. The extensive cinematography used to depict the landscape is nothing if not astounding. Expanse and wide vistas are what capture the imagination before anything else and it is what the audience must contend with as they navigate the film.[17] 'This is part of the oldest land in the world, the Northern Territory of Australia', the narrator explains at the start of the film. The sheer quantity of water, land, mountain ranges and rivers are extraordinary and breathtaking – the 'lonely homesteads' set the scene for the many possible unforeseen interactions that may come about. The land is without a doubt presented as belonging *to* the Aboriginal people and the geological formations and their meanings are imbedded in the long tradition of indigeneity. That the film sets this up at the start does not absolve it of the uneven power dynamics played out in the film but it *does* prioritise and acknowledge the overwhelming nature of the surroundings and the difficulty in harnessing their meaning and value outside of an indigenous Aboriginal epistemology. The first few minutes of the film are committed to prioritising the breadth of Western Australia: they detail the miles of land involved and pronounce on the diversity of the natural habitat. The centrality of the Aboriginal peoples is also expressed at the same time as a confused and perhaps awe-inspired narrator fumbles over the difficulty of locating any precise *beginning* to it all, referring to 'millions of years' to cover up his lack of knowledge. The continued challenge of expressing this epistemology, or even cosmology, and its specificities is what later works such as Wright's *Carpentaria* and Grenville's *The Secret River* attempt.

Where Barbara Creed writes that it is 'impossible to discuss *Jedda* without reference to the stolen generation',[18] this prioritisation forestalls an important discussion into the attempt by Chauvel, and later Grenville and Wright, to *put together* the indigenous Aborigines with their land and their surroundings. Though it is clear that Creed must look to examine the removal from that very land, the connection and how we understand it is also important – in fact, we do not see how we make sense of one without the other. The ways in which connections are made with surroundings is crucial and the extent to which we may be able to appreciate these or not is immaterial.

In the opening scenes of Lawrence's film *Jindabyne*,[19] set in contemporary Australia, we are left in no doubt as to the prominence of the land and the possibilities it holds – both threatening and thrilling. The film opens with a wide view of the desert, a fence, boulders and rocks and an open vista bifurcated by a single road with a single car travelling upon it. On raised ground nearby lurks a menacing figure watching the landscape, waiting, it seems, for the car to come closer. There is something quite terrifying, unrelated to the subsequent events, in *abstracting* the land in this way as it seems to reveal its vulnerability to human crime or desires.

This sense of the land as exposed to human action is a powerful one as it reminds us of the ways in which any understanding of the environment is immediately affected by the events that take place on the land. It could be accidental that we start with the landscape or we could be being asked to consider the very material dimension of terrain or of how space is demarcated and in this case, it may be that it presents opportunities – *all kinds* of opportunities. Shockingly, however, when the man hails down his victim on pretence of spotting a problem with her car, what he actually says to her to explain his erratic behaviour is 'it all comes down from the power station' suggesting that the power station nearby has the ability to *change* minds in some way. That we see this same fear later on when another character flees in fear from the pylons suggests the unintended or unknown consequences of the invasion of something else into this land. Something happens to these two characters – though they seem to have little in common – that *they do not understand* and this something has very real consequences on their behaviour. Narratives that contain unsolved mysteries or that are involved in conveying the costs of secrets and obfuscation are somewhat suited to the story worlds of postcolonial nations. The active participation of the environment in upholding these narratives is not coincidental.

The emphasis on the ways in which people can be changed by their surroundings and how this environment can impact on behaviour is here imagined as a perceived threat, on an organic level. It would appear then that the consequence of the engagement is not always immediately perceptible: in other words, it can be incremental. As viewers or readers it is not always possible to identify this incrementality in the desire to achieve some value-laden interpretation that points towards the consequences of inaction and advocates futurity through action. In the example of *Jindabyne*, the land has been developed in order to create access and the water that has been diverted has been used to create power. We learn in the film that the original village of Jindabyne was itself flooded in order to make way for a dam, suggesting that displacement is at the core of the community. It would be possible and quite straightforward to conduct an inventory here of the uses and abuses of land and to see these actions as continuations of the imperial project – however, might it be more productive to try and see how these abuses result in unforeseen changes that have unintended consequences that reverberate back into the community? Thus, the experience of the land and what it offers up is not immediately perceptible to us. For example, in the short fishing trip (preceding the main fishing trip of the film) that Gabriel Byrne's character Stewart takes with his son at the lake that now covers up the old town, they bring up a clock which he calls a 'clock-fish' in part trying to limit the disappointment but also, interestingly, producing a *new* object for us to consider. A reconfiguration of the natural environment will produce newness. Newness in the film is a difficult concept however and all the characters struggle with it as they often appear at such odds with their surroundings. When the character Claire, played by Laura Linney, mourns an unwanted pregnancy by the side of the road, the immense landscape brings no relief and offers up no comfort. The presence of the land acts to decentralise the characters that otherwise struggle not to continually see themselves as the core. For us, as viewers, these are strong clues as to the importance of the environment and the perils of ignoring it.

In Grenville's 2005 novel *The Secret River*, an 1817 colonial map is included at the start, no doubt standing in for cartographic conquest. It also seems to reveal a great and awe-inspiring expanse and in doing so, questions the very presumption that this land can in any meaningful way, be *had*: we are obliged to look at it and decide for ourselves the ways in which this terrain could or should be subjected to navigation.

The map serves to visually place the protagonist and convict Thornhill *in his place*, regardless of the extent to which he chooses to see himself in any particular way. Thornhill is shocked at how alien his surroundings are upon arrival in New South Wales and notes that 'above him in the sky was a thin moon and a scatter of stars as meaningless as spilt rice. There was no Pole

Star, a friend to guide him on the Thames, no Bear that he had known all his life: only this blaze, unreadable, indifferent'.[20] Grenville's challenge here is to reveal to us a place that is not indifferent to all but appears indifferent to *those who cannot read it*. Those who can read it are framed provocatively by Grenville as so ingrained in it as to be almost indistinguishable from it. Seeing an indigenous Aboriginal for the first time, Thornhill is taken aback by his eyes, 'set so deeply in his skull that they were invisible, each in its cave of bone. The rock of his face shaped itself around the big mouth, the imposing nose, the folds of his cheek'.[21] The man's features are understood in geological terms that would seek to return the Aboriginal to his place at the same time as this place is gradually equated with death, darkness and endless threat. This is echoed in critical work that seeks to redistribute our focus in relation to the colonised subject. In her work on colonialism and nature, Val Plumwood[22] argues for our clear understanding of the extent to which

> an encompassing and underlying rationalist ideology applying both to humans and to non-humans is [...] brought into play in the specific processes of European colonisation. This ideology is applied not only to indigenous peoples but to their land, which was frequently portrayed in colonial justifications as unused, underused or empty – *areas of rational deficit*.[23]

Importantly however, it is the manner of this portrayal that can help us to understand the extent to which these justifications were contiguous and never quite complete. What the attempted representation of indigenous space in *The Secret River*, *Jindabyne* and *Jedda* reveal is the extent to which this justification had to be reiterated and fought over continually in the face of the imposing and ever-present landscape. Plumwood accentuates how the significance of the 'imposition of the colonizers' [...] visions of ideal landscapes [...] see indigenous culture as "primitive", less rational'.[24] We are interested in revealing how postcolonial responses to these issues play out and what the imagined consequences are for a colonial context that continually imposes its vision of an ideal landscape. In her description of the land that became Sydney, Grenville is unforgiving, calling it a 'sad scrabbling place [...] a half-formed temporary sort of place'[25] and in *Jindabyne*, the camera watches the group of friends fishing both before and after they find a dead aboriginal girl in the water, seemingly resolute in their commitment to ignoring the changed reality of their surroundings. In *Jedda*, the sheer distance covered by Marbuk and Jedda as they move further and further away from the cattle ranch is testament to the inability to imagine its total exploitation. The land, it seems, exceeds the limitations of capture.

Attempts to 'tame' the land are however continuous, bolstered by any number of ideologies. As Huggan and Tiffin argue, in Australia, North America, New Zealand and South Africa, genuine curiosity about and respect for indigenous cultures, philosophies and religions was rare, and even the most well-intentioned of missionaries, settlers and administrators tended to conceive of themselves as conferring (or imposing) the gifts of civilization upon the benighted heathen with little or no interest in receiving his or her philosophical gifts in return.[26]

In Nicolas Roeg's 1971 film *Walkabout*, we do however see a curiosity about indigeneity develop but it is slow and often tortured, buffered by fragmented signs of an unwelcome modernity. Where curiosity is embraced more fully as it is in Weir's 1975 *Picnic at Hanging Rock*, it can have devastating effects as it jars against the profound conservatism of an idealised landscape. In both these cases, however, philosophical gifts are precisely what is conferred: gifts surrounding the experience of time, the conception of place and the boundaries of the 'real'. In one particularly memorable moment, the young boy in *Walkabout*, who follows the indigenous Aboriginal who guides him and his sister through the red desert, visualises *his* ancestors walking through that very landscape, no more certain of their destination than he. This chronotope in the film perhaps celebrates the unchanged qualities of that land and presents an alternative to the boy's trajectory which inevitably leads away from this scene as he seeks a way out, back towards 'civilisation'.

Wright's novel *Carpentaria* (2008) is particularly attuned to the extent to which the predictability of nature is unquestioned, until the cooperation ceases.

> It takes a particular kind of knowledge to go with the river, whatever its mood. It is about there being no difference between you and the movement of water as it seasonally shifts its tracks according to its own mood. [...] In one moment, during a Wet season early in the last century, the town lost its harbour waters when the river simply decided to change course, to bypass it by several kilometres.[27]

In both of these examples, natural surroundings, or the environment, can and do change and what they find in their path may or may not be affected. Some land is for passing through and other land is for exploitation but as Wright's example illuminates, even activity around natural sources does not guarantee predictability. In *Walkabout*, what we see is that it is not possible to predict *what* the landscape will reveal.

What much of this literary and filmic postcolonial activity allows us to experience is nothing short of the huge range of relational experiences with space and land. Though the town of Desperance in *Carpentaria* may sometimes have a river, the local Aboriginal family lives in the 'human dumping ground next to the town tip [...] All choked up, living piled up together in trash humpies made of tin, cloth and plastic too, salvaged from the rubbish dump'.[28] These particular Aboriginals are, in the pioneer legends of Desperance, *'not really part of the town at all'*.[29] This incredible opening forces an encounter with a community that is far from the romanticised images of their somewhat intuitive relationship to the land. The dumping ground is potentially the new sacred land, providing for the needs of its inhabitants. This scene produces an extraordinary vision of a recycled habitat able to rival any image of a natural environment.

Compare this to Sally Thornhill in *The Secret River* who is disgusted at the native trees that she does not recognise and:

> wonder[s] aloud that they did not know enough to be green, the way a tree should be, but a washed-out silvery grey so they always looked half dead. Nor were they a proper shape, oak shape or elm shape, but were tortured formless things [...].[30]

It seems that being part of a landscape, or not being able to accept another's landscape, or being seen to be in the wrong landscape, form a consistent concern. The association and connection to the land, whatever that connection may be and however it may be expressed, is one that continually reconfigures modes of belonging and ownership in the colonial and postcolonial context. Bob Hodge and Vijay Mishra argue that, in the context of indigenous Aboriginals today, the choices, broadly, appear to be between 'trying to re-establish traditional ways of life, as close to their traditional territories as is now possible' and attempting to live as 'urban dwellers or fringe dwellers in country towns'.[31] *Carpentaria*'s focus on the latter is a reimagining of this experience of fringe dwelling and it is the landscape upon which lives will be played out and understood that is emphasised. Sally Thornhill will, however, continue to reject the trees in a bid for belonging.

Carpentaria fits in events around the geology and weather systems that encircle the town of Desperance: dust, rains, winds, electrical storms, floods. And sometimes in the narrative, the concrete features of the town do not feature at all. Like Grenville's depiction of Sally's inability to see the trees, Wright emphasises the choices behind seeing for the Aboriginals as well. In discussing the metamorphoses of Desperance, she writes that 'the Pricklebush mob saw huge, powerful ancestral creation spirits occupying the land and sea moving across the town, even inside folk's houses, right across any piece of the country'.[32] The ancestors here function like the camel-riding colonisers in the boy's fantasy in *Walkabout*. These images occupy the space and thus render the land *mutable*. Any material victory over the space and the land understood in colonial terms is subjected to reconsideration as it can be seen to occupy a variety of philosophical and social contexts. For Sally Thornhill, the trees are not right, but they are definitely there. For the Pricklebush mob, the houses may be there but there is something else *overlaying* them that only they can see. And for the boy in *Walkabout*, the camels fold an otherwise absent ancestry into what seems an inhospitable and unknown land. In all cases, the landscape is always reimagined according to need.

In *The Secret River*, the very act of dividing the land is understood as somewhat at odds with the landscape itself, regardless of, as Reid argues, the 'belief in the link between labour, land and reformation [that had] informed [colonial] policy from the start'.[33] Grenville writes that the early settlement bestowed to the freed convicts 'had an odd unattached look, the bits of ground cut up into squares in this big loose landscape, a broken-off chip of England resting on the surface of the place'.[34] Contrary to any sense that settlement and colonisation could be driven forward by an expansionist philosophy alone, what Grenville is attuned to and attempts to draw out is the intensive imaginative labour required to become *acquainted* with the new surroundings. Regardless of the, sometimes abhorrent, actions of the convicts-turned-settlers, this struggle to acquaint is viscerally rendered. It is not necessarily the case that we are to read this as an apology for conquest, as has sometimes been argued, but rather to inhabit the space of its very naissance. In *The Secret River*, Thornhill and his wife continue to train and manage the land around them so that it can fit an idea of 'England' but they are painfully aware of the futility of this. After the fateful and horrific massacre of the indigenous population of the Hawkesbury River, Thornhill knows that 'every tree, every leaf, every rock seemed to be watching'.[35] In the wake of the massacre, it seems as though there is 'no more trouble from the blacks [and] new settlers had taken up land on every bend'[36] but we know from Thornhill that the land observes him – this he *has* learnt. In *Jindabyne*, the jittering camera watching the men fishing stands in for a watchful eye – it is the tree, leaf and rock that Thornhill fears manifest. In *Picnic at Hanging Rock*, the girls are being watched as they explore the rock, their curiosity and amazement evoked through disconcerting music and chaotic camerawork.

In *The Secret River*, Thornhill believes that:

> a person was entitled to draw any picture they fancied on the blank slate of this new place [...] [but his wife Sal's] garden did not thrive. The roses never put their roots down. They clung to life, but were little more than stalk. The daffodils were planted but no trace of them was ever seen again. The turf yellowed and shrivelled and finally blew away in wisps of dry straw.[37]

Contrary to expectation, the land cannot always be bent until it yields to desire and will. As Sue Kossew[38] notes in relation to *The Secret River* and her understanding of the novel as an attempt to balance 'blame and admiration', 'the space of the settler colony [...] was also necessarily a place of violent encounters that *left scars on the land* and on the psyche of the people, both Indigenous and non-Indigenous Australians'.[39] This later conclusion is productive as it allows us to reflect on the very configuration of that land as a powerful injunction of the future relationship to it.

In other words, by working backwards from their particular socio-historical contexts, works such as *The Secret River* and *Carpentaria* are able to reintroduce the unanticipated consequences of this violent encounter: a particular form of displacement that nevertheless attends to its fate with a surprising clarity. As Kossew writes, 'the cultivation of the wilderness in the form of a garden is often an important trope in narratives of settlement [but Sal] is unable to think herself into the Australian landscape or climate'.[40] It is possible to imagine that she can think herself into it and refuses it. It is also the case that the landscape is here shown as *unwilling* to yield to her needs in the same way as it will keep a watchful eye on Thornhill. This is to say that it may have to work both ways. It is intriguing to have this dimension be given so much narrative attention: Grenville's rendering of this rejection is palpable and unforgettable. The settler may get what they want but they cannot fully understand the price they have had to pay. Their energetic superficial rejection of all that does not fit into their world view continues to exist at the margins – just at the periphery of their vision.

By contrast, in *Carpentaria*, the extraordinary description of a car convoy snaking its way along an ancient Dreaming track is evocative in its refusal to romanticise this ritual:

> The spiritual Dreaming track of the ceremony in which they were all involved, moved along the most isolated back roads, across the landscape, through almost every desert in the continent [...] The men in this moving mirage of battered vehicles felt they had well and truly followed the Dreaming. Travel has become *same, same* and mandatory, as the convoy moved in reptile silence over the tracks of the travelling mighty ancestor whom they worshipped through singing the story that had continued for years.[41]

Here the cars are one with the tracks, creating and dividing the sand as they follow the designated and imagined paths. Unlike the road in *Jindabyne*, which carries fear and death, here, the battered old cars find renewed sacredness in a pilgrimage that has been undertaken in a different form. We are not only here emphasising that the landscape is adaptable and malleable, able to withstand human change and desires. Rather, what these examples teach us is that both a forceful certainty and a habituated understanding of the environment can be overturned. The ability of the characters to identify their relationship towards the environment is visible in the extent to which they adapt towards it.

In *Picnic at Hanging Rock*, we again see the compulsion to order a landscape that has no need for such alignment. The girls at the start of the film, offered an afternoon's reprieve from their boarding school, are so very excited to visit the rock and seem at ease with their understanding of it as mysterious. It is not necessary, as Douglas Keesey argues, to see the Hanging Rock as 'a darkness at the heart of white civilisation [where] this unsettling emptiness becomes a blank screen for the projection of dread and desire concerning the inhospitable Other, culture's defining opposite'.[42] Such an interpretation exposes the land to an ideology not consistently applied to it in the film and it is certainly not a discourse that many of the characters subscribe to. The idea of the rock, held by some, and the experiencing of it by others are not one and the same. This is crucial as the film attempts to perform an experiment in resilience – resilience to the very ideas of *what* the Rock might stand for. Its magnificence at the start of the film is awe-inspiring and the trip is arranged for the girls so they might learn something about geology – it is not initially terrifying to the girls who picnic there. Its endorsement by some and vilification by others has as much to do with how they come to it as how it appears to them. The film does not mention indigeneity or Aboriginality and it is impossible to derive this connection from the action within the film. We are better off looking at how the land is sensed, touched and experienced by all in order to gain an understanding as to its presence and also to begin to fathom the limits of that understanding, arranged as it is through relations with this land.

Whichever interpretation we subscribe to, one thing is certain: the rock's existence is evidence of a *before*. Wright notes, in relation to *Carpentaria*, her decision not to 'just write a tale of Aboriginal people suffering the effects of colonisation, becoming marginalised in their own country' as this 'would assume that only the past 200 years mattered, that Australian history starts only with the arrival of white Europeans'.[43] Instead, she insists that *all* times in Australia are important and that the 'colonisation story is not the whole story'.[44] The integration of encounters with the land, as exemplified above, chimes with this. The indigenous population *and* the natural habitat are there in advance of an encounter, already creating interconnected modes of seeing. The colonial encounter may alter the placement towards this space and the land itself plays out its acceptance, rejection or indifference of this change.

Postcolonial reflections on this change are more apposite than they imagine, for in showing the encounter, they show up what needed to be there in order for the encounter to be fractious. In other words, the picnic needs the rock but the film shows us how little the rock requires the picnic. This, in a sense, is *part of the rest of the story*. In *Jindabyne*, the dead girl's body, found by the fishing group who wait until their expedition is over before revealing their finding, presents a stark reminder of how rationality attempts to trump the surreal. The camera in the trees watches and waits for the men to decide what they will do. This world view is woven into the film itself, as it is in *Picnic at Hanging Rock* where girls and women also go missing and are not always found. We might be afraid, and we should be afraid, because this guerrilla mode of exploration is terrifying. *Jindabyne* makes a self-conscious link between the Anglo-Christian world of some of its protagonists and how those very same characters move in a space that is understood otherwise by the indigenous community. The dead girl belongs to the indigenous Aboriginal community who are horrified at the delay in reporting the body. What we see, however, is that the men are somewhat affected by being out at the fishing spot. They do not seem privy to social codes and for a short time, some fundamental complex social expectations cannot be fathomed or acted upon. For a time, the film plays with our *sense of time* and also with a certain ethical responsibility that is expected of the men. The environment seems to disrupt the men's context of social responsibility and cross-cultural accountability. The narrative itself seems to want to wreak havoc with our understanding of linearity – this happens and then after this, another thing should happen. For the men who are fishing, they understand the girl as dead and therefore what matter when she is reported dead? Bruno David argues in his work *Landscapes, Rock-Art and the Dreaming* that

> unlike Christian thought, the Dreaming is based on a view of the cosmos as an interrelated network without subjects or objects. There is not a world 'out there.' It is rather an existence that is defined by the relationship of everything that is and that was [...] In discussing the various dimensions of the Dreaming, therefore, the categories should not be seen as interacting parts [...].[45]

The actions of the group deface an inheritance that acts on them all, even if they are unable to understand it. While they continue to fish, the very air around them signals their moral bankruptcy.

In the context of Wright's writerly aims in *Carpentaria*, what is and what was have the capacity to coexist but they must be recognised as such, and the past must be given legitimacy to exist and have purpose in the present. Often it is the de-legitimisation of the past that can lead to the scarring of the land, and the land often bears the reminder and traces of this past. In *Rabbit-Proof Fence*, Doris Pilkington writes that:

> seasonal time and not numbers is important in recounting this journey. Consistent with Aboriginal storytelling style, seasonal time and the features of the natural environment are more important to recounting this journey than are the western notions of time and distance. I have though worked to synthesise these different forms of knowledge to give readers the fullest insight into this historic journey (xiii-xiv).[46]

Here, we witness the labour that must go into attempting this 'synthesis'. 'Seasonal time' and the 'natural environment' must somehow be twisted in order to metamorphose into 'notions of time and distance'. In other words, the philosophical gift needs to be translated before it can be conveyed. What is lost here, however, is vast: the very narratives that can occupy a variegated understanding of time where all stories can influence all stories needs to be rendered chronologically where cause and effect operate in one direction. It is no wonder the environment cannot, in the colonial imaginary, ever be seen as more than a sum of its potential as *resource*, whether symbolically or materially. In this context, the past is intrusive rather than a *guide*. This is not an idea that is exclusive to the indigenous Aboriginal cosmology. The repercussions of remaining blind to any alterities expressed in relation to the environment work to cement a particular idea of history and of the land in relation to the progress of that history. 'Time' as Pilkington writes,

> was also marked by activities of cultural and ceremonial significance [and listeners to stories would] know that this was the time when traditional rites and rituals were performed. So in these communities time is based on practical events, incidents and seasons.[47]

These ideas are not in themselves unfamiliar and, to a certain extent, are relevant in any cross-cultural context. However, in the colonial and postcolonial context, such reminiscences reinforce the past of the indigenous community, and the playing out of that past on the land, through references to places and paths as well as geographical and other landmarks. It is these landmarks that we *see* across postcolonial cultural activity to varying degrees, whether or not fictional protagonists are given the ability or capacity to experience this. The call to attempt to view landscape as terrain is articulated multiple times in all of the texts and films studied here. This simultaneous multiplicity disinvites any attempt to evoke social and cultural hierarchy. How do we arrive at this juncture, however?

This question of capacity is explored in some detail in *Picnic at Hanging Rock*. The characters are all given particular abilities that allow them to sense their place in a context that we are perhaps encouraged to view as alien. Perhaps it is as a consequence of multiple viewings, but on closer inspection it appears that the girls themselves and the accoutrements that keep them alive – the school, the headmistress, the servants, the clothes – are indeed what is alien. So powerfully does the film centralise the rock and so fitfully does it permit it to intrude our viewing capabilities that it almost appears as an attempt to rise to Wright and Pilkington's challenge to present *all* times. Marek Haltof argues that in the film's opening shots, the rock 'is photographed like an old Gothic castle; as in Gothic novels or horror films, it dominates the region and awaits its new victims'.[48] This interpretation sets the rock up as vampyric, requiring its energy from others. This is not borne out by the film itself, however, where the sound that surrounds the rock points to its very own ecosystem – it is there and has been there for a long time. It does not appear to need anyone or anything. Haltof goes on to argue that, in any case, 'the Australian landscape in [the] film is the source of meaning – a distinctive characteristic which has its own discursive function'.[49] While this may seem a very appealing reading, the 'meaning' suggested here is not always accessible in a discursive and linear sense and it is this inaccessibility and the fear and insecurity that it induces that is made palpable.

This is not to mythologise or make incomprehensible any landscape within and against which the films and texts are positioning themselves but rather to suggest that the presence of the surrounding land and the space that the characters inhabit is not wholly comprehensible to all in the same way. These multiple experiences serve to construct a tension that is then read through a particular perspective. In certain contexts, repetition of this reading then naturalises the 'landscape [as one] filled with mystery and ruled by forces beyond human comprehension'.[50] Any criticism, however, that succumbs to the perceived hierarchy of human comprehension ceases to be in dialogue with the very difficult but absolutely necessary injunction to participate in Wright's investigation of 'all times'.

In other words, we argue that the films and texts do attempt this as they keep the landscape in the foreground. Any and all attempts to prioritise how human relations are affected or how the landscape is read is a viewer/reader decision. A different decision could prioritise the human to landscape interaction outside of any expectation. In Elizabeth Povinelli's work on the long-running cases of native titles in *The Cunning of Recognition*, she argues that while Australian Prime Minister John Howard accepted the need for reconciliation, he

> explicitly rejected all attempts 'to embroil' the Australian people 'in an exercise of shame and guilt,' describing most settler atrocities as 'mistakes' and assigning these mistakes to a past in which the 'overwhelming majority of the current generations of Australians' had no personal involvement.[51]

These claims are thoroughly undermined by the successive generations of writers and filmmakers who have sought to precisely reveal the extent of *involvement*. Rather more elegantly than Howard, these artists have understood involvement in more flexible terms than physical land-grabbing and even where this is the case, as in *The Secret River*, the compulsion surrounding this behaviour is explored and the depth of shame and guilt are taken for granted. Here, we can understand involvement as continued misappropriation and misunderstanding. If the very question of land cannot be resolved, it is perhaps not surprising to find this preoccupation at the heart of much of the cultural work – to present it, to represent it, to negotiate it, to relate to it somewhat. Most of all, however, to *show* it – to have a map, to film the rock, to focus on the insects, the ants and the reptiles, to describe the sky, the trees, the sand. It is possible to imagine that this acceptance is the first step in negotiating alterity – the films and texts seem to want to prioritise this in any case, regardless of where some of the criticism has led us.

For example, in Jonathan Rayner's[52] informative article on Lawrence's film, he argues that *Jindabyne* is

> the narrative of the discovery of a murdered woman's body by four men on a fishing trip [that] foregrounds two perennial staples of Australian filmmaking: the attractions and problems of male-to-male relationships, and the provocations of gender conflict in social and familial contexts.[53]

While this may be the case, the film itself is not interested in any of this at the outset. It sets itself up squarely in what appears to be a lonely landscape. The *clues* as to why the group in the film struggle to understand why they may have crossed certain 'ethnicity-based characteristics'[54] in their misunderstanding of the murder do lie in these first few scenes. The struggle in reaching out to the Aboriginal community is difficult to understand without accepting the presence of a world view and the damage to that world view that has not been acknowledged. It is not only played out in the contemporary dynamics of community and family but also in the context of an unacknowledged otherness. *Jindabyne* to us also conjures up a response to the 'white-vanishing trope' that can be more readily associated with *Picnic at Hanging Rock* and *Walkabout*.

This trope, associated with the 'paradigm of recurring stories in non-indigenous Australian textuality about disappearing whites'[55] is, in *Jindabyne*, turned on its head as it is the Aboriginal girl who has disappeared and the surrounding community that must navigate this loss on their terrain. Tilley argues that in the colonial context the 'hostile-land idea [...] facilitated the co-development of the pioneering and bushman myths. In these almost exclusively masculine myths, an unfriendly landscape provides the foil to create heroes of white-settler "battlers"'.[56] The landscape in *Jindabyne* is, however, *potentially* hostile to *all*, regardless of whether they can see this or not. It is potentially hostile to all because it precedes them all and its abilities are therefore unknown. We find this idea of *precedence* particularly challenging as it underpins so much of the discussion around authenticity in indigenous contexts. It can also problematically be used to argue for a terrain upon which to place what Gareth Griffiths has called 'recovered "traditional rights"'.[57] In other words, arguments and discourses that seek to validate indigenous rights seek to locate those rights in specific locations. While this might temporarily appear to redress the need to remember and legitimate the connection to land in both law and culture, there is the danger that indigenous cultures might also be reduced to this locatedness, thereby distancing their 'right[s] to general social justice and equality'.[58] This problem sometimes speaks to why it is so much more powerful to have the land appear alone – as it does in *Picnic at Hanging Rock*, *Walkabout*, *Jedda* and *Jindabyne*. It is not in all senses there to represent or stand in for an unacknowledged indigenous symbolism or to perform the invisibility of *cultural* alterity. These are valid points but can be seen as dead ends as we might then seek to measure their relative success. Rather, the land is there and the meaning and use of it is the first bone of contention among communities. In her work on contemporary indigenous Aboriginality, Povinelli writes of the changes in orientation to the world as an 'arrangement of existence' which is in no way natural or presumed, and speaks instead of how certain formations and classifications of life come together around social, spatial and ideological discourses (among others) and take shape.[59] In her thoughts on human adaptation to surroundings, Povinelli writes that

> the answer to what a sudden, unexpected change in the arrangement of existence might mean depended on how much a person knew about things, the place, other things in the place, other places, etc. [...] Humans had to learn how to heed such manifestations, and they were assessed in their ability to provide cogent interpretations of them.[60]

This opens up entirely new ways of viewing the interaction in the colony and postcolony. The capacity to understand and be curious about a change in arrangement is undoubtedly beneficial, as we see in *Walkabout* when the children give in to their surroundings and stop trying to order them. In the film, two children find themselves abandoned in the desert after a bewildering incident where a father appears to try to harm his children. The girl and boy initially struggle with their surroundings as they try to retain some order but soon find themselves lost and without water. They meet a young Aboriginal boy who gives them help when they ask for it but he does not appear to be overly concerned with their predicament. This is important as it suggests that the sense of being lost cannot *but* be subjective. The film plays with this notion, as it seems to make their existence less and less visible in relation to their surroundings.

The girl and boy follow him around until they become a loose trio. It is important to consider that it is not that the girl and boy surrender to the Aborigine's knowledge but rather, they all gradually reorient themselves entirely until they are all each other's new surroundings and they eventually do things for each other's sake. In *Picnic at Hanging Rock*, the arrangement is constantly at work but it seems to rotate around the rock that is understood and captured in so many ways – as opportunity, as adventure, as release, as threat, as danger. And also, as itself and none of the above. *Walkabout* presents the most challenging viewing experience as the film deliberately fluctuates in the ways it wants us to see the desert. Where certain cinematic choices emphasise *disorientation*,[61] it seems more likely that the desert simply becomes visible as a space to be walked through rather than understood. It does not impose an orientation but in human terms it does need to be navigated. This is a thrilling perspective on the film as the boy, girl and Aborigine all move through the space in group, arranging themselves along the way and seemingly willing to rearrange themselves with regards to what they meet and encounter. It is difficult to understand the observation by Suneeti Rekhari that

> the refusal of white culture in both *Jedda* and *Walkabout* to accommodate Aboriginal culture, or even to coexist with it, refers directly to a large portion of Australian identity representations, which returned to a familiar end, the triumph of colonial and neo-colonial attitudes.[62]

The films' engagement with these themes cannot be judged solely by their endings. As we have shown above, both films speak to concerns that precede the more politically demanding requirement of equal representation. In other words, they are in dialogue with questions of land and landscape, presence and absence, the possibilities of belonging. The girl appears disenchanted after her return to the city in *Walkabout* and dreams of the Aboriginal boy. In *Jedda*, Jedda and Marbuk's death does not fulfil some colonial prophecy of the indisputable natural 'end' of the Aboriginal race. It comes after a devastating error by Marbuk to enter into unknown territory – a landscape he has no time to familiarise himself with.

Think how different this is from the rigidity we see explored in *The Secret River* where a deep consciousness, formed in the class hierarchies at the heart of Empire, are transported and kept alive in the heart of the convicts. This rigidity is challenged but it remains firm. There is no rearrangement in *The Secret River* and in Grenville's imaginings of this story, there is no place for the idea of this to even emerge. Rather, there is an acknowledgement of the other's place but no attempt to orient to that place.

This orientation or arrangement is also at play in Morgan's autobiography *My Place*, which tells the story of a family's reckoning with the ideas that surround heritage and, in the words of Arlene A. Elder, 'historical precedent'.[63] In this book, the various family members are forced to consider the very idea of Aboriginality as identity and thus all struggle to fathom what shape this might take. This is a very powerful narrative as it works against premeditated assumptions of belonging. The story centres around Sally Morgan who recounts her journey towards a better understanding of the shame but also celebration of indigeneity in a contemporary Australian context. Each character or person has to find *their* place and these differ wildly. We can't see how the book reveals a 'traditional Aboriginal heritage'.[64] Rather, the book presents a variety of, in Povinelli's words, *'manifestations'*, or 'signs',[65] that are then attended to with patience and curiosity. Where the grandmother Daisy can read the natural signs around her as proof of her indigeneity, the call of the birds for example, Sally, the protagonist, requires more *tangible* signs such as the affiliation she discovers between her drawings and that of other Aboriginal family members', as well as listening to and recording experiences and narratives of extended family, some of whom have returned to 'ancestral' lands and others who still live in traditional farms. The book's success lies in its multiplicity (we also hear the voice of Sally's uncle and her mother in the story) and its *inability* to direct the reader towards one overarching experience located in one single place or thing. Some of the most illuminating experiences are the ones that provide 'endless and excessive transformation of the subject positions within the hybridised'[66] for as long as we are interested in the dynamics of the postcolony then this is crucial to representation.[67]

So far we have presented the possibilities inherent in what it might mean to pay close attention to the environment that narratives find themselves in – in particular the natural environment and surrounding land. We understand the struggle over land to be one of the defining features of the longevity of certain colonial tropes in the postcolonial cultural imagination. It is worthwhile to look closely at texts that seem to want to re-establish this struggle as they also perform an archiving of sorts in that they attempt to produce contexts where the imposition of the logic of a colonial framework or the allure of a certain type of dualistic postcolonial critique might actually perform a *disservice*. In other words, we would like to advocate a new starting point for coming face-to-face with otherness: to arrive at a text with a full appreciation that the impulse to provide critique is, by now, ingrained as we work politically in the context of identifying misrepresentation. This can often lead us far away from experiencing alterity. It is the case, of course, that encounters with alterity and our awareness of otherness occur within the dynamics of a confluence of discourses: cultural, gendered, economic and ethnic, to name but a few. It is also the case, however, that being aware of the extent to which these discourses influence our experience is taught to us by the texts themselves in the ways in which they reveal the limited and bound attributes of all perspectives and frames. At the same time, this inspires us to proceed with more dynamic and open readings.

Take, for example, Nadine Gordimer's *The Conservationist* (1974), which is open in the sense of capturing a historical moment in which the legacies of colonial tenure over a particular land are radically contested and inconclusive. Two main experiences and conceptions of the disputed land of apartheid South Africa are dramatised by the book's distinctive voices and forms. There is the abstracted and paradoxical fantasy of productivity and conservation of the farm's owner, the 'white' industrial mogul Mehring. Then there are the rather different – though, since the events of the novel are refracted largely in free indirect style through Mehring's brash but circumscribed perspective, mostly unspecified – attachments of his 'black' foreman Jacobus and of the farm workers. The action of the novel, such as it is, gets underway with the return of 'the owner of the farm' to find a group of children cradling a clutch of guinea fowl eggs.[68] Mehring may breathe 'the dry, cool and perfect air of a high-veld autumn' (C, 3) as he crosses a field of alfalfa, but the failure of his persistent efforts to achieve intimacy and a kind of sensuous knowledge of the land is demonstrated time and again by the book's own form. He shares no lingua franca with the children. His discussions with Jacobus are painfully protracted and halting. Mehring reaches for colonial stereotypes to describe Jacobus's tendency to controvert or ignore his instructions as signs of his obstinacy or cunning, but the novel itself does not pretend to explain Jacobus's outlook or understand his relationship with the farm.

The narrative voice switches between an abstracted realist mode, peering uncomprehendingly at the farm from an elevated and dispassionate vantage, and a second-person mode in which Mehring and the reader are both addressed as 'you' but are still situated at an alienated distance from the land.

> A whole clutch of guinea fowl eggs. Eleven. Soon there will be nothing left. In the country. The continent. The oceans, the sky.
>
> (C, 3)

This crucial interjection, ramifying from the starkly foregrounded and multiply suggestive image of the cradled eggs, may be an omniscient narrator's critical insight into how, for the sociopathic pig iron salesman Mehring, the living world is simply a resource to be colonially plundered. It may be Mehring's own syntactically pared down and impressionistic interior monologue summarising his schizophrenic attitude to nature: raw material to be pillaged or else a plantation to be appreciated and conserved. Either way, for Mehring and for the novel, and also for the novel's readers who are consistently placed claustrophobically inside Mehring's viewpoint, no other way of conceiving or inhabiting the living world is detailed.

Mehring loves the land but not the people, which for J.M. Coetzee is the original sin of South Africa's white population: excessive affection 'toward what is least likely to respond to love' such as 'mountains and deserts, birds and animals and flowers' and an absent 'fraternity with the people among whom he lives'.[69] Mehring's conservationism is the flip side of his alienated and instrumental relationship with the earth. He is a well-off city man who has bought the farm because he has a vague 'hankering to make contact with the land' (C, 17). The farm is used mostly to amuse his friends and lovers and because the losses are deductible from income tax. He flatters himself that he 'was not a sucker for city romanticism' because a 'farm is not beautiful unless it is productive' (C, 18). Antonia, Mehring's former lover who has now left the country and whose reproaches he keeps compulsively harking back to, has told him he makes a fetish of 'Development', the living world being grist to 'one great big wonderful all-purpose god of a machine' (C, 89). This risibly unconvincing justification of 'racial capitalism', plus the gradual breakdown of Mehring's relationships in the novel with Antonia and with his liberal son, his inability to communicate with his workers, and his sense of alienation from a farm that obviously functions effectively without his presence are all of a piece with his increasing alienation from the living world, whether he is soaring thousands of feet above it in a jet bound for Japan or separated from the farm by a flood. The land and its inhabitants are coterminous in Mehring's mind, objects to be labelled, resources to be commanded and exploited, and spectacles to be enjoyed. His own origins, as his German name suggests, are in South Africa's mandated possession South West Africa (which he is dismayed to find his son calling Namibia). Their elderly relatives may know 'everything about plants and animals' but Khan Canyon has been sealed off by a uranium mine and the Damara have been 'removed' to a 'Reserve', just as the Herero were 'removed' and exterminated decades before by their murderous German colonisers (C, 113). The point here is that whether the land is regarded as a Romantic or sometimes erotic spectacle, transformed by genocidal clearances into an exploitable terra nullius, treated as an industrious hobby by a hard-headed businessman or even escaped altogether by white liberals seeking to avoid military conscription or political guilt, the white citizen's attachment to the land is shown to be alienated and tenuous.

It is very important to stress, however, that the novel contains no vision of a more reciprocal and durable relationship to the land. The focus is on the comprehensive discrediting of Mehring's claims of ownership. His efforts to 'tidy' the farm, conceal the unsightly and impoverished dwellings of his workers and make it over into an extension of an Edenic European pastoral landscape by planting chestnut trees are a failure: 'the two small trees now stand like branches children have stuck in sand to make a "garden" that will wither in an hour' (C, 271). Indeed Coetzee's discussion of South African pastoral art, from early visions of the Cape of Good Hope to the imagination of an Afrikaner 'nation of farmers', focuses on 'the topos of the garden, the closed world entire to itself' derived in part from 'the Judaeo-Christian myth of Eden',[70] with all its connotations of 'simplicity, peace, immemorial usage',[71] a land rescued from decay and wilderness. This is a productive landscape, as Mehring insists, but it occludes black labour and the substantive (as opposed to merely picturesque) presence on the land of those who once possessed it. *The Conservationist*, Coetzee goes on to suggest, is a critique of these occlusions perpetrated by white pastoral, since the body of the murdered black man who is callously buried on Mehring's farm by indifferent policemen at the start of the novel 'as if nothing has ever happened' (C, 128), returns to the surface after the flood. What this re-emergence signifies is simply the failure of South Africa's white minority and of its apartheid ruling class to sustain a pastoral ideology capable of justifying its hegemony by effacing the democratic claims of the majority, a failure made starkly visible in this period by the Soweto Uprising of 1976, by the Black Consciousness movement and by increasingly militant opposition to the racist regime. Something clearly *has* happened here, that something being the murderousness of South African history since colonisation.

If Mehring's increasing confusion and isolation betoken his weak and short-lived occupancy of the land, then the storm that floods it, that separates Mehring from the land and his workers and that brings the murdered body to the surface is itself loaded with symbolic significance. This reckoning arrives from Mozambique, as the apartheid regime under Vorster in the 1970s with its 'Total strategy' against internal and external subversion must have expected its principal challenge to come from the insurgent and newly independent states on its borders. Our final image of Mehring is of a diminished and befuddled figure stretched out with a prostitute in a garbage-strewn layby, menaced by possible thieves and petrified by the prospect of his own disgrace. This ignominious and puzzlingly out-of-focus penultimate scene takes us away from our intimate proximity to Mehring's singular voice to an oddly collective voice imploring us from a suddenly established distance to 'Come and look' at 'Mehring, down there' (C, 320), with pity or perhaps contempt for a suddenly belittled and superannuated ruling class. The succeeding and final scene shows the orderly community of farm workers lowering the anonymous murdered man in a wooden box into the 'soft and thick' soil, the sheer richness of the earth testifying to a long history of tenure and cultivation and its pliability to a careful, skilful inhabitation of the land.

> The one whom the farm received had no name. he had no family but their women wept a little for him. There was no child of his present but their children were there to live after him. They had put him away to rest, at last; he had come back. He took possession of this earth, theirs; one of them.
>
> (C, 323)

The solitariness and uncertain identity of the dead man is counterbalanced here by a formidable community confident in its rituals and its possession of the land, which stretches into the future. Yet the distanced and unknowing perspective of the novel is retained in these last lines. '[H]e had come back' recalls the ANC slogan Mayibuye iAfrika! (Africa come back!), yet this is an image composed, as it were, from outside. The community are 'they' not 'we', not least because, as Neil Lazarus argued in 1986, the paradigmatic labour of the white South African writer, in this period at least, is to express her double alienation from her own racial community and from the insurgent masses.

> It would be too much to claim that these white writers [like Gordimer as well as Coetzee, André Brink and Breyten Breytenbach] write *for* the revolution. Such a task is no longer theirs, if, indeed, it ever was. Instead, they write *against* apartheid, where the core of their resistance consists in the practice of truth and in contestation of the legitimacy of official ideology.[72]

Incompatible experiences and conceptions of the land are not resolved in *The Conservationist*. The abstracted, alternately Romantic and rapacious, perspective of Mehring is adopted, explored and then hollowed out. That is all. 'The revolution I am involved in as a writer', according to another dissident white South African novelist, 'is a revolution in the conscience of my people'.[73] *The Conservationist* has little to say about the conscience of white South Africans except to infer that, notwithstanding André Brink's own courage and literary significance, this kind of searching analysis is a sideshow abutting the infinitely more important, though uncomprehended and independently undertaken as well as hopefully revolutionary, emergence of an alternative way of inhabiting the land, led this time by the people whom white South Africans dispossessed. A more durable and reciprocal inhabitation than Mehring's delusions of ownership is hinted at; its existence and its inevitable triumph are signalled and even urged. But it is not for this novel, for ethical as much as political reasons, to say what that alternative might be.

David Dabydeen's novel *Disappearance* (1993) also enjoins reflection on how history is inscribed in space. In this chapter we are emphasising the range of relational experiences of space and land. We should add, therefore, our conviction that Dabydeen's novel attends to the rival ways in which imaginings of a community's – or in this case a nation's – past and of its future are inseparable from the portrayal and imagination of territory. Directly political questions of ownership and belonging beseech attention to what we have been calling the experience of landscape, which involves abstract visions of place as well as closer, more material and even sensuous experiences of, for example, terrains, landscapes, topographies and flora. The novel paints a disquieting vision of England and of English history. The country is shown to be in thrall to a conservative – albeit warlike and embattled, as well as ethnocentric – pastoral dream of durability, order and whiteness. This is also a troubled England, therefore, figured symbolically by the crumbling cliffs of the novel's South coast setting and formally by the jumbled temporality of the novel's structure as well as by its characters' overt anxieties about race and imperial decline: 'the Empire had ended and what was left was palsied decay, like the state of the cliff'.[74] The novel's unstable and frankly messy temporal and spatial structure, which shuttles repeatedly between the narrator's past in Guyana and his present in a village in Kent, show how neither places nor periods are neatly separable. At a precise and meticulously registered moment in the country's history, namely the consolidation of the Thatcherite project in the early 1990s, a conservative vision of England is ironically in the course of being eroded, symbolically and in actuality. What will replace it, according to this intriguingly doleful and inconclusive text, is either an exceedingly combative rearguard assertion of ethnic and cultural 'purity' (epitomised by the 'dangerously patriotic sentiments' (D, 137) of the fascistic Mr Curtis) or, an eventuality the novel seems much less confident in forecasting, perhaps by a nation capable of looking its imperial history in the face and remaking itself along more inclusive and egalitarian lines.

It might seem odd for the crumbling cliff faces of the novel's fictional Kent village of Dunsmere to figure the early 1990s as a period of crisis for conservative visions of England and Englishness. After all, despite the defenestration of Prime Minister Margaret Thatcher by her ministers in 1990, the election of John Major's Tory government in 1992 presaged a radical entrenchment of Britain's new neoliberal settlement with the opening up of vast areas of the public sector to 'the market' and exploitation by private companies. Stuart Hall influentially characterised the Thatcherite project as a radically contradictory amalgam of traditional conservative themes, such as the family, law and order, militarism, the authority of the state and imperial nostalgia, with a brasher and more anarchic emphasis on individual liberty from the constraints of social bonds and government regulations.[75] This last plank of the Thatcher platform might equally be seen, as David Harvey's *Brief History of Neoliberalism* sees it, as an ideology of freedom belied by the much greater levels of social and economic insecurity and inequality, and the enfeebled social services brought about by such policies, or by the military and police power required to implement them. 'Freedom', for Harvey, is therefore an alibi for the anti-democratic and radically inegalitarian goal of restoring conditions for the profitable accumulation of capital by cutting taxes for the wealthy, hampering the powerful trade unions of the post-war period, encouraging consumer debt, handing over the assets of the state to rentiers and monopolists, and encouraging the City to stoke speculative booms in asset prices, stocks and so on.[76] So Thatcherism, that especially bellicose avatar of a fully global movement in the 1980s and 1990s, to reverse the gains of social democratic movements in the overdeveloped world and of liberation movements in the underdeveloped world, stands revealed as an essentially *counter-revolutionary* or 'revanchist'[77] project to restore everything from profits, inequality and social order to fantasies of national and imperial greatness, which is exactly how *Disappearance* portrays this anguished and uncertain period.

This is a novel that uses representations of space to think about the uses to which history is put and to think critically, in particular, about these restorationist visions of England's past. History, the novel posits, is always interested and constructed. What sort of narratives, it asks, do we tell in order to make sense of history and to navigate the cultural and political travails of the present? How did the counter-revolutionary project of Thatcherism conscript the past as an ally? And how might this recruitment of memories and fantasies of the past in the service of a restorationist political project in the present be effectively combatted? One reason why the novel seems so preoccupied by such questions, as Lucienne Loh[78] has argued, is the state-decreed transformation in this period of history into heritage and, as the novel illustrates, of heritage into pastoral visions of the land. Socialist historians like Patrick Wright, Raphael Samuel and Robert Hewison have characterised the National Heritage Acts of 1980, 1983 and 1997 and the setting up of the Department for National Heritage in 1992 as part of an official policy of conservation and restoration. If history has been seen by young Rudge in Alan Bennett's play *The History Boys* as 'one fucking thing after another', and by Marxists such as Walter Benjamin as one fucking thing after another alleviated by opportunities for resistance and occasionally for revolutionary transformation (the history of all hitherto existing society being the history of struggle, according to Marx and Engels), for English conservatives in this period and in this novel the past, by contrast, whether it is manifested in buildings or values or even social structures, is seen as something to be preserved in aspic.[79]

> National Heritage involves the extraction of history – of the idea of historical significance and potential – from a denigrated everyday life and its restaging or display in certain sanctioned sites, events, images and conceptions. In this process history is redefined as 'the historical', and it becomes the object of a similarly transformed and generalised public attention [...] Abstracted and redeployed, history seems to be purged of political tension; it becomes a unifying spectacle, the settling of all disputes. Like the guided tour as it proceeds from site to sanctioned site, the national past occurs in a dimension of its own – a dimension in which we appear to remember only in order to forget.[80]

What Patrick Wright is describing here, as we read him, is an ideology, evident as much in the popular culture of Raj Revivals and the flag-waving jamborees of royal weddings and the 1982 Falklands War as in official policies on urban development, conservation campaigns and the state-sanctioned homophobia of Section 28. That ideology aims not so much to conserve the past as concoct the past, in the same way that Eric Hobsbawm and Terence Ranger talk, in a really useful oxymoron, of inventing traditions.[81] The goal and effect is to censor the past by robbing it of its paradoxes and struggles and in so doing gain an advantage in the cultural and political struggles of the present. Instead of asking which past or whose past is being remembered in a particular ritual or memory or representation, the past is portrayed as something that is simply given and uncontroversial. History is not an arena of struggle, a multidimensional narrative to be thought through and contested but, figured as heritage, a continuum to be obediently safeguarded and maintained.[82]

In *Disappearance*, as Loh has cogently argued, this restorationist vision of the past is expressed above all by a reverence for the English countryside. The villagers of Dunsmere are committed to a pastoral vision of social order and hierarchy, of stability and ethnic homogeneity that is assailed symbolically by the encroaching waves and also challenged more ambiguously by the disconcerting but also, paradoxically, energising presence of the novel's narrator, a thirty-three-year-old unnamed Guyanese engineer charged with shoring up the coastal defences. What his stay makes possible, therefore, is an as yet unresolved (and, the novel's ending ominously implies, perhaps unresolvable) conflict between the amnesia and complacency of conservative (as well as Conservative) restoration and a quite different view of the past that tries hard to trace the many connections between English history and the crimes and outcomes of imperialism and thereby endeavours to open up a more egalitarian (and thus radically un-conservative) future. The novel engages but does not quite overcome a backward-looking construction that is objectionable precisely because it closes off various forms of change and transformation in the present and future.

So, images of the apparently timeless English countryside in *Disappearance* are part of a mourning or rather a melancholia, to use Paul Gilroy's Freudian term, for a lost Empire and its partly mythical social, racial and geographical order.[83] When our narrator visits Hastings with his garrulous landlady Janet Rutherford, she perceptively remarks that the daggers and other weapons unearthed by day-trippers on the beach are usually deprived of their complex and contestable meanings by being rapidly incorporated into a discourse of 'our heritage' (D, 92). The violent past thus 'takes on a certain glamour', the way the 'horror' of prehistoric 'biting-machines' become mere dinosaur bones, curiosities sketched by schoolchildren in a museum. Constructing the past as 'heritage' is a particularly slanted way of imagining the nation, its landscape and history. It makes history look like a narrative of continuity with an absence of radical change, something naturalised and grounded in inheritance, a story of property therefore, with a genetic element. Since the narrator and Mrs Rutherford find themselves in Hastings, myths of the 'island nation', from John of Gaunt's hyperbolic visions of 'This precious stone set in the silver sea/ Which serves it in the office of a wall,/ Or as a moat defensive to a house' in Shakespeare's *Richard II*, to Winston Churchill's island nation fighting on the beaches, are also at stake.[84]

But what other narratives of English history are being hinted at here? Loh's focus is on the ways in which Dabydeen's novel and texts like Caryl Phillips's *A Distant Shore* and V.S. Naipaul's *Enigma of Arrival* unearth the connections between the English countryside and the great biting-machine of British imperialism. We wish to place the emphasis instead on Dabydeen's central metaphorical device of the eroding coastline. For Loh,

> Dabydeen's *Disappearance* dislocates the *spatial* politics that have conventionally designated discourses about immigration as a largely metropolitan concern from which the various institutions and celebrants of rural England generally endeavour to distance themselves [...] [S]uch attitudes – bolstered particularly through narrowly defined beliefs about cultural, ethnic and racial essentialism housed within the heritage discourses institutionally sanctioned during the 1980s – frequently occlude histories that materially embed the English countryside within the violence and exploitation of British imperialism.[85]

Loh's skilful reading emerges from a distinguished anti-pastoral tradition in literary criticism associated most prominently with Raymond Williams' classic *The Country and the City*. She presents *Disappearance*, correctly we think, as a counter-pastoral text. The country, for Williams, has been seen in classic pastoral works such as Philip Sidney's *Arcadia* (1590) and Milton's *Lycidas* (1637) or in the sub-genre of sixteenth- and seventeenth-century country house poetry (one of Williams' main targets) and later in more politically conflicted ways in, say, Wordsworth and in Housman's *A Shropshire Lad* (1896) as a space outside history, a place of innocence, social harmony and tradition that contrasts favourably with the corruptions and worldliness of the city.[86] Williams analyses the country as a place constructed by and in history, specifically the history of the systematic dispossession of the English peasantry by enclosure since the sixteenth century. 'It is not easy to forget', for the materialist critic at least, Williams writes, 'that Sidney's *Arcadia*, which gives a continuing title to English neo-pastoral, was written in a park which had been made by enclosing a whole village and evicting the tenants. The elegant game was only at arm's length – a rough arm's length – from a visible reality of country life'.[87] What Williams merely hints at and Loh wonderfully amplifies is the fact that pastoral fantasies have also occluded the violence of colonial dispossession, visions of a bounded and harmonious as well as essentially timeless rural space shutting out the fraught history of colonial dispossession in which so much of the wealth of the British ruling class originates. Loh therefore shows that Dabydeen's narrator's discomfiting presence, plus his startled exposure of the villagers' militant investment in fantasies of cultural and racial homogeneity, place the messy history of empire at the centre of these conservative delusions of rural peace. This is what Rob Nixon has called 'postcolonial pastoral, writing that refracts an idealized nature through memories of environmental and cultural degradation in the colonies'.[88]

Yet there are two main landscapes heavily freighted with symbolic and ideological meaning in the novel. The narrator and Mrs Rutherford view them both from 'a raised mound of the cliffs'. On one side there is the 'green valley dissected into fields of barley and wheat' showing a long history of settlement and cultivation, 'a settled order', though one whose careful division into separate properties hints at 'centuries of plunder'. 'Nothing, it seemed, had happened to the village in living memory', though further back what had happened was clearly murder and theft. In front of the pair is 'the sea reaching for the shore, recoiling, pressing forwards again, a constant anxiety, like a disturbed patient pacing his room, or fidgeting within a straight-jacket' (D, 85). We want to think further about this insistent spatial metaphor of coastal erosion that Dabydeen uses in order to invite critical reflection on the extreme vulnerability of the pastoral space in which this revanchist conservative ideology is so invested. Our argument, in a nutshell, is that the novel presents British conservatism in the 1980s and 1990s as a doomed rearguard effort, like the coastal defences overseen by the narrator, to counter the inevitable erosion of these bogus certainties of national, cultural and racial homogeneity. The alternative to heritage discourse is not just a more clear-sighted conception of England's colonial past but a vision of the past that allows for a different kind of future, one that incorporates postcolonial subjects and does not seek to separate the island off from the continent and the globe to which the ever-encroaching tides connect it.

The name of the fictitious village of Dunsmere is a combination of the Gaelic prefix meaning 'fort' (like the semi-circular stone fort of Dún Aonghasa hundreds of feet above the cliffs on Inismór in the Aran Islands in County Galway) and the suffix 'mere' that refers in any number of European languages to a body of water. So the name ostensibly refers to a beleaguered and defensive space while its diverse etymology recalls something of the trans- or perhaps pre-national connectedness of early medieval Europe. Dunsmere also recalls Dunwich, the tiny hamlet in Suffolk in the East of England, 'Britain's Atlantis', that was one of the largest towns and trading ports in medieval England before most it was washed away by tidal surges in the thirteenth century. And the proximity of Dunsmere to Hastings allows the narrator to meditate not only on 'the havoc wrought by the sea' but also on a mythologised history of victimhood, 'piracy and plunder by foreign barbarians' (as the narrator semi-ironically puts it) and the 'wave upon wave' of violent raids (D, 26). The Norman Conquest itself, secured of course at William I's victory at the Battle of Hastings in 1066, echoes through the novel as it does through every narrative of English history. Representations of the Norman Conquest have been put to various political uses. Most obviously, there is the chauvinistic and self-congratulatory narrative of English exceptionalism, in which the English flatter themselves that they have resisted foreign invasion for the best part of a thousand years. This is the variant of English nationalism that continues to find expression in jingoistic stunts like the *Sun* 'newspaper' projecting its masthead and 'SEE EU LATER' on to the equally ideologically freighted location of the white cliffs of Dover in March 2017 to mark the triggering of Article 50 and the UK's departure from the European Union. On the other hand, there is the potent but ambiguous myth of the Norman Yoke, the narrative of English history that sees class oppression originating in the Norman usurpation of the Saxon monarchy. Feeding into the Robin Hood myths and into radical political discourse from the medieval period through the radical currents in the Civil War and the writings of Thomas Paine, the removal of the Norman Yoke of class rule becomes the objective of a radically egalitarian and republican politics. As Joe Kennedy argues, however, the myth of the 'Norman Yoke' itself has also recently fed into reactionary ideas about 'authentic' Englishness. Today it is visible most obviously in the defensive postures of the 'hostile environment' and in culture-war rhetoric about deracinated metropolitan elites but also in the patriotic bluster of 'Blue Labour' centrists who think that anti-immigration policies are the best way to address the 'legitimate concerns' of the 'traditional' (a euphemism for 'white') working class. The myth is invoked more explicitly in Paul Kingsnorth's Brexity 2014 novel *The Wake*, written in a form of Old English and focusing on a Saxon smallholder's terrorist campaign against his new Norman masters. Kennedy shows how 'the idea that the "real English" have been oppressed by an alien ruling class since 1066 is a way of turning very specific concerns about class and property into specious ones about cultural sovereignty'.[89] This is a way of channelling real economic discontents into cultural grievances, as has happened in Britain, and especially England, since the injection of the Brexit poison in 2016. There are multiple ways of utilising the past politically therefore, though the dominant ones are still, alas, chauvinistic narratives of exceptionalism on which separatist and imperialist endeavours have been based.

What is missing, of course, is any understanding or narrative of the past that will allow the narrator and postcolonial subjects to claim and articulate a place in England, which is presumably why he himself 'disappears' at the end of the novel in a mood of disappointed resignation to return to Guyana. The reader and the narrator learn several things from the latter's conversations in the book-lined and African artefact-festooned drawing room and in the meticulously tended garden of his elderly landlady. One is the powerful and durable commitment of the English to pastoral visions of beauty, property and purity in which the nation is figured as a carefully bounded and ruthlessly cultivated garden. Another lesson is the appalling, and therefore largely repressed, story of empire, slowly revealed by Mrs Rutherford's revelations of her estranged husband's history of sexual abuse in African schools. The narrator's exasperating and ill-tempered exchanges with his Irish foreman Christie, who may or may not be performing the ironical part of stage Irishman, also drives home this message about the significance and the durability of imperialist power relations. This is a novel in which those relations are confusingly compounded by the narrator's alarming prejudices about the indolence and haplessness of his Guyanese compatriots and by his merely temporary sojourn at Mrs Rutherford's, at the same time as they are radically undercut by Christie's sardonic presence and the pleasing historical irony or inversion of a black West Indian engineer directing an obstinate group of white workers as they shore up the sea defences of a Kentish village. Whether strolling the cliffs with Mrs Rutherford's irascible pooch, marvelling at the 'mythic power' (D, 68) of her garden or feeling browbeaten beneath the Malian masks displayed on the whitewashed walls of her cottage, the narrator is not, as little by little he and we realise, 'in the presence of a venerable England' inhabited by 'keepers of the ritual of lighting up the darkness' (D, 15). These myths and amnesias are defence mechanisms against change and seemingly disruptive social forces and threats.

As we have said, the incessant movement of the narrative backwards and forwards through time and hither and thither through space (between the past in Guyana and the present in Kent) shows how neither places nor periods are neatly separable. But this kind of dense interconnectedness is difficult to locate at the level of content in this narrative of confusions, misunderstandings and departures. Since the history of Britain and of the Caribbean are so densely intertwined (because, as Dabydeen has put it, 'Britain depended upon us heavily for its material and cultural advance'), the possibility of surmounting these ideologies of belonging depends on the elaboration of what Dabydeen calls 'a kind of vision: our cultures have become so intimately enmeshed over the centuries, that you cannot be Guyanese without being British, and you cannot be British without being Guyanese or Caribbean'.[90] But this vision of postcolonial inclusion and connectedness is only gestured at very tentatively in the novel. The narrator succeeds in shoring up the village's defences literally (with the sea wall, though he admits that it will one day collapse) and the nation's defences symbolically (since he obligingly disappears at the end of the novel). Indeed, the novel appears to vindicate Dabydeen's own view that whatever possibility there is for inclusion and transformation in Britain's cities there is no possibility that this 'deep England' can be colonised in return: 'I can't live in the English rural landscape. I don't feel committed to England [...] Migration is too young a process for us to evolve into the landscape and creolize it' by naming its flora and fauna and thus overcoming the landscape's use as a series of icons in the arsenal of English nationalism and imperialism.[91]

The flowers in Mrs Rutherford's garden are, for her, 'rooted in English history' with their vernacular names and their special uses and connotations, the way the seed heads of teasels recall Roman colonisation and red poppies immediately evoke military sacrifice; for the narrator, by contrast, this exorbitantly patriotic investment makes them 'tired symbols of some monumental stupidity' (*D*, 65), a verdict as damning as it is unspecific. Indeed, it takes the narrator's outsider perspective to notice the ruthless exclusion of 'people black like myself' from 'a garden they could never possess, being holed up in poverty and city slums'. He observes on his trips to London that immigrants and their descendants 'live mostly in boxes made of concrete or brick, high up in the air, where the only evidence of nature was pollen irritating their noses'; he sees 'rows upon rows of tower blocks flowering from asphalt and garbage' (*D*, 68). 'Nature' is named, occupied and owned by those who flatter themselves that they are the land's native inhabitants, privileges that postcolonial subjects are denied. This is a situation that the narrator's radically defamiliarising idiom can make us see and regret but which, in this novel at least, seems frustratingly difficult to shift.

Two possibilities are countenanced by the novel. One is that Britain, or rather England, will continue to invent its own past in a way that stymies its future. The other possibility is that England and Britain as a whole will find in the past the resources for devising and implementing a substantively different, more egalitarian and genuinely *post*colonial condition. Alas, the first seems more likely. Several years before the start of the novel Mr Curtis, a fellow villager who appears now to have retreated into a state of bitter reclusiveness, started a grassroots organisation to save his house and the village from the waves. The narrator rummages through a cache of newspaper clippings towards the end both of his sojourn and of the novel, the consequent revelations about Mr Curtis's 'dangerously patriotic' (*D*, 137) Committee for the Defence of Dunsmere providing the culmination of his and our insight into the repulsive truth concealed by his initial delusions about a 'venerable England'. Having inched his house away from the cliffs using jacks and scaffolding poles, the King Canute-like Mr Curtis had subsequently sought to inspire the whole village to order back the tides in a packed meeting in the Church Hall. He berates his opponents as 'cowards' (*D*, 130) and promotes jingoistic myths of 'foreign invasions' and 'barbarians from Europe who laid waste to the villages in acts of unimaginable sadism'. The campaign is in part a blatant and parodic figure for the belligerent nationalism of Thatcherism, that other destructive but doomed defensive action against European assailants and '*collaborators*', the '*enemy within*' as Mr Curtis calls his faint-hearted compatriots and as Thatcher dubbed the striking miners of the NUM.[92] Indeed, Mr Curtis's campaign and the assorted complacencies of the villagers closely and mockingly reproduce the inflated rhetoric of high Thatcherism. Mr Curtis '*spoke of courage, of the soul of the nation that had survived two world wars and triumphed* *over tyranny, and of the corruption of virtue by unpatriotic bureaucrats and time-servers'* (D, 132, emphasis in original). Mrs Rutherford congratulates the narrator on the completion of his coastal scheme ('"you should rejoice in the visibility of your handiwork. Rejoice!"' [D, 154]), echoing Thatcher's notoriously hyperbolic announcement of the conquest of the penguin-populated archipelago of South Georgia in the early stages of the Falklands War as she elbowed aside the Defence Secretary John Nott on the steps of 10 Downing Street: 'Just rejoice at that news!' The crumbling state of the cliff, the Defence Committee argues, resembles the 'disintegration of family values' and 'the disgraceful state of the nation as a whole'. Aggressively combatting rumours of national '*decline*', the Defence Committee, like the Thatcherite junta provoking insurrections in the inner cities and resorting to military-style policing operations in the coalfields of South Yorkshire, 'plunged the village into a state bordering on civil war' (D, 135).

Sounding virtually the full panoply of her characteristic themes, from 'family values' to belligerent jingoism and imperial nostalgia, the Defence Committee's desperate rhetoric mirrors the equally anxious and, as we have been arguing, effectively counter-revolutionary aspirations of the Thatcherite project. The novel brings down the curtain with the narrator's admission that Dunsmere's sea defences are doomed sooner or later to be inundated. Moreover, the revelation that these callow villagers have been browbeaten into supporting a doomed defensive scheme by a bellicose windbag who resembles 'the ferrety Enoch Powell' (as Jumpy Joshi calls that poster boy of Tory racism in another scathing tour d'horizon of Thatcher's Britain, Salman Rushdie's *The Satanic Verses*) as much as he does Thatcher, constitutes a bracingly uncompromising critique not just of the illiberal priorities of the British state but also of the vacuous nostalgia, credulity and fearfulness of the people.[93] The Committee for the Defence of Dunsmere is a composite of thuggish racism, bourgeois provincialism and doomed but destructive revanchist fantasies of reclaimed territory and of a restored social and racial order. It's therefore a kind of stand-in for, or even a baleful prophecy of, any number of reactionary political platforms, including not just Thatcherism but also the National Front and the current English Defence League, the UK Independence Party (and its spin-off the Brexit Party) as well as a painfully triumphant post-Brexit Toryism in which oligarchic interests are fused with Powellite xenophobia.

If the narrator gradually learns to question the timeless certainties of the English countryside and the idea of race and of belonging that it symbolises, then he is also struggling to come to terms with his 'shame' over his own origins in what he presents problematically as the wild backlands of Guyana. He seems to concur with the view that if England represents order, then Guyana is disorder, reproducing as he does so Orientalist tropes of backwardness, stasis, despotism and incapacity for self-government. Yet Guyana, he realises, is a place of violence, dispossession and poverty and by the conclusion he is committed to constructing a different kind of country in the future with the aid of his own knowledge and technical expertise. This is a tentative affirmation of a future freed from the burdens of the past. There is no celebration of Guyana however, no idealised or sentimentalised affirmation of a racial or national heritage, perhaps because militant assertions of naturalised or biological forms of identity allied to exclusionary spaces and carefully censored histories are the most grievous legacy of colonial power: 'I'm *me*', the narrator informs us disarmingly, 'not a mask or a movement of history. I'm not black, I'm an engineer!'

In the final lines of the novel, as the train carrying the narrator away from Dunsmere leaves the station, he takes from his pocket a flower he had 'picked by the wayside on my first day at work'. Now flattened and brittle, 'yet still retaining some of its violent colour', he holds it 'carefully in the cup of my hand, appalled that the slightest movement could cause it to flake and disappear' (*D*, 157). This is a radically ambiguous as well as ambivalent ending. Does the unnamed flower betoken an uncoupling of the land from the designations with which the likes of Mrs Rutherford and Mr Curtis have monopolised it? Alternatively, does its beauty symbolise the durable pull of English pastoral fantasies to which even the narrator seems attached? Is its 'violent' colour a surreptitious reminder of the bloodshed and brutality of both the rural and especially the colonial past? Desiccated and deceased, artificially or fortuitously preserved and soon to vanish, can the flower be read as a premonition of the imminent disappearance of those fantasies? Is the narrator's gentle appreciation of this forgotten flower a hopeful mark of his increasing affection for a place that has effectively excluded him? Is it treasured therefore as a reminder of his equally fragile but affectionate friendship with the surprisingly hospitable Mrs Rutherford? What is about to disappear at the end of *Disappearance* is the land, the inevitable erosion of which, we have been arguing, is an extended spatial metaphor for the wearing away of the complacencies of English nationalism and imperialism. Whether that disappearance will prompt rearguard efforts to shore these things up or whether it will commence the pulling down of these defences and a working through of the legacies and actualities of nationalism and imperialism, is a question that is left unanswered by the narrator and by the novel, as it remains unanswered in the 'hostile environment' of contemporary Britain.

The term 'hostile environment' refers, of course, to the aims of the 2014 Immigration Act that removed the protection from enforced removal of Commonwealth citizens who arrived in the UK before 1971 by requiring them to provide detailed proof of their residence. The Act requires landlords, bank clerks, health workers and others to check people's immigration status. Without these pieces of paper, British citizens have been denied work, access to healthcare, security in old age and in some cases they have been deported. The government had been warned repeatedly for years that the policy would affect this group of British citizens in this way, warnings that were ignored. A policy designed to turn us all into border guards and snoops has spread anxiety among immigrants and their descendants and compounded the long-standing fear that they must constantly assert and prove their right to belong. Needless to say, the government's response to public outrage has been woeful, though interestingly it does seem to have made a mistake in appearing to believe that the woes of a few elderly citizens born in the Caribbean would not prick the nation's conscience and would be a very small price to pay for outflanking anti-immigrant parties to the right of the Tories. Fifty years since the ferrety Powell's 'rivers of blood' speech, people have been talking about the contributions made by immigrants who came here to work, raise families, build communities and transform a country blighted by insularity and racism and that greeted the Windrush generation with hostility and often violence.

These are the rival possibilities facing the country – insularity and openness. They are neatly encapsulated and made available for critical scrutiny by the ambiguous spatial metaphor and by the competing historical narratives of *Disappearance*. All of Dabydeen's fiction in this phase of his work, especially *The Intended* (1991), is tellingly marked by this kind of radically conflicted and ambivalent attitude to the nation's future. There is a commitment to displaying formally and in other ways the sheer bamboozling but often also exhilarating messiness and impurity of identities, communities and histories. Yet Dabydeen's narrators seem curiously unwilling to renounce intensely dubious preoccupations with the colonised or neo-colonised world's supposed barbarity and muddle or to overcome their desire for assimilation into a nation symbolised by great literature, orderliness and pristine whiteness. But, nonetheless, the future remains unwritten in these teasingly inconclusive texts and the authority of these frequently unselfconscious chroniclers is methodically hollowed out: 'I only know *now*, and what used to be', *The Intended*'s narrator tells us in conclusion, but not what is to come.[94] We learn about the impossibility of purity and the extreme difficulty and inadvisability of assimilation on the terms of a dominant culture that is discredited and clapped out. Creative and critical energies question purity and exclusionary forms of belonging. As C.L. Innes argues in her *History of Black and Asian Writing in Britain*, visions of Britain (and especially, as *Disappearance* shows, visions of England that mistake that country for the whole of these islands) must 'be continually invented and reinvented' to accommodate new perspectives and experiences. This process of reinvention, we suggest, takes place through our understandings of history and our portrayals of space and place.[95]

In conclusion we wish to stress two things. First, experiences of the land are relational. There are so many different ways of occupying, experiencing, imagining and representing the contested territories in which colonial power relations are fought out. The various texts we have been reading do not try to encompass or think through them all. That is the second thing we want to point out. Other experiences and modes of inhabitation, we've been saying, often remain simply other in the sense of being unknown. Territory can never be grasped or mapped in its entirety. Nor can conflicts over land and place be precipitately or definitively resolved, or at least the various texts that we've been reading do not try to do so. What the texts share is this sense – plain to us all perhaps, especially in a century in which conflicts over shifting and shrinking territory and over potentially scarce resources will impose themselves even more insistently than ever before – that human beings see and experience the land in clashing and perhaps incompatible ways. As the marvellously perceptive and obstreperous Alsana Begum puts it in Zadie Smith's *White Teeth*, the 'real difference between people was not colour' or gender or faith but 'was far more fundamental. It was in the earth. It was in the sky. You could divide the whole of humanity into two distinct camps', those 'who live on solid ground, underneath safe skies' and those whose vulnerability to monsoons, earthquakes and catastrophic storms betokens a precarious dependency on nature.[96] But a process that is underway in the earth and in the sky is robbing the earth's ruling classes of the delusion that they can escape the bonds of nature and the burdens of solidarity. Our experiences of land may be relational, historically inflected and both politically and economically varied, but in the next century the warming climate will remind us starkly of the existence of a common world.

Notes

1 Graham Huggan and Helen Tiffin, *Postcolonial Ecocriticism: Literature, Animals, Environment*, London: Routledge, 2010.
2 Ibid., p. 17.
3 Fawzia Afzal-Khan and Kalpana Seshadri-Crooks, *The Pre-occupation of Postcolonial Studies*, Durham, NC: Duke University Press, 2000.
4 See Amitav Ghosh, *The Great Derangement: Climate Change and the Unthinkable*, Chicago, IL: University of Chicago Press, 2016.
5 Eyal Weizman and Fazal Sheikh, *The Conflict Shoreline*, Brooklyn, NY: Steidl in Association with Cabinet Books, 2015.
6 Ibid., p. 36.
7 Huggan and Tiffin, *Postcolonial Ecocriticism*, p. 18.
8 Witi Ihimaera, *The Whale Rider*, Auckland: Reed Books, 1987.
9 Kate Grenville, *The Secret River*. Edinburgh: Canongate, 2006.
10 Erin James, *The Storyworld Accord: Econarratology and Postcolonial Narratives*, Lincoln, NE and London: University of Nebraska Press, 2015.
11 Ibid., p. xv.
12 Ibid., p. 4, emphasis added.
13 Ibid., p. 27.
14 Sally Morgan, *My Place*, London: Virago, 1987.
15 *Jedda*, 1955, dir. Charles Chauvel.

16 Q&A with Barbara Creed, CIDRAL public lecture, 'Darwin and the Cinema: Evolutionary Aesthetics, the Emotions & Sexual Display in Film', May 2012, University of Manchester.
17 The cinematographic wide vista is a feature of many films of course, including westerns.
18 Barbara Creed, 'Breeding out the Black: *Jedda* and Stolen Generations in Australia', in Barbara Creed and Jeanette Hoorn (eds), *Body Trade: Captivity, Cannibalism and Colonialism in the Pacific*, New York: Routledge, 2001, pp. 208–230.
19 *Jindabyne*, dir. Ray Lawrence, 2007.
20 Grenville, *The Secret River*, p. 4.
21 Ibid., p. 5.
22 Val Plumwood, 'Decolonizing Relationships with Nature', in Bill Ashcroft, Gareth Griffiths and Helen Tiffin (eds), *The Postcolonial Studies Reader*, Second Edition, London: Routledge, 2005, pp. 503–506.
23 Ibid., p. 503, emphasis added.
24 Ibid., p. 504.
25 Grenville, *The Secret River*, p. 77.
26 Huggan and Tiffin, *Postcolonial Ecocriticism*. pp. 7–8.
27 Alexis Wright, *Carpentaria*, Edinburgh: Constable, 2008, p. 3.
28 Ibid., p. 4.
29 Ibid., emphasis in original.
30 Grenville, *The Secret River*, p. 90.
31 Bob Hodge and Vijay Mishra, 'Aboriginal Place', in Bill Ashcroft, Gareth Griffiths and Helen Tiffin (eds), *The Postcolonial Studies Reader*, Second Edition, London: Routledge, 2005, pp. 359–363, p. 359.
32 Wright, *Carpentaria*, p. 50.
33 Kirsty Reid, *Gender, Crime and Empire: Convicts, Settlers and the State in Early Colonial Australia*, Manchester: Manchester University Press, 2007.
34 Grenville, *The Secret River*, p. 82.
35 Ibid., p. 322.
36 Ibid., p. 327.
37 Ibid., 333.
38 Sue Kossew, 'Voicing the "Great Australian Silence?" Kate Grenville's Narrative of Settlement in *The Secret River*', in *The Journal of Commonwealth Literature*, 42:7 (2007), 7–18.
39 Ibid., p. 8, emphasis added.
40 Ibid., p. 13.
41 Wright, *Carpentaria*, p. 104.
42 Douglas Keesey, 'Weir(d) Australia: *Picnic at Hanging Rock* and *The Last Wave*', in *LIT: Literature Interpretation Theory*, 8:3–4 (1998), 331–346, 332.
43 Stephen Moss, 'Dream Warrior', *The Guardian*, 15 April 2008.
44 Ibid.
45 Bruno Davis, *Landscapes, Rock-Art and the Dreaming: An Archaeology of Preunderstanding*, Leicester: Leicester University Press, 2002, p. 25.
46 Doris Pilkington, *Rabbit-Proof Fence: The True Story of One of the Greatest Escapes of All Time*, White Plains, NY: Hyperion Press, Two Editions, 1996, 2002, pp. xiii–xiv.
47 Ibid., p. xiii.

48 Marek Haltof, 'The Spirit of Australia in Picnic at Hanging Rock: A Case Study in Film Adaptation', in *The Canadian Review of Comparative Literature*, 23:3 (1996), 809–822, 817.
49 Ibid., p. 821.
50 Ibid., p. 821.
51 Elizabeth A. Povinelli, *The Cunning of Recognition: Indigenous Alterities and the Making of Australian Multiculturalism*, Durham, NC: Duke University Press, 2002, pp. 161–162.
52 Jonathan Rayner, 'Adapting Australian Film: Ray Lawrence from *Bliss* to *Jindabyne*', in *Studies in Australasian Cinema*, 3:3 (2009), 295–308.
53 Ibid., 301.
54 Ibid., 302.
55 Elspeth Tilley, 'The Uses of Fear: Spatial Politics in the Australian Whiter-vanishing Trope', *Antipodes*, 23:1 (2009), 33–41, 33.
56 Ibid., p. 38.
57 Gareth Griffiths, 'The Myth of Authenticity', in Bill Ashcroft, Gareth Griffiths and Helen Tiffin (eds), *The Postcolonial Studies Reader*, Second Edition, London: Routledge, 2005, pp. 165–168, p. 166.
58 Ibid., p. 166.
59 Elizabeth A. Povinelli, *Geontologies: A Requiem to Late Liberalism*, Durham, NC: Duke University Press, 2016, p. 59.
60 Ibid., p. 59.
61 Liz Watkins, 'A View from Elsewhere: Ellipsis and Desire in *Walkabout* (Nicolas Roeg, 1971)', *Parallax*, 16:2 (2010), 107–117, 113.
62 Suneeti Rekhari, 'The "Other" in Film: Exclusions of Aboriginal Identity from Australian Cinema', *Visual Anthropology*, 21:2 (2008), 125–135, 127.
63 Arlene A. Elder, 'Silence as Expression: Sally Morgan's *My Place*', *Kunapipi*, 14:1 (1992), 16–24, 17.
64 Ibid., p. 17.
65 Povinelli, *The Cunning of Recognition*.
66 Gareth Griffiths, 'The Myth of Authenticity', p. 168.
67 Ibid., p. 168.
68 Nadine Gordimer, *The Conservationist*, London: Bloomsbury, 2005 [1974], p. 1. Subsequent references to the novel after given after C in brackets in the main text.
69 J.M. Coetzee, 'Jerusalem Prize Acceptance Speech (1987)', *Doubling the Point: Essays and Interviews*, Cambridge, MA: Harvard University Press, 1992, pp. 96–99, p. 97.
70 J.M. Coetzee, *White Writing: On the Culture of Letters in South Africa*, New Haven, CT: Yale University Press, 1988, p. 3.
71 Ibid., p. 4.
72 Neil Lazarus, 'T.W. Adorno and Contemporary White South African Literature', *Cultural Critique*, 5 (1986–1987), 131–155, 155, emphasis in original.
73 André Brink, *Mapmakers: Writing in a State of Siege*, London: Faber & Faber, 1983, p. 53.
74 David Dabydeen, *Disappearance*, Leeds: Peepal Tree Press, 2005 [1993], p. 118. Subsequent references are given after D in brackets in the main text.
75 Stuart Hall, *The Hard Road to Renewal: Thatcherism and the Crisis of the Left*, London: Verso, 1988, pp. 39–56.

76 David Harvey, *A Brief History of Neoliberalism*, Oxford: Oxford University Press, 2005, pp. 5–38.
77 We take this term from Neil Smith.

> However much camouflaged by economists' diagrams and equations and the homilies of conservative, social individualism, neoliberalism was also a quite direct strategy of class struggle. A weapon of reaction and revenge – revanchism – it was designed to take back for the ruling classes and their professional and managerial consorts the 'losses' that twentieth-century 'liberalism' has visited on them.
> (Neil Smith, *The Endgame of Globalization*, London: Routledge, 2005, pp. 143–144)

78 Lucienne Loh, *The Postcolonial Country in Contemporary Literature*, Basingstoke: Palgrave, 2013, p. 88.
79 Karl Marx and Friedrich Engels, *The Communist Manifesto*, Harmondsworth: Penguin, 1971 [1888], p. 79. Walter Benjamin, 'Theses on the Philosophy of History', *Illuminations*, ed. Hannah Arendt, trans. Harry Zohn, London: Fontana, 1992 [1940], pp. 245–255.
80 Patrick Wright, *On Living in an Old Country: The National Past in Contemporary Britain*, London: Verso, 1985, pp. 69–70. See also Robert Hewison, *The Heritage Industry: Britain in a Climate of Decline*, London: Methuen, 1987; and Raphael Samuel, *Theatres of Memory: Past and Present in Contemporary Culture*, London: Verso, 2012 [1994].
81 The contributors to Hobsbawm's and Ranger's collection are interested in how state authority is reinforced by the careful censoring of the past in manufactured myths of longevity and continuity in, for example, European nationalisms of the nineteenth century, colonial East Africa and Victorian India. *The Invention of Tradition*, ed. Eric Hobsbawm and Terence Ranger, Cambridge: Cambridge University Press, 2012 [1983].
82 An even more topical example of how political possibilities can be closed off by a stale longing for an invented past is the British austerity cult vividly excoriated by Owen Hatherley's *The Ministry of Nostalgia*, London: Verso, 2016. In everything from retro architectural and interior design trends to 'Keep Calm and Carry On' merchandise and its ubiquitous tongue-in-cheek offshoots, Hatherley traces a politically detrimental conflation of post-war austerity with the current Tory version. If the original wartime poster, aimed for distribution in the event of a German invasion, was intended to stiffen the sinews of a people's war against fascism while wider austerity nostalgia recalls the resultant construction of the welfare state, full employment, the building of comprehensive systems of health care and education, plus a massive programme of social housebuilding, the contemporary version means the exact opposite of all that – tax cuts for the wealthy, benefit cuts for the most vulnerable, bank bailouts and the destruction of what remains of the public sphere and collective provision. Nostalgia, once again, amounts to a politically consequential bowdlerisation of the past.
83 Paul Gilroy, *After Empire: Melancholia or Convivial Culture?* London: Routledge, 2004.

84 Robert Colls has written compellingly of the persistent investment in English art of these ideas of an untainted landscape outside of the history of class and colonial dispossession.

> English history increasingly became identified with a certain look of the land. People were invited to view territory as 'landscape' – a right and a wrong way of looking. Strangely, English landscape painters had found their golden age during the heaviest years of parliamentary enclosure. Their invitation to view the countryside turned the countryside into just a view. Those who did the painting and those who did the viewing, therefore, repossessed not the land but the meaning of the land. 'Emparking' was a fine word for a kind of enclosure that turned land into landscape by clearing out all those who lived there [...] All the books about rural England which followed in the wake of enclosure and were simultaneous with the agricultural depression of 1870–1940 knew the same: that if the land was to be valued in meaning as well as in money, then it had to look pretty. As pretty as a picture, in fact.
> (Robert Colls, *Identity of England*, Oxford: Oxford University Press, 2002, pp. 235–236)

85 Loh, *The Postcolonial Country*, p. 88.
86 Though for Williams pastoral is almost always an ideological distraction from social and economic injustices and struggles in any given era, its elegiac craving for a prelapsarian state of social and natural harmony is also an expression of discontent with the corruptions and unhappiness of the present. Pastoral is both ideological *and* critical.
87 Raymond Williams, *The Country and the City*, London: Hogarth Press, 1985 [1973], p. 22.
88 Rob Nixon, 'Environmentalism and Postcolonialism', in Ania Loomba, Suvir Kaul, Matti Bunzl, Antoinette Burton and Jed Esty (eds), *Postcolonial Studies and Beyond*, Durham, NC: Duke University Press, 2005, pp. 233–251, p. 239.
89 Joe Kennedy, *Authentocrats: Culture, Politics and the New Seriousness*, London: Left Book Club, 2018, pp. 159–160.
90 David Dabydeen interviewed by Wolfgang Binder, *Journal of West Indian Literature*, 3:2 (1989), 67–80, 72. 'In almost all his works,' as C.L. Innes has argued, 'Dabydeen sets up a linguistic and aesthetic struggle between the cultural traditions and experiences framed by the Western canon and histories and experiences which he as the descendant of a Guyanan plantation worker seeks to express.' Long poems and poem cycles like *Slave Song* (1984), *Coolie Odyssey* (1988) and *Turner* (1994) reflect on the long interconnections between the English artistic canon, British history and the colonial history of slavery and indentured labour. C.L. Innes, *A History of Black and Asian Writing in Britain, 1700–2000*, Cambridge: Cambridge University Press, 2002, p. 240.
91 David Dabydeen, Interview with Kwame Dawes, *The Art of David Dabydeen*, ed. Kevin Grant, Leeds: Peepal Tree Press, 1997, pp. 199–221, pp. 218–219.
92 One of the definitive accounts of the unsuccessful year-long strike by the National Union of Mineworkers in 1984–1985, and of the violence, smears and

skulduggery used to defeat it, is Seumas Milne's *The Enemy Within: The Secret War Against the Miners*, London: Verso, 2014.
93 Salman Rushdie, *The Satanic Verses*, London: Vintage, 1988, p. 186.
94 David Dabydeen, *The Intended*, Leeds: Peepal Tree Press, 2005 [1991], p. 173, emphasis in original.
95 Innes, *A History of Black and Asian Writing in Britain*, p. 244.
96 Zadie Smith, *White Teeth*, Harmondsworth: Penguin, 2000, pp. 210–211.

Bibliography

Benjamin, W., 'Theses on the Philosophy of History', in Hannah Arendt (ed), *Illuminations*, trans. Harry Zohn, London: Fontana, 1992 [1940], pp. 245–255.
Brink, A., *Mapmakers: Writing in a State of Siege*, London: Faber & Faber, 1983.
Coetzee, J.M., *White Writing: On the Culture of Letters in South Africa*, New Haven, CT: Yale University Press, 1988.
Coetzee, J.M., 'Jerusalem Prize Acceptance Speech (1987)', *Doubling the Point: Essays and Interviews*, Cambridge, MA: Harvard University Press, 1992, pp. 96–99.
Colls, R., *Identity of England*, Oxford: Oxford University Press, 2002.
Dabydeen, D., 'Interview by Wolfgang Binder', *Journal of West Indian Literature*, 3:2 (1989), 67–80.
Dabydeen, D., 'Interview with Kwame Dawes', in Kevin Grant (ed), *The Art of David Dabydeen*, Leeds: Peepal Tree Press, 1997, pp. 199–221.
Dabydeen, D., *The Intended*, Leeds: Peepal Tree Press, 2005 [1991].
Dabydeen, D., *Disappearance*, Leeds: Peepal Tree Press, 2005 [1993].
Davis, B., *Landscapes, Rock-Art and the Dreaming: An Archaeology of Preunderstanding*, Leicester: Leicester University Press, 2002.
Elder, A.A., 'Silence as Expression: Sally Morgan's *My Place*', *Kunapipi*, 14:1 (1992), 16–24.
Ghosh, A., *The Great Derangement: Climate Change and the Unthinkable*, Chicago, IL: University of Chicago Press, 2016.
Gilroy, P., *After Empire: Melancholia or Convivial Culture?* London: Routledge, 2004.
Gordimer, N., *The Conservationist*, London: Bloomsbury, 2005 [1974].
Grenville, K., *The Secret River*. Edinburgh: Canongate, 2006.
Griffiths, G., 'The Myth of Authenticity', in Bill Ashcroft, Gareth Griffiths and Helen Tiffin (eds), *The Postcolonial Studies Reader*, Second Edition, London: Routledge, 2005, 165–168.
Hall, S., *The Hard Road to Renewal: Thatcherism and the Crisis of the Left*, London: Verso, 1988, pp. 39–56.
Haltof, M., 'The Spirit of Australia in Picnic at Hanging Rock: A Case Study in Film Adaptation', *The Canadian Review of Comparative Literature*, 23:3 (1996).
Harvey, D., *A Brief History of Neoliberalism*, Oxford: Oxford University Press, 2005, pp. 5–38.
Hatherley, O., *The Ministry of Nostalgia*, London: Verso, 2016.
Hewison, R., *The Heritage Industry: Britain in a Climate of Decline*, London: Methuen, 1987.
Hobsbawm, E. and Ranger, T. (eds), *The Invention of Tradition*, Cambridge: Cambridge University Press, 2012 [1983].

Hodge, B. and Mishra, V., 'Aboriginal Place', in Bill Ashcroft, Gareth Griffiths and Helen Tiffin (eds), *The Postcolonial Studies Reader*, Second Edition, London: Routledge, 2005.

Huggan, G. and Tiffin, H., *Postcolonial Ecocriticism: Literature, Animals, Environment*, London: Routledge, 2010.

Ihimaera, W., *The Whale Rider*, Auckland: Reed Books, 1987.

Innes, C.L., *A History of Black and Asian Writing in Britain, 1700–2000*, Cambridge: Cambridge University Press, 2002.

James, E., *The Storyworld Accord: Econarratology and Postcolonial Narratives*, Lincoln, NE and London: University of Nebraska Press, 2015.

Keesey, D., 'Weir(d) Australia: *Picnic at Hanging Rock* and *The Last Wave*', *LIT: Literature Interpretation Theory*, 8 (1998), 3–4.

Kennedy, J., *Authentocrats: Culture, Politics and the New Seriousness*, London: Left Book Club, 2018.

Khan, F.A. and Crooks, K.S., *The Pre-occupation of Postcolonial Studies*, Durham, NC: Duke University Press, 2000.

Kossew, S., 'Voicing the "Great Australian Silence?" Kate Grenville's Narrative of Settlement in *The Secret River*', *Journal of Commonwealth Literature*, 42:2 (2007), 7–18.

Lazarus, N., 'T.W. Adorno and Contemporary White South African Literature', *Cultural Critique*, 5 (1986–1987), 131–155.

Loh, L., *The Postcolonial Country in Contemporary Literature*, Basingstoke: Palgrave, 2013.

Marx, K. and Engels, F., *The Communist Manifesto*, Harmondsworth: Penguin, 1971 [1888].

Milne, S., *The Enemy Within: The Secret War Against the Miners*, London: Verso, 2014.

Morgan, S., *My Place*, London: Virago, 1987.

Moss, S. 'Dream Warrior', *The Guardian*, 15 April 2008.

Nixon, R., 'Environmentalism and Postcolonialism', in Ania Loomba, Suvir Kaul, Matti Bunzl, Antoinette Burton and Jed Esty (eds), *Postcolonial Studies and Beyond*, Durham, NC: Duke University Press, 2005, pp. 233–251.

Pilkington, D., *Rabbit-Proof Fence: The True Story of One of the Greatest Escapes of All Time*, White Plains, NY: Hyperion Press, 1996, 2002.

Plumwood, V., 'Decolonizing Relationships with Nature', in Bill Ashcroft, Gareth Griffiths and Helen Tiffin (eds), *The Postcolonial Studies Reader*, Second Edition, London: Routledge, 2005.

Povinelli, E.A., *Geontologies: A Requiem to Late Liberalism*, Durham, NC: Duke University Press, 2016.

Povinelli, E.A., *The Cunning of Recognition: Indigenous Alterities and the Making of Australian Multiculturalism*, Durham, NC: Duke University Press, 2002.

Rayner, J., 'Adapting Australian Film: Ray Lawrence from *Bliss* to *Jindabyne*', *Studies in Australasian Cinema*, 3:3 (2009), 295–308, DOI: 10.1386/sac.3.3.295_1.

Reid, K., *Gender, Crime and Empire: Convicts, Settlers and the State in Early Colonial Australia*, Manchester: Manchester University Press, 2007.

Rekhari, S., 'The "Other" in Film: Exclusions of Aboriginal Identity from Australian Cinema', *Visual Anthropology*, 21:2 (2008), 125–135, DOI: 10.1080/08949460701857586.

Rushdie, S., *The Satanic Verses*, London: Vintage, 1988.

Samuel, R., *Theatres of Memory: Past and Present in Contemporary Culture*, London: Verso, 2012.
Smith, N., *The Endgame of Globalization*, London: Routledge, 2005.
Smith, Z., *White Teeth*, Harmondsworth: Penguin, 2000.
Tilley, E., 'The Uses of Fear: Spatial Politics in the Australian White-vanishing Trope', *Antipodes*, 23:1 (2009), 33–41.
Watkins, L., 'A View from Elsewhere: Ellipsis and Desire in *Walkabout* (Nicolas Roeg, 1971)', *Parallax*, 16:2 (2010), 107–117, DOI: 10.1080/13534641003634739.
Weizman, E. and Sheikh, F., *The Conflict Shoreline*, Brooklyn, NY: Steidl in Association with Cabinet Books, 2015.
Williams, R., *The Country and the City*, London: Hogarth Press, 1985 [1973].
Wright, A., *Carpentaria*, Edinburgh: Constable, 2008.
Wright, P., *On Living in an Old Country: The National Past in Contemporary Britain*, London: Verso, 1985.

Websites or other

Q&A with Barbara Creed, CIDRAL public lecture, 'Darwin and the Cinema: Evolutionary Aesthetics, the Emotions & Sexual Display in Film', May 2012, University of Manchester.

Films

Jedda, 1955, dir. Charles Chauvel.
Jindabyne
Picnic at Hanging Rock

2

MOBILITY

The assertion that humans are mobile is a bit of a truism. Whoever thought they weren't? '[W]hereas trees have roots, men have legs and are each other's guests', to use George Steiner's incisive formulation about the inevitability of human movement and the ethical and political responsibilities it enjoins.[1] And global mobility is nothing new. The movement of impoverished and war-stricken populations from Central America to the United States or from and within North Africa and the Middle East are certainly comparable to, say, the flight of Jews from the Russian Empire at the end of the nineteenth century. These movements are positively dwarfed in scale by the enforced transportation of people across newly drawn borders after the world wars and during the Partition of the Indian Subcontinent in 1947 or the migration of tens of millions of European rural workers and their families to the United States half a century before that, let alone the tens of millions of slaves transported to the Americas between the sixteenth and nineteenth centuries. When discussing mobility, one is obliged to do so, therefore, in specific rather than abstract ways. The point that we want to get across in this chapter is that questions about who gets to move, whether those who move do so willingly or unwillingly, how they move therefore, and how different humans, by contrast, are often forced through poverty or other forms of violence to be stationary, are urgent political questions that have been addressed repeatedly in a variety of salutary ways by postcolonial texts. The denunciation of movement by the political Right in addition to attempts with walls and border regimes to thwart movement is clearly an unacceptable dereliction of moral and political responsibility; after all, the plight of mobile populations is usually the direct consequence of the predacious mobility of capital with which fortified first-world societies have enriched themselves. But the undiscriminating acclamation of movement is not very helpful either. It neglects the powerful authorities and structures that mean that many, if not most, humans are prevented from moving by hardship and razor-wire fences. Andrew Smith calls this 'the "free-air-miles" sentiment in postcolonial theory', where 'the postcolonial fascination with migrancy becomes a kind of *alibi*, erected in place of a genuine confrontation with the lives of those at the receiving end of global capitalism's polarizing action'.[2] Even radical critics like Michael Hardt and Antonio Negri problematically celebrate as revolutionary the movements of the 'multitude' across borders. But such people are usually fleeing persecution and poverty only to end up in camps or on the low-wage, poorly housed and victimised fringes of first-world service economies. Their lives have been transformed by mobility but Hardt and Negri's post-imperial utopia of free movement has not been brought any closer to realisation by their movements.

We accept that the right to control one's own movements is an essential aspect of the demand for global citizenship and for a world order that has finally transcended the divisions and inequalities of imperialism, as Hardt and Negri insist.[3] Hardt and Negri suggest that the free movement of people, added to the free movement of capital and commodities, is leading to a utopia of mobility. Yet this event has demonstrably not taken place; the mobility of capital from the Global North to the Global South and the necessitous mobility of labour in the other direction are exacerbating global inequalities rather than smoothing them away and are leading to more fences and border controls rather than fewer, as Giovanni Arrighi has sagely observed.[4] State power is being intensified rather than diminished as a result. 'Contrary to the arguments of a number of scholars and commentators that globalization is undermining the position of the state', as Reece Jones points out in his study of the increasingly violent means by which states fortify their borders, 'the global scale of border violence demonstrates that the state remains the dominant container of political power in the world'.[5]

When people move, they do so for a variety of reasons, in a variety of situations and predicaments, and with a variety of effects and implications. Mobility is not a good thing in and of itself. An invading army, for example, is on the move. Most refugees would probably wish they could have stayed in a safe and prosperous home. Since the abolition of fixed exchange rates in the early 1970s, capital has been exceptionally mobile. Much of it has flowed from African and Latin American economies since the 1980s as a result of the debt and dependency enforced by the 'structural adjustment' regime of the International Monetary Fund.[6] Capital has also gushed, under what Peter Gowan calls the 'Dollar-Wall Street regime', from the surplus economies of East Asia and the Persian Gulf towards US corporations, consumers and government debt or to 'offshore' financial centres in the Caribbean.[7] It is as if the mega-wealthy have followed Wemmick's advice to Pip in *Great Expectations* to get hold of 'portable property'.[8] 'Uneven mobilities' is Mimi Sheller's helpful term for a situation marked by both the unchecked movements of the super-rich and their portable wealth *and* the compulsory imprisonments or forcible movements of the global poor.[9]

A great deal of postcolonial writing clearly celebrates the new and more expansive experiences, identifications and attachments prompted by global mobility, as this chapter will seek to show. But it also stresses the pains and hardships of mobility, the sorrow contingent on leaving a native place with all its social ties and its familiar cultural and linguistic markers, in addition to the enduring obstacles placed in the way of migrants by borders, inequalities and chauvinisms of all kinds. Kamila Shamsie's *Home Fire* (2017), for example, begins with a thrillingly tense description of the petty and humiliating rigmarole faced by Isma, a young British Muslim woman, as she tries to catch a plane from Heathrow to the United States. This novel is indeed a kind of thriller, albeit not one that ends as that highly formulaic genre tends to, with a graphic image of the nation state being secured by heroic action from some external menace like a terrorist conspiracy or a Soviet invasion but of the explosion caused in a park in Lahore by the detonation of a suicide vest strapped to the Antigone-like protagonist Aneeka and her lover, the Home Secretary's son! A 'home fire', of course, is an archetypal image of safety, contentment and hospitality. But the national 'home' of Britain in this novel is also *on* fire, being symbolically consumed by the actions of its appointed guardian, the Sajid Javid-like Muslim Home Secretary Karamat Lone, who has stripped Isma's brother of his citizenship when he left to work for the media arm of Islamic State in Syria. Lone's retro-certainties in a speech to his old school in Bradford about some sort of normative ideal of Britishness, to which immigrant communities must be badgered and compelled to aspire, are shown to be a myth that camouflages the real complexity of the overlapping identifications and attachments of all citizens including, in this novel, young British Muslims.[10]

Home Fire is a loose contemporary retelling of Sophocles' *Antigone* in which a radicalised 'traitor' throws in his lot with the Caliphate while his sister reports her brother to the authorities and the other sister conspires to rescue her reckless sibling by seducing the Home Secretary's gullible son. The novel thus explores the potential conflicts (for Aneeka and Parvaiz and, from a different standpoint, for Lone) between family, faith and the security-fixated state. In particular, the novel dramatises, as *Antigone* of course does, a tension between, on the one hand, the laws of the state that enforce loyalty and obedience and, on the other, natural or perhaps religious laws concerned instead with notions of personal conscience and justice. Less obvious, perhaps, is the novel's attention to the potential compatibilities (for Isma) between family, faith and a more inclusively defined vision of the collective. The durable craving for a secure 'home' is articulated in the novel, most eloquently and surprisingly, by the obnoxious braggart Farooq, who first radicalises Parvaiz and recruits him for Islamic State. 'You know this country,' he tells Parvaiz, à la Farage or Trump, 'used to be great' before (sounding now more Corbyn-like) it was destroyed by welfare 'reforms' and the crippling of the National Health Service. When was that? asks Parvaiz.

> Not so long ago. When it was understood that a welfare state was something you built up instead of tearing down, when it saw

migrants as people to be welcomed, not turned away. Imagine what it would be like to live in such a nation. No, don't just smile. I'm asking you to do something: imagine it.[11]

It is in part the hopeless anomie of life in Brexit Britain, with its precarious low-paid work and its relentless trashing of the collectivist legacies of the nation's social democratic past (symbolised by the siblings' former involvement in the campaign to prevent the closure of their local library), that fires cravings for purposeful attachments and a meaningful collective life. These are aspirations that might find expression, the bellicose Farooq's disarmingly nostalgic and patriotic rumination implies, in the very different visions of Islamic restoration, making Britain great again or possibly even reviving dimly remembered social democratic aspirations. No easy answers to these complicated political quandaries are offered by a novel in which it is precisely the existence and even intensification of borders, inequalities and chauvinisms that drive the novel's thrilling action. Its final image of the lovers' doomed embrace is one of conflict and conflagration.

One of our favourite examples of a text that strives to think through and explain different kinds of political radicalism (in this case, competing visions of 'purity') is *Pure* (2012), the reliably idiosyncratic Timothy Mo's alternately grim and comical tale of terrorist conspiracy in Southern Thailand.[12] The novel relates in the first-person the outlandish adventures of Snooky, a Malay ladyboy or katoey who is arrested in a drugs bust and forced to go undercover by her British and Thai handlers to report on a gang of inept, small-time jihadists. The intensely satirical humour is generated when Snooky reports back irregularly and irreverently on the group's activities via her modified laptop. Her missives are saturated with the idiom and reference points of mass culture that repeatedly deflate the purist delusions of the po-faced militants. Mo's novel might therefore remind many readers of Chris Morris's 2010 film *Four Lions*, in which a group of four young British Asian Muslim men from Sheffield, plus their pal Barry (under the preposterous nom de guerre Azzam al-Britani), plan an attack on the London Marathon. Their cack-handed efforts to link up with Al-Qaeda, the flat vowel sounds of their deadpan Yorkshire accents and their humdrum working lives relentlessly puncture this confused gang's pompous fantasies about martyrdom and devotion. So, too, do the hopelessly eclectic cultural reference points that animate their inventive repartee, made up of bathetic daydreams about the rubber dinghy rapids at Alton Towers, cravings for takeaway chicken wings, and crackpot conspiracy theories about 9/11 downloaded from YouTube. This film, which frequently resembles surveillance footage, with its jerky tracking shots and rapid close-ups, does not neglect to show the incompetence and stupidity of the functionaries of the British state that match the witless bungling of the wannabe jihadists. In the final scene, as the credits start to roll, MI5 agents are about to torture the terrorists' leader's innocent brother in a shipping container at an RAF base temporarily transferred by dint of a paper flag to Egyptian sovereignty.

The theory that comedy stems from incongruous juxtapositions is vindicated in Mo's *Pure* when the increasingly Stockholm Syndrome-afflicted Snooky desperately tries to hide the hilariously lewd tattoo on her lower back ('insert penis here') from Shaykh, her dashing but unsmiling jihadi mentor. *Pure* thus parodies these fantasies about hygienically unspoiled cultures and faiths, which include both Shaykh's ridiculous fantasies about a pan-Islamic theocracy and the colonial reveries of Snooky's patriotic and absurdly donnish spymaster, the conceited Oxonian and Anglo-Catholic Victor Veridian, whose fictional Brecon College is responsible for miseducating several Asian despots. When the brainwashed Snooky (aka Ahmed) cuts her hair, takes testosterone to stimulate the obligatory beard and removes her tattoo with battery acid, *Pure* exposes the sheer absurdity as well as the cruelty and the element of chilling self-deception invested in these ideologies of purity. Purity cannot be achieved, as the dirty finger marks that inevitably stain the papery white dust jacket of the hardback edition will prove. Similarly, the ironies and witticisms as well as the admixed registers and multiple and distorted perspectives of the novel itself time and again subvert Shaykh's algebraic certainties. Purity is a worthless ideal, albeit one that leads in this novel to the deaths of hundreds in a nightclub in Phuket, one that is confected by humourless powers that cannot tolerate a world that has been pleasingly mixed up and moved about.

One more example of postcolonial fiction's capacity to present two contrasting visions or possibilities of mobility in the same text is *Banjo* (1929) by Claude McKay, the Jamaican pioneer of the Harlem Renaissance. This is a recognisably modernist novel with its picaresque, consciously plotless tales of black male 'vagabonds' in the big commercial city of Marseille, a port 'that the world goes through'.[13] Most interesting for our purposes is the way that this cosmopolitan site, a tumultuous locus for the mobility both of immigrant workers and the manifold commodities of world trade, allows for the dramatisation of two contrasting political visions. On the one hand, these men who hustle for work on the docks have been conscripted, to use David Scott's telling term, into a modern regime of wage labour.[14] On the other hand, as Brent Hayes Edwards contends, they consciously reject that regime on which they are intermittently and reluctantly dependent, just as they reject the newfangled system of passports and border controls by which they are ceaselessly harassed and even deported.[15] Ray even dreams of starting an orchestra and the banjo is in fact, as Michael Denning has shown, an image of the way in which vernacular musical forms originated in the ports of the 1920s via the circulation of musical traditions, musicians, discs and instruments along colonial shipping routes. *Banjo* encapsulates a moment before the era of concerted decolonisation and before the Great Depression temporarily retarded the global market for sound recordings, when, according to Denning, hybrid and vernacular musical forms like New Orleans jazz but also samba in Brazil, tango in Buenos Aires and Montevideo, and other hybrid musical forms in Jakarta, Havana, Shanghai and Accra, were first pioneered.[16]

The novel celebrates and partly adopts the lyrical and improvisational forms of jazz, its rhythms of 'repetition, with very slight variations'[17] and (at the level of the novel's extraordinarily rich and inventive idioms) jazz's distinctive timbres. Its very form therefore cultivates the protagonists' 'dream of vagabondage' as well as the 'unquenchable desire' of Banjo (the character) 'to be always going'[18] beyond existing frontiers and constraints. *Banjo* thereby gestures 'toward a larger vision of the planetary', in Mary Lou Emery's words, even as it portrays 'the contradictory violence and creativity of global exchange'.[19] That vision is always accompanied by the actuality of bigotry, violence and exploitation. Strong stirrings of the anti-colonial aspirations that Denning attributes to vernacular music in this period (which accomplished a veritable 'decolonisation of the ear', in his agreeable phrase) are also heard in earnest discussions about Marcus Garvey, the articles in the *Negro World* newspaper and the way the characters' lives and desires are mediated and hampered by racist ideologies and belittling discourses about the 'primitive'. Dissonant off-stage noises reach the characters from the Cardiff race riots, the Amritsar massacre and the bankruptcy of Garvey's Black Star shipping line. Bridget T. Chalk argues that the novel's plotlessness is a formal rebuke to the administration and rigidification of identities under imperialism, including by the interwar passport system.[20] This is by no means *only* a utopian text therefore, since it is conspicuously baulked (not least by the glaring dearth of substantial female perspectives) in its efforts to picture a concrete alternative to what Ray, the novel's guiding consciousness and intrepid intellectual calls, à la D.H. Lawrence, the 'machine civilization' of modern imperialism.[21] But its jazzy form, its protagonists' penchant for 'play' rather than alienating work, and its celebration of 'vagabondage' as a veritable *mode de vie* posit, for Ray at least and for the novel's readers who are carefully positioned in sympathy with his aspirations, a potential (if not yet actual) substitute for the hierarchies and inequalities increasingly exerted by a world divided like our own by Empire, race, nation and class.

> It seemed a most unnatural thing to him for a man to love a nation – a swarming hive of human beings bartering, competing, exploiting, lying, cheating, battling, suppressing, and killing among themselves; possessing, too, the faculty to organize their villainous rivalries into a monstrous system for plundering weaker peoples [...] A patriot loves not his nation, but the spiritual meannesses of his life of which he has created a frontier wall to hide the beauty of other horizons.[22]

This chapter therefore maintains that physical and intellectual movements across actual and imaginary horizons of all kinds can be tremendously salutary, bringing into view perspectives and forms of attachment and identification that are truly global or at least post-national. This is what the novels analysed in this chapter do. So, while we obviously favour a certain kind of mobility (the voluntary mobility of peoples across actual and imaginative borders) and while global citizenship is clearly an extremely attractive idea, we want to look at the complexities, multiplicities and frequent contradictions of mobility in the contemporary world and therefore in contemporary postcolonial texts.

To speak of mobility now of course is to address, most importantly, the large exoduses of peoples in various parts of the globe as a result of war, climate change and the extremes of impoverishment resulting from neoliberal policies. No recent novel, to our minds, has addressed this kind of mobility as fruitfully or as radically as Mohsin Hamid's *Exit West* (2017). 'All over the world', as *Exit West*'s disarmingly composed narrator reminds us, calmly placing our protagonists' movements in bigger world-historical and world-ecological perspectives, 'people were slipping away from where they had been, from once fertile plains cracking with dryness, from seaside villages gasping beneath tidal surges, from overcrowded cities and murderous battlefields'.[23] The title is an extremely succinct abbreviation of the plot, in which Nadia and Saeed, a young couple from an unnamed city somewhere in Asia that has been taken over by 'militants' (with echoes of Aleppo in Syria and Mosul in Iraq but also of Hamid's own Lahore) do indeed 'exit' westwards through magic portals towards Mykonos, London and eventually California. 'Exit West' is also a kind of stage direction. So the overdue departure from the stage of world history of 'the West' is being ordered or proclaimed here: *Exit West*, pursued not by a bear but by the millions of now mobile disenfranchised and grievously exploited citizens of the non-Western world. But as Neil Lazarus reminds us, 'the West', as it is usually employed, is a vague geographical rather than a precise political concept and one that therefore usually confuses us about the real origins of power in the contemporary world.[24] In our view it is not so much 'the West' whose departure is being announced or implored in the novel and its title but the concept itself, the canard or ideological chimera of 'the West', and therefore the dangerous but increasingly popular ideological belief, which the concept usually supports in conservative political discourse, that the supposedly exceptional societies, guiding values and economic arrangements of 'the West' must be protected by force and walls from influxes of migrants.

This is a work, then, about the potential dissolution, or at least the radical transformation, of the 'Western' nation state as a form or institution of centuries' standing in the context of migration and other forms of enforced global mobility. It reveals the dubiousness of territorial definitions of citizenship and subjectivity. Other categories dismantled by the novel include those we usually employ to make sense of globally mobile migrants: the refugee (who, according to the 1951 UN Convention, is a person outside the country of his or her nationality owing to fear of persecution); the asylum seeker (a person applying for refugee status); and the economic migrant (usually but reductively seen as a voluntary migrant). Nadia and Saeed do not seem to belong to any of these classifications. They have not been granted refugee status or even been given the opportunity to apply for it. Nor are they economic migrants exactly, for they are fleeing a government takeover by 'militants'. Perhaps they can be placed in the category of the educated and tech-savvy young professionals who are for Paul Mason part of the vanguard leading the generalised revolt against neoliberalism and its global depredations.[25] These are the 'graduates with no future' for whom structural inequality, bankrupt states and stagnant growth offer only 'austerity until death, but with an upgraded version of the iPhone every few years'.[26]

For *Exit West*, the mobility of populations as a result of climate crisis, state violence, extremes of inequality and constrained life chances represents a challenge to the fortified border walls now being erected by, for example, the Trump administration in the United States and by the European Union. In both these cases, we venture to suggest, the protracted crisis of financialised capitalism since 2008 and the resultant 'austerity' measures that have compounded problems such as inequality, insecure work, personal indebtedness, stagnant wages and living standards, have brought about an efflorescence of reactionary anti-immigrant, racist and even crypto-fascist political movements. Neoliberalism is retreating behind border walls, with popular rage directed inwards at minorities and welfare 'scroungers' and outwards at migrants and refugees. Yet, unusually and extremely auspiciously, *Exit West* construes the mobility of populations as a political opportunity not as a threat. It permits readers to glimpse the alternative to recrudescent nationalisms: solidarity with (not violent antipathy towards) migrants, appreciation of (rather than armed hostility to) the reality of the global mobility of populations and, ultimately, the radical reconstruction of the overdeveloped societies of 'the West' along lines of equality, not hierarchy and exclusion.

There are nearly 70 million forcibly displaced people around the globe, according to the UNHCR, of whom around 40 million are internally displaced and around 25 million are refugees. Most refugees are hosted in non-'Western' countries such as Turkey (with three and a half million), Lebanon, Uganda and Iran. The real numbers are presumably far higher, since these numbers apply only to those people who conform to the official definitions. They do not include the even vaster, but in fact unknown, number of 'economic migrants' who are usually presented in, for example, the British media as interlopers or else as impostors or hapless victims of traffickers, to be expelled or 'returned' at the earliest opportunity. Most migrants may not be forcibly displaced but their journeys away from the depredations of climate disaster and poverty are hardly painless. Their enormously dangerous travels and the inhospitable nature of their destination, a country (Britain in this case) that can offer them little other than a global lingua franca and low-paid service sector work, attest to the direness of the prospects that they have fled. So the terms that are usually employed to categorise mobility are themselves potentially misleading. Poor people are not voluntary migrants. And migration is not an exclusively 'first-world problem'.

The unidentified city where *Exit West* begins is effectively any location from which people might flee in fear of violence or in pursuit of greater prosperity and freedom. To the end of exploring mobility in order to controvert the sensationalist and alarmist narratives put about by the news media, Nadia and Saeed are presented in ways that defy widespread preconceptions about migrants and about Muslim migrants in particular. Theirs is a highly unorthodox love story. They part unexpectedly towards the end of the novel, at which point Nadia is in a same-sex relationship with her friend from the food cooperative in Marin. These are migrants' stories that do not claim to be representative, for there is of course no such thing as *the* migrant story or *the* migrant experience. It is the feverishly melodramatic TV news anchors, not our consistently unflustered narrator, who say that the war was 'adding to an unprecedented flow of migrants that was hitting the rich countries, who were building walls and fences and strengthening their borders, but seemingly to unsatisfactory effect' (*EW*, 71). The figure of the migrant, usually seen thus in the mass and thereby dehumanised as part of a menacing 'horde' or 'swarm', is carefully individualised by the novel.

Nadia, for example, is 'always clad from the tips of her toes to the bottom of her jugular notch in a flowing black robe', not, however, because she is devout, still less because she is oppressed, but 'so men don't fuck with me' (*EW*, 16), a statement that is appealingly subversive of media clichés about young Muslims. This 'black robe' is acknowledged to be a complex and versatile signifier of, among other things, liberty and self-determination. Saeed prays more often and with greater dedication during the course of the novel, though definitely not because he is a zealot but because prayer too has multiple purposes and meanings: 'Young men pray for different things of course, but some young men pray to honour the goodness of the men who raised them, and Saeed was very much a young man of this mould' (*EW*, 201). If for hostile governments and unsympathetic media outlets prayer as well as beards and abayas are symbols and instruments of oppression and segregation, in *Exit West* they defiantly denote the exact opposite. Saeed prays, for example, in remembrance of his parents and in awareness of the inevitable burden of mortality and loss: 'this loss unites humanity, unites every human being, the temporary nature of our being-ness' (*EW*, 202).

The arrival in the European Union in 2015 of around a million migrants and refugees, many of whom were fleeing the civil war in Syria and the vast majority of whom crossed the Aegean Sea from Turkey to Greece, was mostly spun by the media and by many politicians as a crisis or emergency. *Exit West* disputes that construction. A 'crisis' implies something from which we need protection provided by the state, a threat to an otherwise trouble-free and smoothly functioning order, one that must be repelled or expelled. The unflappable tone of *Exit West* manages to present the arrival on European shores of large numbers of people fleeing the catastrophe in Syria and wars in Iraq, Afghanistan and Libya, that were in large part caused by ill-conceived 'Western' 'interventions', not as a crisis but as an opportunity for introspection about the practices and priorities of 'Western' states. Moreover, 'crisis' wrongly implies something extraordinary and unusual, whereas the flight of large numbers of people from poverty, war and climate change is an established fact of history, the refugee being as old as the nation state itself: ever since there have been nation states with citizens or subjects there have been those human subjects whom nations have not considered to be legitimate nationals and have therefore persecuted and expelled, whether one is referring to the Rohingya Muslims fleeing from Myanmar to Thailand, Malaysia and Bangladesh at the start of the twenty-first century or to the Huguenots fleeing to all parts of Europe in the seventeenth. Migration, according to *Exit West*, is not a novel phenomenon, let alone an unprecedented one. It is not even the 'new normal'. What Nadia and the novel's readers learn is that migration and the consequent transformation of loyalties and identities are simply unalterable facts of history and of human life: 'everyone migrates, even if we stay in the same houses our whole lives, because we can't help it. We are all migrants through time' (*EW*, 209).

The novel's equable tone is crucial here. *Exit West* resembles a kind of fable in which violent and catastrophic events that happened 'in those days' (*EW*, 98) and 'back then' (*EW*, 1) are being narrated calmly from a position of distance and hindsight. It is as though the surreptitious concession to political optimism of familiar dystopian novels, like Margaret Atwood's *The Handmaid's Tale* and George Orwell's *Nineteen Eighty-Four*, whose appendices speak of their nightmarish dystopias in the past tense, has been applied to the whole novel with its fairy tale-like 'Once upon a time' mood. The style is throughout curiously unshockable and serene. Whether it is the death of Nadia's cousin 'who, along with eighty-five others, was blown by a truck-bomb to bits, literally to bits, the largest of which, in Nadia's cousin's case, were a head and two-thirds of an arm' (*EW*, 29), the death of her former lover (*EW*, 31), the everyday misogynistic abuse to which she is subjected (*EW*, 30) or even the grim spectacle of a group of boys playing football with a human head (*EW*, 82), everything is narrated with the same sang-froid and a slightly fussy insistence on exact detail. We claim that the incongruous combination of matter-of-fact tone and outlandish events does not reduce but in fact amplifies the shocking and outlandish quality of such happenings. It also represents an effort not to be overwhelmed by the understandable and inevitable responses of grief, fear or horror and to establish the kind of analytical distance required for reflection and explanation.

The style is frequently chatty and colloquial as well, even at times rather flat and seemingly extemporaneous, even slightly clichéd and inelegant. 'Back then', we are informed on the first page, before the 'militants' seized control of Nadia and Saeed's city, 'people continued to enjoy the luxury of wearing more or less what they wanted to wear, clothing and hair wise' (*EW*, 1). Our narrator frequently resorts to the lacklustre shorthand 'going forward' (*EW*, 13, 185). This is the kind of no-nonsense business English, a sort of basic lingua franca or easily picked up and universally grasped Esperanto, that Nadia and Saeed themselves might have heard at the evening classes on corporate identity and product branding where they meet. The unruffled tone works to deprive events portending the dissolution of the nation state of their capacity to shock and disconcert us, even as the rudimentary and plain-speaking English adopts a language of global accessibility and interconnection. Moreover, the often extremely long and circuitous sentences with their abrupt changes of direction, their continual commas, and proliferating conjunctions and clauses serve to join up apparently separate realities and experiences, as though the digressive syntax is itself breaking down barriers and divisions. A single sentence, such as the two-pages-long description of a young Austrian woman braving racist mobs to join a march in solidarity with migrants in Vienna after 'militants' mount a terrorist attack, encompasses a history of that city that instructively places the violence of the present in the longer context of the city's far more violent past, a detailed sketch of a personal dilemma that neatly illustrates the political alternatives between violence and solidarity, comically random digressions and juxtapositions of different global locations connected in real time by online streaming (*EW*, 104–106).

The novel's portable structure achieves something similar. The main narrative is regularly and abruptly interspersed with short tales of other people who have passed through the magic portals, including a woman in a bedroom in a prosperous suburb of Sydney where a figure tumbles unseen from a doorway in her wardrobe (*EW*, 5); a sinister figure who follows two Filipina women who have just emerged from a dark alleyway in Tokyo, menacingly 'fingering the metal in his pocket as he went' (*EW*, 28); an accountant in Kentish Town in London contemplating suicide whose second bedroom turns into a portal and who is inspired to start an exciting new life in Namibia (*EW*, 126–128); and an elderly gentleman from Brazil who passes repeatedly through a portal to Amsterdam and begins a romantic relationship with a Dutchman. The novel's straightforward juxtaposition of these impressionistic vignettes therefore allows for the diverse experiences and possibilities of global mobility to be hinted at, to the extent that the adjustments to this new world, while they may be violent and onerous for many, are for others 'unexpectedly pleasant' (*EW*, 172). The episodic structure, like the winding and extended but never convoluted syntax, also enables the novel form itself to be made over into 'a device for the presentation of simultaneity', in the useful phrase from Benedict Anderson's classic study of the cultural constructions of the nationalist imagination.[27] *Exit West* provides 'a complex gloss upon the word "meanwhile"', only this time portraying, not the anonymous but connected activities of subjects within the circumscribed confines of the nation state, but the simultaneous and connected, if extremely varied, activities of subjects moving about on a veritably global canvas.

The portals through which Nadia and Saeed and others are magically teleported to distant parts of the globe are a kind of metaphor for the ease, or at least frequency and possibility, of global mobility. Readers do not see the arduous travels that most migrants undergo, the physical exertion and privation, the terrible perils and calamities of sea crossings in the Mediterranean or desert crossings in the Sahara, the dangers of exhaustion and abuse and death, the depredations of people traffickers and so on. Migrants simply emerge unexpectedly to be symbolically reborn '[w]ith a final push [...] [,] trembling and sliding to the floor like a newborn foal' (*EW*, 5). The science or technology of these more or less instantaneous transportations of human beings are not explained to us by our phlegmatic narrator, who seems as unperturbed by these incredible doorways as his characters.

There are no digressions on quantum physics since this is not a realist novel or, rather, it is something like a magic realist novel, provided we understand by that, perhaps over-used, term something like its Latin American progenitors understood by it, that is, a striking juxtaposition of the imperturbable tone of a realist narrator with the exaggerated outlandishness of fantastic processes and events. Hamid's magic portals are figures, as Theo Tait suggests, 'for a world in which distance has grown smaller and travel easier'. The portals' ubiquity and rapidity as well as the narrator's characteristically composed account of their appearance and their effects points up, as Tait goes on to assert, the absurdity of the 'curious custom of treating human beings as belonging to a sub-species just because they, as it were, walked through a door'.[28] They are metaphors, to be thoughtfully and calmly considered, for an emerging world in which the mobility of populations and the expiry of the reactionary ideologies that seek to detain and administer those populations have finally come to pass.

These doors 'that could take you elsewhere, often to places far away, well removed from this death trap of a country' (*EW*, 69) are also perhaps a kind of allusion to and a technique derived from science fiction or children's literature. They are equal parts *Star Trek* transporter and wardrobe door from C.S. Lewis's Narnia Chronicles. The man whose second bedroom turns into a portal to Namibia feels that 'the nearby blackness unsettled him, and reminded him of something, of a feeling, of a feeling he associated with children's books, with books he had read as a child, or books that had been read to him rather, by his mother' (*EW*, 127). In children's literature, of course, there is no dubious opposition between reason and fantasy. The fantastic element is accepted not resisted, embraced as a kind of revelatory imaginative possibility rather than a failure or a fanciful divergence from 'the way things are'.

So the doors also enable a kind of imaginative travel beyond the ideological constraints of the present, which is why they recall those other mysterious rectangular technologies of communication and movement, the novel form, and, as Tait notes, mobile phones, which are indeed described by the narrator at one point as 'portals' (*EW*, 55). Smartphones are as ubiquitous in the novel as they are now in our daily lives.

> In their phones were antennas, and these antennas sniffed out an invisible world, as if by magic, a world that was all around them, and also nowhere, transporting them to places distant and near, and to places that had never been and would never be.
>
> (*EW*, 35)

Phones are 'magical' enablers of communication and imaginative projection. They allow Saeed 'to access Nadia's separate existence' (*EW*, 36) and citizens of the underdeveloped world to 'see on some small screen people in foreign lands preparing and consuming' in places where 'there was sex and security and plenty and glamour' (*EW*, 39), thus surmounting, if not physically then imaginatively, the borders and divisions set in place by social and economic inequality.

Phones are also 'mesmerising'. Saeed hides and restricts 'all but a few applications' and rations his screen time to an hour a day (*EW*, 36). It is not true, therefore, as Tait alleges, that *Exit West* falls prey to 'a kind of technological optimism' that would not be out of place in a TED talk. Adam Greenfield worries that potentially liberating technologies such as the smartphone actually 'leave existing modes of domination mostly intact'.[29] Their users are stressed out by the need to constantly upgrade, to master new bodies of knowledge, to stand ready 24/7 for unnecessary work and wasteful consumption and thus to overfill our increasingly regimented days with virtual chores. Owners of smartphones, almost everybody basically, are also haunted by the knowledge that these gizmos have been assembled by wage slaves in Shenzhen while some of their components have been mined by hand in the Congo. They are doomed in a breakneck cycle of rapid obsolescence to be dismantled and transformed into toxic e-waste dumped in, for example, the Agbogbloshie slum in Accra where the food chain is contaminated by the metals extracted from discarded electronic devices shipped from Europe.[30] The smartphone is not necessarily a device for effecting communication, as Saeed's addiction shows, or for overcoming the legacies and actualities of imperialism, as Apple's exploitative supply chains illustrate and as the residents of Agbogbloshie who burn the plastic casing of old iPhones to retrieve and sell the copper wiring might attest. So the novel is actually quite attentive, in the way that TED talks rarely are, to the rival possibilities of technological change.

On the one hand, various 'magical' four-sided devices effect actual and imaginative connection. On the other hand, new technologies compound existing inequalities. As Grégoire Chamayou shows in his 'philosophical investigation' of drone warfare, new military technologies like the drones that patrol and bomb the militant-occupied city or the robots that besiege the migrants in 'dark London' reassert or prolong social and geographical divisions. Drones too are 'networked machines' (*EW*, 81) in the sense of being operated remotely from some base in the Nevada desert or in the even more disquieting sense of cooperating together on unmanned platforms in pursuit of algorithmically determined lethal strikes. The massive expansion of drone warfare by the Obama administration against militant groups in Afghanistan, Pakistan, Somalia and Yemen has transformed what was once a surveillance technology into a lethal remote-controlled or even autonomous weapon. The attraction, of course, for the user is that drones impose a sense of permanent insecurity on the enemy (and on civilian populations) while eliminating the risk of American casualties. Yet Chamayou shows that drones are woefully ineffective (since they fail to isolate militants from the communities in which they operate) and that they induce a permanent 'siege mentality' and a damaging state of terror in the civilian population over which these devices endlessly hover. 'It would be mistaken to limit the question of weaponry solely to the sphere of external violence,' writes Chamayou. 'What would the consequences of becoming the subjects of a drone-state be for the state's own population?'[31] *Exit West* provides an answer to this question. Drones, whether they are used in Pakistan, Afghanistan or the Palestinian territories, thereby compound divisions between a dominant population unconscionably distanced from the consequences of its own violence, prey to the delusions of 'unstoppable efficiency' and 'inhuman power' nurtured by these murderous but profoundly stupid weapons, and a permanently stressed and beleaguered subject population, robbed of agency and humanity by 'the kind of dread that a small mammal feels before a predator of an altogether different order, like a rodent before a snake' (*EW*, 151).

In such ways, the novel prepares and eventually poses an essential political question of our age: what kind of cultural and political transformations are required if we are to embrace rather than resist global mobility? Having first purchased access to the mysterious portal that more or less instantaneously transports them to a camp on the Greek island of Mykonos, Nadia and Saeed's next magical teleportation takes them to a kind of gigantic squat in central London comprised of one or two million migrants from all parts of the globe. For several weeks they camp out in an unoccupied mansion in Kensington and Chelsea. That borough has itself become a symbol, of course, since the conflagration at Grenfell Tower in June 2017 (not long after the novel's publication) of the gigantic social and economic inequalities in the heart of the capital city.[32] This 'dark London', described by the newspapers as one of the 'worst of the black holes in the fabric of the nation' (*EW*, 126), is a vivid image of the truly global social and economic inequality to which mass migration is in part a response.

The response of 'native' Londoners and of the state authorities to this 'black hole' is central to the novel's larger meditation on the perils and possibilities of mobility. On the one hand, the migrants are met with demonstrations of solidarity and with practical assistance. Soup kitchens, aid agencies and earnest young doctors minister to new arrivals. Occupied houses set up their own 'councils' and defence committees that resemble nothing so much as revolutionary forms of direct democracy. For instance, the council in Nadia and Saeed's house requisitions and rations provisions before a planned attack by the security forces and gives the lion's share to the children. In addition, however, violent 'nativist' mobs attack migrants and there are riots 'to reclaim Britain for Britain' (*EW*, 132). This area of London is overflown by fighter jets and patrolled by soldiers, armoured vehicles, sinister robots, helicopters and drones.

Exit West thus dramatises the necessity and urgency of a fateful political choice that Hamid himself has spelt out very eloquently elsewhere in his response to the 2015 migration 'crisis'. Hamid and his novel cleverly reframe the choice not as one about whether European states are content to welcome refugees, since the mobility of populations (as the novel's images of instantaneous teleportation show) has been made far easier and more appealing than ever before, but rather whether those states are willing 'to become the sorts of societies that are capable of taking the steps that will be required to stop the flow of migration'. For that to happen, borders need to be hardened, aliens must be harassed and expelled, and the nation state turned unapologetically into a 'hostile environment' that deters those who are not 'native-born' with threats of violence.

> In such a Europe, the essence of Hitler's thousand-year Reich will not have been defeated; it will merely have suffered an interruption that lasted a few decades [...] All Europeans, including the people of Britain, must ask themselves if they wish to live in such societies. They need to dispense with the delusion that theirs can remain pleasant countries and unattractive countries at the same time. If they decide that no, in the end they do not have it in them to do what would need to be done, to become the kinds of people who would repel migrants – horrify migrants, terrify migrants – then

they will need to plan for a future of large-scale migration. And it seems to me that the first step needs to be to articulate a vision of an optimistic future as a migrant-friendly society.[33]

The novel closely reproduces these concerns and phrases. The expected slaughter of the migrants by the army is called off. 'Perhaps they had decided that they did not have it in them to do what would have needed to be done', for 'the doors could not be closed [...] and they had understood that the denial of coexistence would have required one party to cease to exist' (*EW*, 164). 'Decency' wins out, or 'bravery, for courage is demanded not to attack when afraid' (*EW*, 165).

So, Hamid is convinced that states like Britain will need to be changed radically in order to overcome the fear of migrants and repudiate 'violently nostalgic visions' of taking back control or making the homeland great again or pulling up the drawbridge, discouraging migrants with fences and walls and with the deterrence of punitive violence and with the defensive assertion of ideologies of racial and national belonging. Those societies must make a leap of the imagination. This is a momentous choice of course, for Hamid's warning about the recrudescence of fascism makes clear the sobering possibility that the violent persecution, exclusion and internment of migrants echoes the crimes of Europe's totalitarian past. In *Exit West*'s near-future London, 'nativist extremists' form paramilitary 'legions'; the 'fury' of these 'nativists' reminds Nadia of 'the fury of the militants in her own city' (*EW*, 156), the novel being convinced (correctly in our view) that the xenophobic fury of European nationalisms and the similarly chauvinistic fanaticism of Islamist militancy are commensurate and mutually reinforcing. Recalling the Nazi pogrom of November 1938, there are rumours of 'a coming night of shattered glass' or Kristallnacht in this 'migrant ghetto' (*EW*, 159). Hannah Arendt, the preeminent theorist of totalitarianism of course, also worried in her magnum opus on that subject that the challenges posed by stateless and 'redundant' populations might be dealt with by 'solutions' that recalled the methods of totalitarian movements.

> The danger of the corpse factories and holes of oblivion is that today, with populations and homelessness everywhere on the increase, masses of people are continually rendered superfluous if we continue to think of our world in utilitarian terms. Political, social, and economic events everywhere are in a silent conspiracy with totalitarian instruments devised for making men superfluous [...] Totalitarian solutions may well survive the fall of totalitarian regimes in the form of strong temptations which come up whenever it seems impossible to alleviate political, social, or economic misery in a manner worthy of man.[34]

Are we, the novel asks bluntly, prepared to countenance the recrudescence of fascism, in admittedly altered circumstances and forms, in a process of violent deterrence and fortification that is rendering certain human beings rightless as well as expendable, in which refugees are treated as a threat and a danger and even a kind of sub-species that nation states need to ward off like a deadly virus? In her home city, Nadia worries that if they flee then she and Saeed 'might be at the mercy of strangers, subsistent on handouts, caged in pens like vermin' (*EW*, 90), which is of course what now happens to migrants and their children on the US border with Mexico. That the US, whose president refers to immigrants as 'animals', does in fact imprison people in cages is an instance less of the novel's prescience and more of the rapidity and thoroughness with which first-world border regimes are succumbing to the logic of violence and exclusion that *Exit West* diagnoses.[35]

Nations, we're told by the novel's contemplative narrator, are 'like a person with multiple personalities' (*EW*, 155). But which version of the nation state will prevail in a world in which '[w]ithout borders nations appeared to be becoming somewhat illusory' (*EW*, 155)?

> Even Britain was not immune from this phenomenon, in fact some said Britain had already split, like a man whose head had been chopped off and yet still stood, and others said Britain was an island, and islands endure, even if the people who come to them change, and so it had been for millennia, and so it would be for millennia more.
>
> (*EW*, 156)

The novel's composed tone counsels acquiescence in the historical fact that nations endure even as they change radically, both because mobility is incontrovertible and because the cost of preventing mobility is, frankly, politically and morally inconceivable.

The best way to read the novel, therefore, is as an attempt to construct utopian alternatives to the nation state form and to the last-ditch defence of the nation state by fascistic 'nativists', alternatives that have eluded us thus far, the novel suggests, because we tend to see migrants mainly as a threat and a problem.

> It has been said that depression is a failure to imagine a plausible desirable future for oneself, and not just in Marin, but in the whole region, in the Bay Area, and in many other places too, places both near and far, the apocalypse appeared to have arrived and yet it was not apocalyptic, which is to say that while the changes were jarring they were not the end, and life went on, and people found things to do and ways to be and people to be with, and plausible desirable

futures began to emerge, unimaginable previously, but not unimaginable now, and the result was something like relief.

(*EW*, 216)

By construing mobility as something other than a crisis or a catastrophe, *Exit West* effectively answers Fredric Jameson's call for cultural and imaginative work that shatters the twin dominion, as he puts it, of dystopia and regression, the two alternatives that have captured and hindered our thinking about the future. The novel makes us 'able again to think politically and productively, to envisage a condition of genuine revolutionary difference'.[36]

The final third of the novel thus becomes a detailed exploration of the cultural, institutional and even infrastructural changes required to adjust to the gradual dissolution or at least radical transformation of the conventional nation state form. A gigantic new city, the 'London Halo', is being built by and for new arrivals, who pay a 'time tax' whereby a portion of the income and work of new arrivals goes to existing residents. This task brings migrants into contact with the foreman and other 'natives', from whom they learn to understand their new home, 'its people and manners and ways and habits' 'though of course their very presence here meant that its people and manners and ways and habits were undergoing considerable change' (*EW*, 178). This new world is by no means a utopia. There are enormous political and cultural disruptions and conflicts, including bombings by migrants and nativists, though the changes 'seemed less than apocalyptic' and Nadia senses that, in Britain at least, 'existence went on in tolerable safety' (*EW*, 168). Cooperatives are established in Marin in California and a 'plebiscite movement' agitates for the creation of a regional assembly for the Bay Area, elected on the basis of one member one vote 'regardless of where one came from' and that might supplant or at least complement existing democratic institutions (*EW*, 219).

There are also profound cultural changes appropriate to this post-national world. Just as Nadia has learned from her Nigerian comrades in their occupied mansion that there is no such thing as the English language (*EW*, 144), with English existing in multiple spoken and written forms, her subsequent adventures in Marin in California demonstrate the way that everything from human sexuality to cuisine and music can be creatively expressed and combined in numerous ways in conditions of cultural cross-fertilisation. The unexpected move through yet another portal to Marin illustrates not only the growing compulsions and pleasures of mobility but also something like a 'great creative flowering', a 'new jazz age', no less, of hybridised musical expression. If the novel has already stressed the contingency and the incessant multiplicity of nations and their identities it now, very auspiciously, identifies the same qualities in cultural expression of all kinds.[37]

Migration and transformation are simply unalterable facts of history and of human life. Mobility is inescapable, fashioning as it does a confusing and often fraught reality that must be acknowledged. It is also pleasurable and generative of all kinds of exciting cultural and political possibilities. It comprehensively dismantles the distinction between natives and migrants or between, as the novel phrases it, those who migrated recently and those whose forebears migrated longer ago. The novel attends to the pains as well as the pleasures and possibilities of mobility. Saeed continues to grieve for the father he feels he has abandoned, for example: 'when we migrate, we murder from our lives those we leave behind' (*EW*, 94). Yet there is a muted utopianism to the whole performance. The direct forms of democracy and the cooperative enterprises described towards the end of the novel presume a model of rights and of citizenship that is no longer bound up with territoriality. It is not so much that refugees should become citizens; rather, the novel intimates, citizens should become refugees, that is, mobile members of multiple political communities engaged in more complex forms of belonging, citizenship, cooperation and decision-making. It is not that migrants should adapt to a given nation state but that nation states should adapt to migrants, that is, by abandoning their age-old and constitutive distinction between citizens and non-citizens. In the future, the world will resemble the community of migrants gathered in Mykonos, minus the state of radical precarity, in which 'everyone was foreign, and so, in a sense, no one was' (*EW*, 100).[38]

We should frankly acknowledge, therefore, that in forecasting or at least imagining a decentralised world of direct control by workers and communities of their own lives and labour, of new taxes, administrative arrangements and forms of redistribution, of accommodated migrants and socialised housing as well as hybridised forms of cultural expression, Hamid's novel is anticipating a specifically socialist future. In this context, socialism would mean simply, in Immanuel Wallerstein's words, 'a program for the decommodification of everything'.[39] This is by no means an inevitable future. Democratisation and decentralisation, the proliferation of cooperative ways of living and working, the 'elimination of the category of profit' so that production might be geared more towards socially and ecologically desirable ends, the abolition of state-authorised distinctions between citizens and non-citizens, plus the phasing out of wage labour, though not necessarily of money and competition (since even socialist economists recognise the need for 'a certain amount of capitalism between consenting adults', in Erik Olin Wright's witty phrase[40]), are possibilities that *Exit West* places before us with a utopian but also urgently political insistence.

'Location, location, location, the estate agents say. Geography is destiny, respond the historians' (*EW*, 9). *Exit West* is a novel about a stage in human history in which geography is no longer destiny. In Britain, for example, which by the end of the novel is undergoing an arduous phase of cultural and physical reconstruction in response to the indubitable realities and opportunities of migration, a recognition of this fact might involve a final reckoning with the legacies of the country's imperial past. Paul Gilroy has insisted that the dominant relationship with this past is still melancholic, that is, characterised by Britons' anxious inability to reconcile themselves to the loss of empire and to the discrediting and abandonment of empire's ideologies of racial hierarchy and national exceptionality. The refusal to work through feelings of 'discomfort, shame and perplexity' about imperialism and imperialism's legacies and continuities leads to a kind of forgetting or repression, Gilroy contends. What follows is 'an additional catastrophe: the error of imagining that postcolonial people are only unwanted alien intruders without any substantive historical, political, or cultural connections to the collective life of their fellow subjects'.[41] The radical reconstruction of British national identity as well as of the country's social and economic structures and political institutions necessitates an adjustment, of the kind pictured by Hamid's novel, to the fact that Britain, as Robert Winder suggests, is 'a country settled at a deep level by immigrants' since the first Jutes, Saxons and Romans and not just in the last few decades by arrivals mistakenly construed as 'challenges' and 'problems'.[42] Britain has always been a migrant society and is a migrant society now more than ever. The utopian goal is to recover from post-imperial 'melancholia', to put behind us exclusionary ideologies of race and nation and land, and face up to and ultimately embrace the consequences of the world's interconnectedness.

We are convinced that the European Union has yet to rise to the challenge of global mobility. One political possibility rejected in the novel but adopted by the EU since 2015 is the reinforcement and militarisation of borders. The EU pursues the free circulation of goods and commodities but not of people. In the EU, alas, democracy and solidarity are more honoured in the breach than the observance. The financial crisis since 2008, for example, was met by the political and economic elites of the core states and by the EU's technocratic bureaucracy as an opportunity to entrench division and inequality. It is not enough to state that the EU is a powerful supra-national bloc without a demos, a set of institutions without a people, and that therefore those in charge of its mostly unaccountable institutions fail to observe the principles of community and solidarity. We are asking not only for those principles to be observed *within* Europe's borders. A border is still a border even if it contains 27 comparatively affluent nation states. The final movement of Beethoven's Ninth Symphony and the gold stars on a blue background denote unity between member states but they are still the symbolic paraphernalia of an exclusionary nationalist project, albeit this time on a continental scale.

The EU is not the solution or the answer to the national and racial divisions and exclusions inflicted by imperialism; it is a recurrence of these offences. As Stathis Kouvelakis contends, its 'border regime is an extension of the history of colonialism and domination that Europe and the West have exercised over the rest of the world, and to which "the construction of Europe" now adds a further chapter'.[43] The EU as presently constituted is not a cosmopolitan alternative to the bellicose xenophobia of the Trump administration or to the legacies and actualities of European imperialism. It is an apparatus for enforcing division and inequality. The single currency, for example, has turned the peoples of the EU's southern periphery into servants of their governments' creditors. Why? So that the bad debts accumulated by French and German banks might be transferred to Europe's citizens. Not debt forgiveness but austerity, unemployment and enforced market 'liberalisation'; not unity or shared aspirations but punitive 'fiscal waterboarding'; not the accommodation of migrants but exclusion and scapegoating.[44] Most importantly for our purposes therefore, the EU's response to the growing mobility of populations has been woefully self-serving and short-sighted. Several EU states in 2015 refused to fund Operation Mare Nostrum, the Italian government initiative to rescue migrants and refugees from the Mediterranean Sea. Border patrol operations were increased, FRONTEX (the European Border and coastguard agency) was tasked with militarising the EU's borders and in 2016 a dubious deal was struck with Turkey to prevent refugees and migrants from reaching the EU and to expel those who made it. This agreement with Turkey is in barefaced defiance of international law, which stipulates very clearly that refugees are entitled to remain until authorities have processed their claim and that refugees are not obliged to claim asylum in the first country they reach.

The border regime of the EU includes not just its detention centres, the Evros fence on Greece's land border with Turkey and the watchtowers and razor-wire fences of Melilla and Ceuta (Spain's enclaves in Morocco) as well as the vessels patrolling the Mediterranean but also, as Kouvelakis notes, funding for, and various forms of, collaboration with the security forces, warlords and militias of Libya, Mali and Sudan.[45] To be brief, the welcome relaxation of border controls within the EU's Schengen Area has been accompanied by the intensive consolidation of borders between the EU and North Africa and the Middle East. The response of the EU to the refugee and migrant 'crisis' mirrored its response to the economic crisis (not to mention the climate crisis); it shirked responsibility and deflected the costs on to the victims. The aim, as Costas Lapavitsas observes, seemed to be to contain the financial and migration crises on Europe's periphery while preventing these crises from spreading to the core, where German manufacturing is the only remaining engine of Europe's feeble economic growth. Refugees and migrants already inside the EU were kept trapped in Greece, a country ill-equipped because of its economic devastation to cope with the costs of accommodating them. Those outside the EU are detained in Turkey.[46] To its credit, Germany admitted a million people, Britain, to its shame, very few. Hungary closed its borders. There was little solidarity among member states, in short, and still less between the EU and the people fleeing the blighted lands beyond its borders. The only coordinated response was to treat the refugees and migrants as a security threat and to effectively militarise Europe's Southern border. We agree with Kouvelakis that, at present, the EU is 'a specific institutional entity [...] which confiscates the name of "Europe" to conceal at the symbolic level the operation of exclusion that lies at its core'.[47]

So, perhaps the most salutary but also contentious lesson imparted by Hamid's suggestive fable of mobility is that postcolonialists should definitely *not* mistake the fortified first-world enclave of the European Union for a culture or a society that has surmounted the actual and ideological divisions that imperialism continues to inflict. We proffer no opinions here about Leave versus Remain! But we are convinced that even this important political question is almost nugatory in comparison with Hamid's novel's far more urgent and still more vexed, though as yet unanswered, question of whether European societies are capable of emerging finally from imperialism's shadow. For that to happen, for those societies to become more hospitable, more equal and more democratic plus far more culturally hybridised, radical reconstruction is necessary, of the kind envisioned towards the end of the novel. The EU's cheerleaders, in what Tariq Ali has dubbed the 'extreme centre',[48] uncritically affirm Europe's supposedly progressive history, its enlightened 'values' and benevolent global role and even a shared and exceptional continental identity. These empty notions could hardly be less attractive to postcolonialists who are committed to deconstructing Eurocentric doctrines and myths. 'Europe is literally the creation of the Third World', observed Frantz Fanon, which means that both its material prosperity and its arrogant sense of its own cultural distinctiveness rest upon exploitation and exclusion.[49] It's hard to paint one's face blue and gold with any enthusiasm when one knows that Europe's self-understanding is inseparable from the genocidal exploitation of the rest of the globe.

What is urgently required in the member states of the European Union is not a single currency or balanced budgets or entire nation states enslaved to their governments' creditors or the Frontex border force illegally preventing refugees from claiming asylum, but wholesale social, economic and cultural reconstruction. Notwithstanding Brexit or Grexit or Frexit or Italexit, if the EU is incapable of encouraging this kind of radical reconstruction, of effecting a long overdue departure from all the exclusionary ideologies and structures denoted by a reactionary allegiance to the ideological chimera of 'the West' (Wexit, if you will), then it will not survive and does not deserve to. *Exit West* shows us that the hybridised societies of postcolonialists' dreams are the future products of arduous efforts at transformation, not the flawed and exclusionary nation states and supra-national blocs of the present.

'The novel's engagement with the Syrian refugee crisis (partly responsible for provoking the resurgence in populist, xenophobic responses to immigration)', as Kristian Shaw has argued, 'underscores the desired maintenance of a fortress Europe to guard against undesirable cultural influence and suggests that EU policy merely reinforces Europe's external borders and weakens internal ones, ensuring that an embrace of alterity remains ultimately deferred'.[50] It is not the distention or intensification of borders but their dismantlement that *Exit West* counsels, in reality but first at the level of the imagination. This task, we posit, will involve thinking our way outside many of the national and continental attachments and identifications that we usually affirm when we imagine the possibilities of collective life. The trick is to distinguish between the resurgent populism of the Right (where 'the people' names a strictly delineated national community) and a thankfully renascent but radically dissimilar 'Left populism' where 'the people' consists of all people everywhere who share an interest in constraining the power and wealth of the billionaires and oligarchs. This non- or supranational 'we' would consist of workers, immigrants, the precarious middle class, networked and physically and imaginatively mobile young people like Nadia and Saeed, in addition to all those who for other reasons share an opposition to precarity and a desire for the democratisation of political and economic power, which is what *Exit West* explicitly envisions. For the late French sociologist Pierre Bourdieu, Europe could only remain true to its professed values of solidarity and community if it broke out of the rigid fiscal restrictions of the common currency, democratised its institutions and revised relations with the rest of the world that are currently far too close to the belligerent defence and foreign policy priorities of the US government, as well as too wedded to the unequal trading relationships inherited from Europe's colonial past.

> If they are genuinely to be transformed, it can only be by a vast European social movement, capable of elaborating and imposing an open and coherent vision of a political Europe, rich with all its past cultural and social achievements and armed with a generous and lucid project of social renewal, resolutely open to the entire world.[51]

This is a largely rhetorical appeal. It may name a utopian project. But what the dissolution or wholesale reconstruction of the nation state means in practice as well as an indication of the urgency and scale of that endeavour, essentially the abandonment of the originary distinction between native and migrant and the formulation of much more far-reaching forms of solidarity, are intimated by *Exit West*. The novel accepts and acclaims the perennial but intensifying reality of globally itinerant populations, from its fantastic but dispassionate narratives of mobility right down to the level of its phlegmatic tone, accessible Esperanto and free-wheeling syntax. The brief final chapter, set half a century in the future, in which Nadia and Saeed return to their home city, which is 'not a heaven' but is 'not a hell' either (*EW*, 227), places the apparently catastrophic or dystopian events of the present in a much longer chronological and historical perspective. Thus, *Exit West* imagines a 'plausible desirable future' on the other side of our historical present of inequality, precarity, climate breakdown and national and racial chauvinism.

Nadine Gordimer's *The Pickup*[52] (2001) is committed to showing ways in which in some contexts, free choice and freedom to some become *so* commonplace as to be invisible. Set in the early 2000s in a city in South Africa, the story circles around a young local white woman, Julie, relatively privileged, who encounters a migrant Arab, Abdu, working at a garage, when her car breaks down. The relative ease with which she can move around her city is stark in comparison to his declaration, early on in the novel, that 'I go where they let me in'.[53] This distance is therefore established at the start: where she declares that it is sometimes 'good to get out' of one's country for a spell, he will go 'wherever they let you in'.[54] A tension is thus introduced between the rituals that young and relatively secure cosmopolitan citizens participate in and the rather different concerns of the migrant that divert from and cannot participate in this same laissez faire attitude. Gordimer's is not a social critique, however. Rather, she is attuned to the rhythms and hues of the very experience of various forms of spatial and social freedom (hard won for some in the case of South Africa) and places these alongside the more recent political impetus for her country to make migrants welcome. This dynamic is then played out in a post-apartheid context where the very questions of civic freedom and mobility, in all its forms, still dominate and the memory of a very different social and political structure is still germane. In his work on the forms of anti-apartheid activism, Håkan Thörn argues against becoming too caught up in the rhetoric of border-crossing that accompanied much of the international impetus behind anti-apartheid rhetoric. He reminds us that 'it is just as important to focus and analyze the prevailing importance of old borders and the construction of new ones in this context'.[55] In other words:

> [...] not all people could travel. In fact, the South African borders were closed to a number of people, who wanted to leave or visit the country. And in the sense of cultural or 'racial' borders, not just the politics of the apartheid regime, but also the practice of solidarity work, involved constructing a number of borders between 'us' and 'them'. Such borders were often related to national identities and interests as well as national political cultures.[56]

The idea of crossing borders is at the foreground of many of the interactions in *The Pickup*, and in this context what is at play is the reconfiguration of us and them and a broadening out again of the meaning of borders. Caught up in the global migration movement, South Africa now also has to play a part in the new international obligations to open its borders to refugees and asylum seekers without replaying its older historical, racially inflected border dynamics. As Thörn points out, 'globalization does not necessarily mean that the nation state, understood as a political space, is fading away'.[57] In many ways, *The Pickup* articulates and performs this new interrelated space where the two converge. Within this new political space, however, familiar dynamics return and are played out again.

Comparing this text to the short stories 'Town and Country Lovers'[58] by Gordimer in the 1970s, one can't help but be profoundly affected at the changes that she is exposing. In the short stories, the ability to 'move' between spaces is an all-consuming preoccupation for interracial love stories that are thwarted by the watchful eyes of community and police. Here, the emphasis is on arriving to the loved one and the perils of the journey itself. The stories and their cinematic adaptations are curious and revealing about how restrictions on mobility are overcome and the risks involved in doing so. There, crossing the divide is material as well as social and the lovers are in fear of being found out and charged with the Immorality Act.[59] The difference between those that are able to use their freedom of movement and those that are materially and geographically restricted is stark. Poignantly, the protagonist of the story set in the town, Dr. Franz-Josef von Leinsdorf, is an Austrian geologist working in Africa. He has ostensibly travelled far and wide: 'Peru, New Zealand, the United States [...] layer upon layer, country after country'.[60] So thorough is his ability to execute these moves that he can survive without having to show any 'interest in the politics of the countries he works in'.[61] These first few lines in the story are extraordinary in the way that they casually pick up, without judgement, on the straightforward way in which Franz-Josef can move in the world without hindrance, either physical or political, free to come and go as he pleases. Not required to choose whether he needs to stay or go, the assumption however, among his colleagues, is that he is like 'many of these well-educated Europeans [who] have no intention of becoming permanent immigrants; neither the remnant of white colonial life nor idealistic involvement with Black Africa appeals to them'.[62] Thus, the two most crucial and defining features of the South African political landscape (colonialism and anti-colonial movements) are ones that need not be dealt with at all. When Franz begins an affair with a 'light-skinned' 'coloured' girl working at the supermarket checkout, he seems clear about some of the restrictive policies around interracial relations, but not others. To his mind, she can act as though she is his servant (as though this is not in itself a social problem): 'say I'm employing you' he suggests, whereas her fear, which she articulates as her mother's fear were she to find out, is that they 'get caught'.[63]

Movement and growth for her is the ability to work in the supermarket rather than a factory – thus signalling a progress of sorts: 'With the continuing shortage of semi-skilled whites a girl like this might be able to edge a little farther into the white-collar category'.[64] His fantasy of her social mobility is powerful as is hers when she considers how on quiet Sundays when they secretly venture to the countryside in his car she is almost '*like* a wife'.[65] Gordimer's nuanced treatment of the small and unique ways in which the huge gulf between these two characters manifests is indicative of the extent to which freedom itself is as much structural as it is private. Where he casually reminds her that his Christmas plans involve travelling to the mountain ranges of Italy, her world consists of moving between her work and his home where she finds herself so tired that 'once dinner was eaten she could scarcely keep awake'.[66] These delicate references to where and how the characters move across their days – he to various geological sites in his car, she on foot to her work and then stealthily and carefully back to the home they now share, betray a quiet tolerance of much larger socio-political injunctions that organise movement across the city. Though cognisant that their relationship is prohibited, they adjust to the broader structures that dictate this illegality. Once arrested and separated, what is most jarring is the immeasurable gap in their social standing, not continually apparent in the context of their intimate affair. She travels various distances measured in very different ways, from 'one of nine children of a female laundry worker' to living in the townships, to Frantz's house. The distance she undertakes between the supermarket and his flat is significant as an indicator of her ability to keep moving. Gordimer experiments here with the price of social mobility played out in the context of risky interracial relations. Where the court is unable to prove that they have acted in any way immorally on the night of the arrest, it seems that the true indictment comes from Franz who declares that 'even in his [own] country it's difficult for a person from a higher class to marry one from a lower class'.[67] It is noteworthy to our broader argument that Gordimer here shows how social categories and various forms of discriminatory behaviour can be seen to cut across national lines. In other words, where particular forms of behaviours are seen to perhaps contravene apartheid-era laws, what actually allows these to be enforced and acted upon are also much older ones of class and economic boundaries that have evolved elsewhere and that facilitate and even enable apartheid views to flourish. In *The Pickup*, it is this significant gap in economic potential that appears to sometimes supersede or at least sit alongside the question of colour. In an illuminating conversation between Julie and Abdu on the issue of his expired work permit, Julie wonders what he would do if found out? 'Out' he says, to which her musings of 'Where would he go' are followed by Gordimer's observation that 'there are always solutions in the resources she comes from'.[68] The description of her social context as 'resources' highlights the extent to which she and others like her are surrounded by choices and options that can be *reconfigured* into resources even when they are not directly recognised as such. In this case, people and their professions become recourses (doctors, lawyers, bankers) as they can facilitate movement. Moving towards them or away from them is simple and their accessibility is ubiquitous. Julie's understanding that being 'at the border, at immigration' has no power over her life whereas it structures every move in Abdu's, is a shock and perhaps a reminder that certain ideological and material partitions are never fully revoked in the context of the nation state, notwithstanding its past. In other words, new boundaries and new restrictions on movement come to occupy older spaces.

These restrictions have the ability to shape their relationship, indeed provide it with its right to exist at all:

> To continue in their present state: his situation in itself, alone determined this. He is here, and he is not here. It's within this condition of existence that they exist as lovers. It is a state of suspension; from the pressures of necessity to plan; look ahead. There is no future without an identity to claim it; or to be obligated to it.[69]

This state of suspension allows for the very real and intimate behaviour of lovers to flourish at the same time as it denies any other type of movement for Abdu. The conditions that, however, might enable planning and a futurity are not in existence as long as he remains outside of the legal framework of the state. While it is perhaps obvious that this precarious condition brings some value and can be construed as a freedom of sorts, there is also a fear in being unmoored. This comes across when Abdu asks Julie to introduce him to her mother and father. Gordimer swiftly cuts through any temptation to valorise perceived freedoms (not having to spend time with one's parents) construed out of necessity (not knowing when one might see one's parents again). In another scene, friends of Julie's father announce that they are relocating and this word, 'relocate' is placed in quotation marks, announcing the independent impetus behind it.

> 'Relocate' they're saying. It's the current euphemism for pulling up anchor and going somewhere else [...] The fêted couple are about to be immigrants. Sitting among the gathering Julie is seeing the couple as those – her father's kind of people – who may *move about the world welcome everywhere*, as they please, while someone has to live disguised as a grease-monkey without a name.[70]

This ability and forgone reality is so natural as to be almost unbearable in Abdu's context. Mobility for him is contained within the spaces he inhabits and can move within – his work, her home, their weekends spent in the veld. His own constraint is also visible in her ability to visit her family – to do this simple act without complication. Later in the novel, the ease with which Julie is able to travel to Africa as his wife to be with him (though the overall plan is to eventually emigrate to the US) is bewitching in its simplicity. 'She had made her choice; here it was. She was the one with the choices. The freedom of the world was hers'.[71] This perceived freedom does, however, come under intense pressure as he works tirelessly to realise it for himself also. This is undermined by what we come to understand as the underbelly of certain forms of privilege – the privilege to see the struggle and suffering that a fresh migrant life can bring. Though propelled by a desire to move on, to achieve success and to have a good life beyond that bestowed by family and local community, Abdu is not able to join Julie in her future vision for him and the grim prediction that he will find himself in the US with no money:

> living in a dirty hovel [...] cleaning American shit – she has seen the slums of those cities, the empty lots of that ravaged new world, detritus of degradation [...] at least in her home, that city of the backward continent, lying under a car's guts was a better human grade.[72]

This particular insight is a blow to the migrant dream, so desperately held onto by Abdu. In the crisis that follows, his perception that 'that's where the world was' and that the ideal was worth the sacrifice collides with a knowledge that she has gleaned from her own freedom of movement: a freedom that has revealed untold suffering and indignities. Julie's interesting and surprising interpretation clashes against Abdu's drive to *move on* and to live, if necessary, the immigrant life he has conjured up, as harsh as it may be. Although she manages to secure a loan for both of them from a family friend, which would mean the harsher edges of starting up a new life could be sidestepped, Abdu instead begs her to go and stay with her mother, who lives in California, until *he* is better established. Here, Abdu replays the mythology of penniless migrants working years in order to bring over their wives to the promised land. Completely misunderstanding her plan of them living together in comfort while they establish themselves, Abdu tries to explain that 'I can't take you to live the way immigrants start [...] I must find work, I must find somewhere where you can live'.[73] His insistence that they do it this way – she living in comfort with her mother while he plays out the hardships of impoverished migrant life – is utterly rejected by Julie. Her final revelation, that she intends to stay in *his* country of origin after he migrates to the US, is utterly surprising to Abdu but not perhaps for us. Uninterested in living the same life of her past in California while Abdu forges ahead in the harsh immigrant existence, Julie harnesses the power of her independence to stay put, to stay where she has chosen. This ending is a treatise on the complexity of how we view the privileges of mobility.

In Gordimer's work, we find all of the structural restrictions deployed to ensure that some can move freely while others cannot; where some can see out their visions of the future and others are left waiting and at the mercy of bureaucratic processes. Yet, her work also has a way of querying the very notion of freedom in a globalised world and she is sensitive to not romanticising our understanding of mobility as always already heavily associated with fresh starts and endless opportunity. She also sharply brings our attention to the very different routes undertaken by cosmopolitan citizens who look for opportunities and experiences that might remove them from the old socio-political borders of the colonial past at the same time as postcolonial subjects might still dream of idealised beginnings at the metropolitan centre.

Another text that challenges ideas around the perceived advantages of mobility centred on dualistic notions of freedom versus captivity is Joe Sacco's graphic novel *Palestine* (2003).[74] Sacco's journey to Palestine, originally written and illustrated in a nine-issue comic series, traces the journalist Sacco's adventures in Palestine during 1992–1993. Here, the comic book insists on stretching what we might consider captivity to be and challenges certain depictions of Palestine, in particular Gaza, as an 'open prison'. Although this analogy might reflect a concrete socio-political impetus to jolt a complacent international community into action, it does not permit a more nuanced approach to the context of the occupied territories that is not always figured as one incessantly underpinned by a certain understanding of the Israeli/Palestinian political crisis. While completely attuned to the varying levels of injustice that the Arab-Palestinian community must endure on a daily basis, Sacco is, however, careful to reveal the rather more complex issue of how they navigate this daily life. In a manner akin to Elia Suleiman's *Divine Intervention*, Sacco manages to expand the territory right before our eyes as he details the minutiae of movement. This is a deft magician's trick as it enables the land to be experienced as expansive as a result of those who move across it rather than understood as reductive by those who might only experience it as punitive. In the very first drawing, it is Sacco who is outside, waiting to go in. He is the one who must come here to learn and experience the context that he wants to write about and once he is in, his journey is nothing short of a whirlwind!

One of the most invigorating aspects that Sacco captures is the energy required to keep moving in the face of restrictions, be they political, military or social. In taxis, vans, cars, by foot and sometimes even carried along by people, Sacco is on the move constantly as are his subjects – he goes from visiting the lost land of a Palestinian family to visiting a Palestinian hospital to accidently joining in a protest march. Everywhere you look in *Palestine*, people are on the move: they go to work, own shops, they drive around, they visit friends and family, they go to market, go to school, work in olive groves, visit the mosque, spend time with family members in prison. They also protest and this means that they are out in the open and often vulnerable. Rather than their stasis, it is this constant movement that interests Sacco. Although it is right that so much critique has centred on how Sacco's graphic novel provides a bird's-eye view[75] of the occupation through highlighting all of the ways in which the spaces are restricted through borders and checkpoints and the ubiquitous wall, it is also the case that Palestinians insist on their ability to move within and occupy fully the spaces that are allowed to them and on finding new ways to manipulate the diminishing land actually available to them.

It is in fact this particular feature, taking the time to traverse what might seem impossibly small distances, that disrupts any sense of speed as a feature of mobility in modern life. Here, the ability to move at all is a component of the freedom that is still available rather than always already an example of how the lack of mobility acts as an exemplar of the lack of freedom. We understand the argument and implication that the occupation is everywhere. What Fiona Farnsworth calls 'the collective social absorption of "occupation" as a constant state'[76] is bolstered by an obvious 'architecture of occupation'[77] that delimits the space and shows itself up even in the surrounding restrictive infrastructure that includes soldiers and military vehicles.[78] However, people still move, regardless of whether they are watched or not. One particularly extraordinary scene is teeming with action and contains no commentary. In this image, almost everyone is on the move.

Sacco calls this section 'Refugeeland' and the people certainly seem to be navigating a rain-sodden and badly designed road without adequate drainage. People of all ages populate the image, loading up carts, going to school, playing in the puddles and walking to work. For all of the work around restrictions in relation to the everyday experience of Palestinian society, Sacco's *Palestine* does not actually dwell in this in the same ways that, say, Guy Delisle does in his graphic novel *Jerusalem*.[79] Here, Delisle most affecting illustrations are the ones that detail the extraordinary, almost inhuman patience with which people navigate the often excruciating waits at border crossings. In one of his most visually arresting scenes, he reveals the absurdity of how long it takes to traverse what seems an insignificant space. His sketch of a detour that now has to consider the separation wall exemplifies how much longer it now takes to cross over to the university in Jerusalem.

Rather than dwelling on how long it takes to reach the end point, however, Sacco's *Palestine* reveals *every* instance of mobility itself to be heroic as they hold within them a particular potential. In this case, the actual start and end point of Sacco's drawings of his journeys through Palestine are less significant than the ability to somehow still undertake them. In this context, a relatively 'short' trip that Sacco takes with a couple of acquaintances in Gaza from their home to their family greenhouse feels like a very *long journey* as we begin to understand the various components of what it takes to, for example, move tomatoes from greenhouse to market. In the section aptly called 'Tomatoes', Sacco is taken on a tour of a family's greenhouse near Deir el-Balah (in the Gaza strip) where he learns that 'trucking produce a few dozen miles from Gaza to the West Bank requires six different permits […] the vehicle pass alone needs clearance from five different offices'.[80] This, alongside other restrictions involving taxes and water supply, produce an extremely complex and rather off-putting system within which to attempt any agricultural ventures. Sacco is surprised that 'despite all this, these guys want to prove that Palestinians know how to grow a tomato'.[81] And this is indeed the surprise – that despite knowing that these tomatoes are often not eventually sold as Palestinian products, the *attempt* to nevertheless participate in this broader global market is still ongoing. Regardless of the various obstacles, the pride in the produce does not wane. Sacco captures this poignant moment where the suppliers from Gaza wish for their produce to retain some value outside of Gaza. Sacco also gives over space in his text for a discussion about the complexities around export tax, produce sabotage and the cultural capital interlaced in the labels that are placed on the tomato packaging. An implicit knowledge that Gaza has negative or unproductive associations leads the producers to accept that 'Carmel®Israeli Tomatoes' sell better than those labelled 'Gaza'. This poignant observation pays tribute to the many ways in which potential forms of mobility, in terms of goods and services, are limited and restricted. Though this delimits the extent to which the Palestinian producers can participate in global markets, their understanding of how best to achieve any role within it and the knowledge required to do so is undiminished. Certainly, getting around and also understanding the systems that allow for goods and for people to move around, is a preoccupation for Sacco and shows up in his work. Rather than only foreground the perceived spatial restrictions assumed of the contemporary Palestinian existence, he does take the opportunity to reveal the instances of mobility both in a personal but also a socio-historical sense. What might be recognisably considered freedom of movement is certainly clear in the scenes where Sacco relaxes in Tel Aviv[82] – where not every moment seems riddled with an urgency to either get somewhere, or get something done. Here, roads are clearly demarcated, parents stroll with their children and people sit and chat on park benches. It is not that these moments cannot be had in Sacco's *Palestine* but rather that he focuses instead on those instances where persons struggle for the day when that normalcy may arise and in the meantime, they keep moving.

In another memorable section where Sacco has a meeting with 'a couple of executive members of the Palestinian Federation of Women's Action Committees', it becomes obvious that, for all of the widely held perception that Palestinians undergo similar levels of deprivation and hardship, the women that come to the committees for legal help are often miles apart ideologically from those women appointed to advise them. Complaining that sometimes it is useless to talk about women's rights and notions of equality might come as a surprise for anyone reading Sacco's *Palestine* with a view to further understanding the ways in which the majority of Palestinians experience these restrictions on a daily basis from within their context as an occupied people. Instead, what the federation executives complain about is their inability to get across any notion of equality between the sexes in some spaces in Palestinian society where very traditional norms prevail: 'But in the villages it's different. They still think they're subordinate to men. They'll think I'm talking a foreign language if I tell them they're equal to men [...] Sometimes it seems like we're talking to ourselves.'[83] Here, it becomes clear the distances that some of the women have travelled in terms of being in conversation with broader ideas around a 'rights' discourse and, in particular, with educating women around 'using Islamic law to advance women's rights' even if that sometimes seems counterintuitive.[84] Here, the hard work is to separate the perceived limitations imposed by culture (be that Muslim or Christian in a Palestinian context) from the *actual* rights ingrained in religious law that can often be very advantageous to women when decoupled from traditional societal-based behaviours. It is sobering to read here the sophisticated understanding of the limitations of a 'rights'-based feminist agenda that might seek to decontextualise a sense of what might seem right – in this case a married woman complaining of her abusive husband – to what can actually be done. Here, the journey for the Palestinian activists is an arduous one: they must consider their dreams and hopes, born out of intellectual engagement with a history of international anti-colonial feminist thought and reconcile this with what they are able to offer women seeking help on the ground. We view this as a particularly fraught and bittersweet understanding of mobility: to understand and see when to move in a *particular* ideological and discursive direction rather than remain stubbornly and ineffectively committed to a particular viewpoint: 'Look,' says Rita, one of the women trying to work for reconciling apparently opposing viewpoints, 'I'm a Catholic [...] three years ago I was all for secular laws to protect women, I wouldn't give the idea up. But we can't achieve that now [...]'.[85]

Sacco's interviews and perceptive insights allow us to view the extent to which some Palestinian women have indeed engaged with and helped shape and argue for the implementation of certain global feminist and post-feminist ideals, in particular around the issue of decoupling women's rights from non-secular agendas. These women have travelled quite far in their thinking from certain contexts, such as nationalist ones, that expected and pushed for the secularisation of certain issues around the protection of vulnerable and subordinate family members. However, these women have also travelled wide in the opposite direction – understanding that what can get lost in the overwhelming adherence to a nationalist movement can also mean losing sight of more local and community customs that bind people together.

In the above examples, we have tried to show the extent to which mobility can be thought about even in contexts that at first seem to exemplify its complete absence. Movements of knowledge and of ideas are just as significant as the ability or freedom to move between physical spaces. Also, the capacity and opportunity to imagine other contexts and to engage with broader intellectual ideas is a sign of aspirations to be part of something wider. Paying attention to the ways in which texts represent moments where this aspiration or ability is expressed is vital as it helps us to move away from a critique that only celebrates moments that entirely break free from materially obvious limitations.

The consequences of the various ways in which mobility is experienced is explored in multiple illuminating ways by Elia Suleiman in his much talked about 2002 film *Divine Intervention: A Chronicle of Love and Pain*.[86] Suleiman's exploration of the tension that arises in the context of living with and under occupation in contemporary Palestine is intensely memorable for the ways in which it takes seemingly ordinary moments and turns them into sites for the exploration of how daily life becomes fertile terrain for profound insights into the meaning and experience of various forms of freedom. In Jacqueline Rose's analysis of the film, the aspects that render many of the actions absurd are understood as outcomes of 'a disaster it refers to obliquely – the Occupation is pervasive and glimpsed but as yet unnamed.[87] Something dreadful has happened offstage, but before the story and the filming begins'. This dreadful but unseen power also has the ability to, it seems, alter time as 'every moment feels suspended and slowed down, as the pace of daily life crawls almost to a halt'.[88] While this reading is compelling and speaks to a political critique that would seek to represent the ways in which the unseen occupation has the ability to manipulate the subjective experience of time and to negatively influence any tendency towards envisioning movement and progress, it is also accurate to say that there is a *lot* of movement in the film at the same time as there is an acute awareness of contexts where there should be movement and for some reason, there isn't.

Kay Dickinson writes persuasively on the multiple ways in which 'roads have understandably haunted the film culture of this tiny and potentially easily traversed country'.[89] She describes *Divine Intervention* as a film that 'wind[s] around road systems' and tells the story of a 'love affair at the checkpoint and peppers its storyline with arguments about driveway expansions and car license plates'.[90] Dickinson invites us to resist simply describing the road in Palestinian films as a metaphor for getting nowhere and participating instead in 'a road-building process of sorts' where we can begin to better understand how infrastructure is actually utilised, sometimes in surprising ways. Hugely contested in the Israeli/Palestinian contexts, roads continue to determine what areas are connected to each other and what areas are, as a result, cut off. Dickinson reflects that the 'institution of what is increasingly dubbed an "apartheid road system" has no firm foundation in Israeli law, making the implementation of this infrastructure extremely opportunistic, arbitrary and unregulated'.[91]

It is in fact this opportunistic, arbitrary and unregulated feature of the treatment of infrastructure, and in particular roads, that *Divine Intervention* takes to task, seeking to intervene in the very place where movement is most crucial and where the injunction to keep moving is rudimentary and necessary. As Dickinson notes, 'Palestine can, at times, expertly negotiate the tension between resolute, nationalistic permanence and tactical or enforced transience'.[92] This dynamic, or tension, is worked upon and coaxed out of moments that might, on first viewing, appear as examples of stasis or even as instances of unconscious repetition. In the now often remarked upon scene from *Divine Intervention* of a man waiting by a bus shelter for a bus that will never come, surely what is important is that there *should* be a bus – for there is a bus shelter that has been built for this very purpose. The expectation that there will be a bus is, in essence, a valid one in terms of a structure that seeks to enable the movement of people. In this context, the bus schedule, or lack of one, does indeed reinforce the idea that there is nowhere to go but it simultaneously reminds us that there should be somewhere to move along to. We are not sure that we need to see these scenes as daily deaths[93] but rather as reminders of the daily struggle to continue to enact and engage with that which should function but does not.

Cars, in addition to the road, who uses them and what powers they provide, are used to their full extent in *Divine Intervention*. Residents use cars as spaces of privacy where they do not need to constantly police their innermost sentiments and can speak and act freely against an expectation that they perform a daily nationalist solidarity. Access to a car and to the most ubiquitous problem of a car parking space, is a filmic act of world-shrinkage where the problems faced by the ordinary Palestinian are not far removed from anyone living in a busy town surrounded by congestion. Nevertheless, driving, fixing cars, taking cars away and stopping others from driving are an integral part of the film. In subtle but noticeable ways, Suleiman's use of the car and roads in the film undermines the sense of Palestine as objectively *small* (with nowhere to go) – making size and distance inherently a subjective experience and the right and ability to move in that space, whatever its size, an integral aspect of a progressive and mobile society.

That transport here takes on a wholly unexpected set of signifiers shows how residents of occupation improvise and reshape otherwise banal objects and their uses. In other words, in *Divine Intervention*, a car becomes a space for lovers to meet and also a space from which to start an insurrection (in a memorable scene, a balloon with Arafat's face printed on it is released from the car and crosses the checkpoint). When a frustrated man tears off the licence plates from his neighbour's car, he stops that neighbour from being able to drive.

When a man drives through the street, seemingly greeting his neighbours but inwardly using the foulest language to describe them, he exercises his right to hate those whom we might expect him to love. In a particularly frustrating set of scenes, an Israeli task force comes to fix a patch of road that is constantly being destroyed by a local Arab. He does this in order to make it difficult for them to drive through. Displaying a thorough understanding of how crucial it is to get around and to be able to move quickly, the film focuses on how various modes of transport can perform unexpected roles when they are denied their primary objective – to move people around. It's not so much that the film wants to celebrate small moments of rebellion but rather that the film does make some rather poignant and cutting observations about what is needed for the smooth functioning of daily life. What often brings into focus the truncated purpose of the car is the representation of the ubiquitous checkpoint. Anna Ball writes of the ability of certain directors to change our expectation of what can happen at the checkpoint through what she engagingly calls an 'aesthetics of astonishment'.[94] What is most astonishing of all in Suleiman's film, perhaps, is that there is no attempt by the protagonist to cross the checkpoint at all though there is a commitment to be *by* the checkpoint and to witness the events that occur. This choice stresses the extraordinary, complicated nature of navigating the various checkpoints that, in Ball's words, 'isolate Palestinians both from Israel and from one another'.[95] This lack of mobility to cross is, however, counteracted in the insistence to be in a car nevertheless and to do what is possible within the space that *is* permitted and that can be navigated. As Anna Bernard notes, Suleiman's film 'has helped to further develop a vivid popular imaginary of the experience of crossing – or not crossing – the West Bank checkpoint'.[96]

Speaking of navigation, *Divine Intervention* wastes no time in honing in on what it might mean to *know* a place and to know one's way around it. This is very different from being permitted to move in that space as a result of geo-political decisions. In a scene that is reminiscent of a Monty Python sketch, a tourist in Jerusalem asks for help from Israeli police who are looking after a prisoner in a jeep. Unable to help the tourist find her way to the Church of the Holy Sepulchre, the soldiers get the Arab prisoner out of the jeep and solicit his help. The prisoner, who is a local, knows his way around even though he is not permitted to walk freely or even take off his blindfold. A mental map of the area is so accessible to him that he can guide the tourist easily (in fact he gives her three different routes). This exchange toys with our notion of mobility and freedom of movement as it highlights the paradox of knowing exactly how to get to somewhere that you are not permitted to travel to. Mobility is, here, a commodity and one that is held back, gifted but also mocked.

The freedom to move is calculated differently based on the particular context and the ability to get far and not does not seem to impact on the insistence to get in the car or to wait for the bus – even if the car has nowhere to go and the bus never comes. Reminded by a neighbour that 'there is no bus', the waiting man replies 'I know'. It is not the lack of knowledge that makes him wait, neither is it a bowing down to some sort of nihilistic tendency. Rather, seen in the context of the entire film, every opportunity to point out the curtailment of movement simultaneously expands the very idea of movement itself. In other words, as Dickinson points out, 'Palestinian cinema entices us to reconsider [...] the stamina required for quotidian (versus "spectacularized") existence under occupation'.[97] The sheer energy required to sometimes not seemingly move an inch is captured so poignantly in the multiple scenes of the lovers who meet at the checkpoint and spend their time with their hands entwined, searching and enacting other's feelings. Here, we sense that great distances are covered in terms of meaningful engagements while they sit in a stationary car.

Divine Intervention works hard to capture the pressure points in a context where movement and mobility are subject to reinterpretation. On the face of it, a geographically small space occupied by military personnel and sophisticated infrastructure might seem straightforward to manage. The film shows the refusal of the recipients of this management system to fully acknowledge and orient themselves towards this reality. In turn, the occupation does not itself fully understand the small but utterly destructive actions that incrementally stall its work. The roadwork team constantly come back to fix the broken road, the checkpoint guards that persistently monitor every single movement are anxious, the soldiers who have no sense at all of their geography need help from a local – and all are slowed down by the quotidian existence of those around them who must keep moving, if only to stand still.

The imperative for the citizen who is also a migrant to continue moving to and from the country of origin is of central importance to films such as Moroccan filmmaker Ismaël Ferroukhi's *Le Grande Voyage* (2004). Set in the context of volatile discussions around the role of Islam in secular France, Hakim Abderrezak argues that the film queries whether or not 'we need to revisit the idea of immigration to, and integration in, France?'.[98] Abderrezak argues that, although the film enacts one man and his son's voyage from France to Saudi Arabia by car for the holy pilgrimage, the sense of what it might mean for migrants to travel across to another destination they consider home, in this case a religious home, presents us with particular questions around what mobility might mean. Where we might assume the end point of certain types of journeys, from perceived postcolonial peripheries such as Morocco to imperial centres such as France, to be the cosmopolitan city, with all of its caveats and hidden brutalities for certain forms of migratory experiences, in this film it is the ability to voyage out that gives the father and son the opportunity to understand the significance and import of their voyage in. Once again, we are in the context of what could be viewed as a road movie: 'the road movie is not a new genre in *Beur* cinema [...] To go on pilgrimage by car from France, however, is an original scenario'.[99] Abderrezak deploys a fascinating and expansive term to encapsulate how he sees this journey: disimmigration, or revealing something that was not anticipated in the context of migration. This movement is one that then, to an extent, seeks to look pragmatically to the advantages of the migrant experience and, to an extent, to perhaps question and reject them by choosing to travel away. 'Disimmigration' argues Abderrezak, 'thus becomes a divergent movement made in an unexpected way and to a novel place in order to bury the burdensome notion of *émigré* where it all started'.[100]

Disimmigration, then, alerts us to the ways in which, as political and social contexts continue to prove incapable of arbitrating the 'hazardous narrative of identity and immigration',[101] culture responds by imagining ways out of this seemingly intractable condition. The film challenges what Bekers et al. have termed 'Europe's alleged ownership and transmission of "universalist" Enlightenment principles (civilization, nationalism, human rights, scientific progress, etc.)' and participates in 'the continuing re-examination of the role of the cultural imagination in (re) conceptualizing, the past, present and future of Europe'.[102] In *Le Grande Voyage*, one of the first scenes takes place in a used car depot and, in a subsequent scene, one of the first bits of information we are given is that a father's eldest son has been arrested and has had his driver's licence revoked. Keen to take the Haj and to make his way there by car the father laments that he 'does not know how to drive and [can't] wait another year [until his son is out of prison]'. Cars and driving are clearly central to the disimmigration narrative that is to follow and the father orders his younger son Reda to drive him to Mecca. About the car, 'it can drive around the world', Reda's elder brother tells him of the car he has loaned them for the trip. The journey however, provides Reda's father with the opportunity to cut him off from the world in an unforgettable scene where he throws out Reda's mobile phone: thus begins their journey of defamiliarisation. Reminding him that they are not 'tourists', Reda's father ensures that the trip across Europe turns into a perfunctory one – a question of getting enough miles under their belt before falling asleep in the car, exhausted. The father's insistence that they take back roads where possible and avoid the motorways means that they are exposed to smaller and less known places along the way, with no possibility of taking time over sights. When they stop in the middle of what seems like a fork in the road in the midst of empty fields, Reda takes photos of what he can, desperate to capture anything of this voyage. This is a peculiar and desperate trip – devoid of any of the excitement and thrill of travel and heavy with unspoken desperation to arrive and to escape at the same time. In many ways, it enacts and speaks to the unspoken hardship of migration and to the harshness of travel when not bounded by the comfortable inquisitiveness that often accompanies tourism and journeys. Although Reda and his father have all of the necessary paperwork, passports and visas and do not experience any unwelcome inquiries at the border, their travel is nevertheless haunted by what seems to be their community-bound existence back in France.

When Reda begs his father whether they can stop off in Milan or Venice so that he might get to see these cities, he cries that 'he may never get to see them again in his whole life'. This is a curious statement as Reda is a young man with French citizenship. Yet from what we see of his life, we understand that it is somewhat bound up with what he feels is expected of him.

These representations and observations by Ferroukhi are profound as they speak to the limitations borne out of a particular context and interpreted by individuals who exist in particular migrant communities. Why wouldn't a young French man be able to visit Venice, one might ask? Here, what is at play is a particularly poignant set of dynamics that revolve around the unspoken expectation that the journey of the migrant must somehow stop at a particular destination; that the burden of such an undertaking can only be undergone once. In moving away from France, Reda and his father must not be seen to be seeking to gain anything at all from the countries and nations they move across – they remain itinerant and nomadic until they reach Mecca. The freedom to travel, paradoxically, brings no pleasure. In fact, Reda is incredulous to find that his father still prefers to deal with the underworld of informal exchanges than to participate in more structured forms of citizen participation.

For example, rather than go to an official currency exchange stall, he prefers to haggle with currency hustlers and seems to get a better deal. This particular form of intercultural exchange succeeds because the two men haggling through a peculiar form of sign language and limited vocabulary recognise something in each other, something that Reda does not. The particular migrant experience of having to sometimes exist under the radar is shown up here as one that has become second nature. Reda's awkward and rather fearful reaction shows the complicated nature of such an act outside of any material necessity. It is as though the socio-cultural context that underpins a certain history of migration into Europe brings with it a certain distrust that is then enacted in daily exchanges. Thus, in many ways, the deeper they move into the journey, the more isolated and removed they become, both geographically in terms of the deserted routes and backroads they choose to drive on and socially in terms of the marginalised people they encounter and engage with.

The hardship that they endure, including taking shelter in abandoned freezing bus stops and finding themselves snowed in when they fall asleep in their car, does to some extent mirror a frantic and precarious journey, though in this case the men are both protected by their legitimate and legal status (we often see their passports at checkpoints) and also to an extent by their cultural capital (they continue to speak French and English to strangers as they travel across Europe). The latter, however, acts as a profound hindrance, for example, as they try to enter Turkey. Here, a middleman has to intercede on their behalf in order to convince the police of their intentions. He ends up joining them on the trip, though the father warns Reda that he doesn't trust him. The film makes us acutely aware of the relative nature of freedom and the often-perceived advantages around mobility that are however highly contingent and often rooted in longer and more protracted social histories.

Abderrezak suggests that the father is attempting to '*dés-occident* (de-Western[ise]) Réda'[103] but, more poignantly, the film is trying to de-familiarise the West away from the progressive infrastructure that often stands in for it, such as overdeveloped cities and fast motorways.

The privilege of mobility is not at all what it seems in *Le Grande Voyage*. Rather, the quality of the destination and the complicated and necessarily inherited cultural history of the migratory voyage into Europe and all of the sacrifices that it requires are replayed even on the voyage away. It is as though all voyages are tainted or overcome by that first painful one. In her consideration of Arabic literature of migration to Europe, Johanna Sellman notes that current narratives explore 'the changing meanings of exile as well as citizenship in the context of mass migration' and offer ways in which we can 're-imagine diaspora and mobility'.[104] *Le Grande Voyage* seems to pick up on these points and participates in an enactment of a certain type of vulnerability that comes from being 'outside established networks of support'[105] (753) that exist only in the ethno-national bound spaces back in France. Although understandably much of the current critical focus is on the 'concerns and contexts of contemporary forced and precarious migrations and the border-building practices that states employ in an attempt to limit or manage mobility',[106] what *Le Grande Voyage* performs is a backwards glance at the sacrifices made for that mobility; sacrifices that are not always overcome and replaced but rather sit uncomfortably alongside the perceived benefits of citizenship. Reda's father has been in France for 30 years and so his context of migration is very different to the more contentious and volatile one that has gripped Europe this century. The political and public debates that he and his family inhabit are ones that focus on 'the perceived reluctance to integrate and migrate'.[107] In fact, an acute summary of the conditions that Reda and his family find themselves in provides a broad context within which we can begin to appreciate the particular form of escapism enacted in the film. Gerrits writes:

> The concentration of migrants in the poorer districts of the larger cities and suburbs, the distinct language, culture and religion of many migrants, the congruence of ethnic diversity and disparities in education and income, the relatively high levels of unemployment, social security dependence, and crime among some minority groups, as well as the fear and the realization that the violence and fundamentalism in the Muslim world would be imported into the societies of Western Europe, gave the immigration issue an unprecedented social and political acuity. Together with European integration, the immigration issue generated a stronger emphasis on the political significance of the nation and national identity.[108]

Gerrits' analysis above does not so much present a truth as it highlights the spectrum upon which the lives of migrants can be plotted according to age, gender, ethnicity and religion. Significantly in the film, we do not see overt 'expressions of xenophobia and racist violence'[109] yet the overall context of the film's making is, as Abderrezak argues, 'the major nationwide debate on French identity and the ongoing questioning of the compatibility of Islamic values with secularism'.[110] *Le Grande Voyage*, however, does not place this context in the foreground, letting it emerge rather in the process of the voyage out towards Mecca. It is interesting to see how the start of the film is concerned with all of the markers associated with a marginalised migrant community: Reda's family live in a very small apartment, his parents speak Moroccan Arabic at home, his mother wears traditional dress and is a homemaker. The family do not seem to have very much money and the journey is a frugal one in terms of comfort. Reda himself does have aspirations to do well in school and resents having to take the time off to do his father's bidding. Yet there is a sense that the father is aware of the difficulties that lie ahead for his son and inadvertently perhaps finds a way to reveal to him the various ways in which the migrant voyage does not begin and end where one might expect. The film also espouses, in its ending in Mecca, a very surprising and perhaps unintended possibility: that France was never the end point of migration. In fact, Reda's father dies and remains in Mecca.

Sellman extends this argumentative potential in her analysis of contemporary migration studies where she reflects on the growing body of work (citing Michel Agier, *Borderlands: Towards an Anthropology of the Cosmopolitan Condition* (2016)) that reconfigures what we might have once considered destinations (centres of Empire) into 'points of transit'.[111] Though *Le Grande Voyage* is not a story that tracks the precarious conditions faced by the many displaced migrants undergoing very different forms of journeys today, it does perhaps anticipate some of the continuing social unease within which certain migrant communities continue to exist. Thrust alongside the more conspicuous and urgent conditions of the many migrants attempting hazardous flights, *Le Grande Voyage* reminds us of the constant low-level scrutiny that sits alongside the experience of migrant communities in postcolonial Europe. Even within a context of relatively secure citizenship, aspirations for available socio-economic opportunities seem stymied and stalled.

Conclusion

The above examples ranging from modernist and contemporary fiction, apartheid and post-apartheid texts, to representations of Palestinian contexts and Maghrebi cinema, all show how mobility is engaged with and made manifest in a variety of unexpected ways. Movement itself is conceived of in such different and inspiring ways by the artists, writers and filmmakers that challenge any sense of centre-periphery certitude. Mobility is creatively understood to involve not only the very physical act of traversing space but also configured as a radical opportunity to question any perceived injunction to blindly accept that progress or development occurs in only one direction. Opportunities to question and revisit this directive are at the heart of the experiences discussed in these texts and films. One character's understanding of freedom does not coincide with another community's experience of supposed liberty that fails to bring with it opportunities for social and economic advances. At the same time, in the spatially restrictive context of Gordimer's stories set in apartheid and post-apartheid South Africa and conducted along racial lines, the configuration of mobility is dramatically different for the various characters involved. The very understanding of distances travelled has altogether divergent meanings that are often incomprehensible to the various individuals, even when in intimate relationships. In the context of Palestine, mobility is a daily material concern though at the same time, participation with and contribution to global issues and concepts disclose an intellectual mobility unrestricted by otherwise inflexible physical borders. In the Maghrebi film *Le Grande Voyage*, we see how the opportunity to undertake a very different form of migration voyage works to query the myth of arrival to the colonial centre. Here, by subtly traversing the *periphery* of European cities, the film gestures towards the other more rugged Europe of abandoned bus shelters, deserted hotels and featureless borders. The ability and privilege to move unhindered ironically leads away from Europe altogether, as if in acknowledgement of the thwarted promise of migration.

The texts discussed in this chapter explore the pains and hardships of displacement. They also implore us to recognise the often-unexpected pleasures and illuminations contingent on mobility. These texts toy with and, frequently in a defiantly and sorely needed register of composed hopefulness, foretell the shape of a world that construes mobility not as threat but as promise. The best way to read them is to follow their lead by tracing and then seeking to elucidate the various relationships, networks and connections that they portray. As we shall see in the next chapter, Edward Said used the term 'worldliness' to describe how texts are produced and then subsequently circulate in specific circumstances in the world. It behoves the critic, Said argues, to explain the myriad different ways in which texts register or articulate these originating contexts for various audiences.[112] The value that we attribute to these texts and the pleasure and instruction we have derived from reading and teaching them is inseparable from the ways in which they actively illuminate these worldly origins and consequences and thus work to connect up situations, events, people and other phenomena that might otherwise seem reified or disconnected.

Thus, Hamid's *Exit West*, for example, invites readers to see in specific dramas and lives the confluence of everything from climate change, the migration 'crisis' and inequality to the perils and possibilities of technological change. A more Marxist idiom might call this way of reading 'dialectical', provided we mean by that term something like Theodor Adorno's 'intransigence towards all reification', that is, a refusal to accept that such important phenomena exist or can be understood in isolation.[113] At stake, ultimately, is the ability to think critically about mobility and to cultivate ways of reading that are themselves mobile in the sense of trying to use the occasion of reading as an opportunity to piece together apparently reified worlds. These texts refuse what Rebecca Solnit has called 'the ideology of isolation'. Why, Solnit asks, does the very idea of climate change pose such a threat to the fossil fuel cartels and other beneficiaries of financialised capitalism? Because 'it tells us more powerfully and urgently than anything ever has that everything is connected, that nothing exists in isolation'.[114] Let us insist, as Solnit does, that making such connections also means seeing conflicts and discrepant interests as well as acknowledging the necessity of struggle and action. If the increasing concentration of carbon dioxide and other greenhouse gases irrevocably alters the atmosphere and therefore the future of all life on Earth, then the ideology of 'every man for himself' is immediately proved false and new forms of collective responsibility become urgently necessary. Something similar could be said about migration. Nothing demonstrates the obsolescence or at least the invidiousness of borders and the offensive arbitrariness of state-sanctioned distinctions between citizens and non-citizens more than the spectacle of refugees herded into camps, incarcerated in cages, tortured and enslaved in Libya or callously abandoned to their deaths in the Mediterranean.

The texts analysed in this chapter enjoin a great cognisance or mindfulness of our world's dense interconnectedness. It is an ethic of care or of taking care (in the dual sense of being aware of something or someone and of taking responsibility) that they invite, bearing in mind that the new nationalist movements seeking to beggar their neighbours in an era of economic crisis and climate breakdown as well as the oligarchs and demagogues seeking to orchestrate these distractions and indoctrinations are, like Tom and Daisy in *The Great Gatsby*, 'careless people' 'who smashed up things and creatures and then retreated back into their money or their vast carelessness [...] and let other people clean up the mess they had made [...]'.[115] What new forms of collective action and responsibility arise when texts get us to start thinking critically and carefully about mobility?

Notes

1 George Steiner, *Language and Silence: Essays 1958–1966*, London: Faber & Faber, 1985, p. 228.
2 Andrew Smith, 'Migrancy, Hybridity, and Postcolonial Literary Studies', in Neil Lazarus (ed), *The Cambridge Companion to Postcolonial Literary Studies*, Cambridge: Cambridge University Press, 2004, pp. 241–261, pp. 245 and 258.

3 Michael Hardt and Antonio Negri, *Empire*, Cambridge, MA: Harvard University Press, 2000, p. 400.
4 Giovanni Arrighi, 'Lineages of Empire', in Gopal Balakrishnan (ed), *Debating 'Empire'*, London: Verso, 2003, pp. 29–42.
5 Reece Jones, *Violent Borders: Refugees and the Right to Move*, London: Verso, 2016, p. 67.
6 Walden Bello, *Dark Victory: The United States, Structural Adjustment and Global Poverty*, London: Pluto Press, 1994.
7 Peter Gowan, *The Global Gamble: Washington's Faustian Bid for World Dominance*, London: Verso, 1999. This symbiosis between East Asian surplus capital and US debt is unpicked in Giovanni Arrighi's *Adam Smith in Beijing: Lineages of the Twenty-First Century*, London: Verso, 2007; and Leo Panitch and Sam Gindin's *The Making of Global Capitalism: The Political Economy of American Empire*, London: Verso, 2012.
8 Charles Dickens, *Great Expectations*, ed. Charlotte Mitchell, Harmondsworth: Penguin, 1996 [1861], p. 201.
9 Mimi Sheller, *Mobility Justice: The Politics of Movement in an Age of Extremes*, London: Verso, 2018, p. xi.
10 Kamila Shamsie, *Home Fire*, London: Bloomsbury, 2018, pp. 87–88.
11 Shamsie, *Home Fire*, p. 144.
12 Timothy Mo, *Pure*, London: Turnaround Books, 2012.
13 Claude McKay, *Banjo: A Story without a Plot*, New York: Harvest, 1970, p. 46.
14 David Scott, *Conscripts of Modernity: The Tragedy of Colonial Enlightenment*, Durham, NC: Duke University Press, 2004.
15 Brent Hayes Edwards, *The Practice of Diaspora: Literature, Translation, and the Rise of Black Internationalism*, Cambridge, MA: Harvard University Press, 2003, pp. 204–205.
16 Michael Denning, *Noise Uprising: The Audiopolitics of a World Musical Revolution*, London: Verso, 2015.
17 McKay, *Banjo*, p. 95.
18 Ibid., p. 11.
19 Mary Lou Emery, 'Caribbean Modernism: Plantation to Planetary', *The Oxford Handbook of Global Modernisms*, ed. Mark Wollaeger and Matt Eatough, Oxford: Oxford University Press, 2012, pp. 48–77, p. 59.
20 Bridget T. Chalk, '"Sensible of Being Étrangers": Plots and Identity Papers in *Banjo*', *Twentieth Century Literature*, 55:3 (2009), 357–377, 361.
21 McKay, *Banjo*, p. 321.
22 Ibid., p. 137.
23 Mohsin Hamid, *Exit West*, St Ives: Hamish Hamilton, 2017. Subsequent page references are given in the main text after *EW*. We take the term 'world-ecology' from Jason W. Moore's work. Moore argues that a world-ecology emerged in the sixteenth century as a result of capital's utilisation of the cheap inputs of labour-power, food, energy and raw materials. See *Capitalism in the Web of Life: Ecology and the Accumulation of Capital*, London: Verso, 2015. A good example of the kind of critical work facilitated by Moore's concept of 'world-ecology' is Sharae Deckard's account of the 'irrealist' 'literature of cacao' in the Caribbean and Latin America, 'Cacao and Cascadura: Energetic Consumption

and Production in World-ecological Literature', *Journal of Postcolonial Writing*, 53:3 (2017), 342–354.
24 For Lazarus, '"the West"' comes to stand in for imperialist power; but since what is thus named is preeminently a civilizational value rather than a mode of production or a social formation, the alibi of "the West" serves to dematerialize what it tacitly references'. 'The fetish of "the West" in postcolonial theory', *Marxism, Modernity, and Postcolonial Studies*, ed. Crystal Bartolovich and Neil Lazarus, Cambridge: Cambridge University Press, 2002, pp. 43–64, p. 54. Lazarus has also warned against the hasty conflation of 'postcommunism' and 'postcolonialism' in the discipline, whereby former Soviet bloc countries such as Poland, Lithuania and Hungary are welcomed into the 'postcolonial' fold. The problem isn't that the Soviet Union wasn't an imperialist power, which of course it was, but that the escape from its orbit is sometimes taken to be an escape into the arms of a homogeneously and often uncritically conceived 'West' or 'Europe'. Such blunt terms actually tell us very little about relations of power in the modern capitalist world-system, whether we are using them disparagingly or, as postcommunist postcolonials often do, with a more positive connotation. 'Spectres Haunting: Postcommunism and Postcolonialism', *Journal of Postcolonial Writing*, 48:2 (2012), 117–129.
25 Paul Mason, *Why It's Still Kicking off Everywhere: The New Global Revolutions*, Second Edition, London: Verso, 2013, pp. 66–73.
26 Paul Mason, *Postcapitalism: A Guide to Our Future*, London: Allen Lane, 2015, p. 212.
27 Benedict Anderson, *Imagined Communities: Reflections on the Origin and Spread of Nationalism*, Revised Edition, London: Verso, 1991, p. 25.
28 Theo Tait, 'Some will need to be killed', *London Review of Books*, 16 November 2017.
29 Adam Greenfield, *Radical Technologies: The Design of Everyday Life*, London: Verso, p. 8. See also Jonathan Crary, *24/7: Late Capitalism and the Ends of Sleep*, London: Verso, 2014.
30 'Highest levels of world's most toxic chemicals found in African free-range eggs: European E-waste dumping a contributor', 24 April 2019.
31 Grégoire Chamayou, *Drone Theory*, trans. Janet Lloyd, Harmondsworth: Penguin, 2015, p. 18. See also Andrew Cockburn, *Kill Chain: Drones and the Rise of High-Tech Assassins*, London: Verso, 2016.
32 The perishing in the dreadful inferno at Grenfell Tower of more than seventy predominantly poor Londoners, many from ethnic minorities as well as undocumented migrants, residents whose repeated complaints about electrical surges, flammable cladding and the lack of a sprinkler system were seemingly ignored, provide a grim confirmation of the novel's insistence on attending to the extreme levels of social and economic inequality within as well as between nation states. One upshot of that inequality is a national housing crisis, of which London and specifically the borough of Kensington and Chelsea, in which dilapidated fire hazards, massive social housing waiting lists and mass homelessness exist alongside unoccupied mansions bought by offshore trusts as speculative investments and money laundering schemes, are a graphic encapsulation.
33 Mohsin Hamid et al., 'The turmoil of today's world: Leading writers respond to the refugee crisis', *The Guardian*, 12 September 2015.

34 Hannah Arendt, *The Origins of Totalitarianism*, New York: Harcourt, 1994 [1951], p. 459. Arendt's classic 1951 study shows that European imperialism helped prepare the ground for the voracious expansionism and the violent race hate of fascism. Many anti-colonial writers have stressed totalitarianism's similarities and even its indebtedness to the dictatorship of the colonial state. In his *Discourse on Colonialism* (1950), a jeremiad against the European empires, the Martiniquan poet and politician Aimé Césaire told his readers that Hitler had only 'applied to Europe colonialist procedures which until then had been reserved exclusively for the Arabs of Algeria, the coolies of India, and the blacks of Africa'. Before Europeans were Nazism's victims therefore, 'they were its accomplices'. Aimé Césaire, *Discourse on Colonialism*, trans. by Joan Pinkham, London: Monthly Review Press, 1972 [1950], p. 14. Sven Lindqvist's searing study of the origins of the European genocide, *'Exterminate All the Brutes'*, agrees that 'Auschwitz was a modern industrial application of a policy of extermination on which European world domination had long since rested'. Sven Lindqvist, *'Exterminate all the Brutes': One Man's Odyssey into the Heart of Darkness and the Origins of the European Genocide*, trans. Joan Tate, New York: The New Press, 1996, p. 160. This is a truth recently underscored by the thesis of David Olusoga and Casper Erichsen's important study of the conquest of German South West Africa, *The Kaiser's Holocaust*. Nazism, Olusoga and Erichsen demonstrate, 'was, in part, the final homecoming of theories and practices that Europeans had developed and perfected in far-flung corners of the world during the last phase of imperial conquest'. David Olusoga and Casper W. Erichsen, *The Kaiser's Holocaust: Germany's Forgotten Genocide*, London: Faber & Faber, 2010, p. 3.

35 'Trump calls some unauthorized immigrants "animals" in rant', *New York Times*.

36 Fredric Jameson, *The Antinomies of Realism*, London: Verso, 2015, pp. 308–309.

37 *Exit West* thereby recalls Michael Denning's analysis of the hybrid origins of vernacular music in the globe's colonial ports around the 1920s.

38 Judith Butler has provided a useful definition of 'precarity' as a term that 'designates that politically induced condition in which certain populations suffer from failing social and economic networks of support more than others, and become differentially exposed to injury, violence, and death'. It names 'the differential distribution of precariousness. Populations that are differentially exposed suffer heightened risk of disease, poverty, starvation, displacement, and vulnerability to violence without adequate protection or redress', for example, refugees or sexual minorities prevented from accomplishing 'the breakthrough of certain kinds of gender performances into public space, free of police brutality, harassment, criminalization, and pathologization'. Judith Butler, *Notes Toward a Performative Theory of Assembly*, Cambridge, MA: Harvard University Press, 2015, p. 33.

39 Immanuel Wallerstein, *The Decline of American Power: The U.S. in a Chaotic World*, New York: New Press, 2003, p. 244.

40 Erik Olin Wright, 'Participatory Economics: A Sympathetic Critique', Robin Hahnel and Erik Olin Wright, *Alternatives to Capitalism: Proposals for a Democratic Economy*, London: Verso, 2016, pp. 17–47, p. 40.

41 Paul Gilroy, *After Empire: Melancholia or Convivial Culture?* London: Routledge, 2004, p. 98. See also Robert Spencer, 'The Politics of Imperial Nostalgia',

in Graham Huggan and Ian Law (eds), *Racism, Postcolonialism, Europe*, Liverpool: Liverpool University Press, 2009, pp. 176–196.
42 Robert Winder, *Bloody Foreigners: The Story of Immigration to Britain*, London: Abacus, 2004, p. 1.
43 Stathis Kouvelakis, 'Borderland: Greece and the EU's Southern Question', *New Left Review II*, 110 (2018), 5–33, 22.
44 The Euro is not a genuine single currency, as the former Syriza finance minister Yanis Varoufakis points out, since it has no mechanism for fiscal transfers between states and makes national governments responsible for their own debts. Yet it also prevents heavily indebted countries from regaining competitiveness by currency devaluations. Greece remains trapped in austerity, hardly a beneficiary of solidarity. *And the Weak Suffer What They Must? Europe, Austerity and the Threat to Global Stability*, London: Vintage, 2016, pp. 216–217. Varoufakis is a leading light of the Democracy in Europe 2025 movement (DiEM25) that aims to radically democratise and socialise the EU. Costas Lapavitsas offers a more militant proposal for replacing the EU entirely due to its largely unaccountable institutions and its determination to institutionalise austerity, exemplified by a currency and a central bank that work principally in the interests of the big banks and of German export capitalists. Costas Lapavitsas, *The Left Case Against the EU*, Cambridge: Polity, 2019. The EU has painfully few answers to the existential problem of climate change, to the need to transform the voracious banks into publicly owned vehicles for allocating investment, or to the growing social and economic inequality within the EU that is feeding the rise of the far right, or to the growing inequality between the overdeveloped and underdeveloped worlds that is the major factor in prompting migrants to risk their lives on the Mediterranean. See also Wolfgang Streeck, 'Why the Euro Divides Europe', *How Will Capitalism End? Essays on a Failing System*, London: Verso, 2016, pp. 165–183; and Heiner Flassbeck and Costas Lapavitsas, *Against the Troika: Crisis and Austerity in the Eurozone*, London: Verso, 2015.
45 Kouvelakis, 'Borderland: Greece and the EU's Southern Question', p. 12.
46 Lapavitsas, *The Left Case Against the EU*, p. 119.
47 Kouvelakis, 'Borderland', p. 7.
48 Tariq Ali, *The Extreme Centre: A Second Warning*, London: Verso, 2018.
49 Frantz Fanon, *The Wretched of the Earth*, trans. Constance Farrington, Harmondsworth: Penguin, 1990 [1961], p. 81.
50 Kristian Shaw, 'BrexLit', *Brexit and Literature: Critical and Cultural Responses*, ed. Robert Eaglestone, London: Routledge, 2018, pp. 15–30. 'Populism', by the way, strikes us as an imprecise term to characterise the recrudescence of xenophobic nationalisms, at least when it is unqualified in this way. Too often it is deployed as a catch-all term to describe very different types and levels of political challenge to the hitherto dominant neoliberal consensus on competition, the entrepreneurial state, finance-led growth, the exploitation of immigrants, etc. It conflates progressive alternatives based on the defence of migrants, economic equality and decarbonisation with reactionary projects to protect the status quo behind border walls. All political projects rely on a defence of 'the people'; the struggle to define 'the people', as Chantal Mouffe argues, is what politics *is*. Chantal Mouffe, *For a Left Populism*, London: Verso, 2018.

51 Pierre Bourdieu, *Firing Back: Against the Tyranny of the Market 2*, trans. Loïc Wacquant, New York: New Press, 2003, p. 15.
52 Nadine Gordimer, *The Pickup*, London: Bloomsbury, 2001.
53 Ibid., p. 13.
54 Ibid., p. 13.
55 Håkan Thörn, *Anti-Apartheid and the Emergence of a Global Civil Society*, Basingstoke: Palgrave, 2006, p. 19.
56 Ibid., p. 19.
57 Ibid.
58 Nadine Gordimer, *Life Times: Stories 1952–2007*, London: Bloomsbury, 2010.
59 This law dates back to 1927 and has subsequently been revised many times. Essentially it forbade extramarital or consensual sexual relations to take place between black South African and White South Africans. The amendment in 1957 further forbade all sexual relations between white people and non-white people.
60 Gordimer, *Life Times*, p. 268.
61 Ibid.
62 Ibid.
63 Ibid., p. 272.
64 Ibid., p. 274.
65 Ibid., p. 274, emphasis added.
66 Ibid., p. 273.
67 Ibid., p. 278.
68 Ibid., p. 19.
69 Ibid., p. 37.
70 Ibid., pp. 48–49, emphasis added.
71 Ibid., p. 115.
72 Ibid., p. 230.
73 Ibid., p. 238.
74 Joe Sacco, *Palestine*. London: Jonathan Cape, 2003.
75 Rose Brister, 'Sounding the Occupation: Joe Sacco's Palestine and the Uses of Graphic Narratives for (Post) Colonial Critique', in *ariel: A Review of International English Literature*, 45:1 (2014), 103–129.
76 Fiona Farnsworth, '"What I Saw for Myself": Collating Polyphonic Voices in Joe Sacco's Palestine Narratives', in *Cambridge Journal of Postcolonial Literary Inquiry*, 6:2 (2019), 199–219, 211.
77 Ibid., p. 212.
78 Ibid.
79 Guy Delisle, *Jerusalem: Chronicles the Holy City*, London: Jonathan Cape, 2012.
80 Sacco, *Palestine*, p. 170.
81 Ibid., p. 171.
82 Ibid., p. 261.
83 Ibid., p. 134.
84 Ibid., p. 135.
85 Ibid.
86 *Divine Intervention: A Chronicle of Love and Pain*. Dir. Elia Suleiman, 2003.

87 Jacqueline Rose, *Proust Among the Nations: From Dreyfus to the Middle East*, Chicago, IL: Chicago University Press, 2011, p. 179.
88 Ibid., p. 178.
89 Kay Dickinson, *Arab Cinema Travels: Syria, Palestine, Dubai and Beyond*, London: BFI/Bloomsbury, 2016.
90 Ibid., p. 138.
91 Ibid., p. 141.
92 Ibid., p. 143.
93 Rose, *Proust Among the Nations*, p. 179.
94 Anna Ball, 'Kafka at the West Bank Check-point: De-normalizing the Palestinian Encounter before the Law', *Journal of Postcolonial Writing*, 50:1 (2014), 75–87, 85.
95 Ibid., p. 76.
96 Anna Bernard, 'No Way Through: Approaching the West Bank Checkpoint', *Journal of Postcolonial Writing*, 50:1 (2014), 88–102, 90.
97 Dickinson, *Arab Cinema Travels*, p. 144.
98 Hakim Abderrezak, *Ex-Centric Migrations: Europe and the Maghreb in Mediterranean Cinema, Literature, and Music*, Bloomington, IN: Indiana University Press, 2016, p. 26.
99 Ibid., p. 31.
100 Ibid., p. 35.
101 Ibid.
102 Elizabeth Bekers, Maggie Ann Bowers and Sissy Heff, 'Imaginary Europes, Phantoms of the Past, Conceptions of the Future?', in *Journal of Postcolonial Writing*, 51:2, 127–131, 128, 131.
103 Abderrezak, *Ex-Centric Migrations*, p. 33, emphasis in original.
104 Johanna Sellman, 'A Global Postcolonial: Contemporary Arabic Literature of Migration to Europe', *Journal of Postcolonial Writing*, 54:6 (2018), 751–765, 751.
105 Ibid., p. 753.
106 Ibid.
107 Andre Gerrits, *Nationalism in Europe since 1945*, New York: Palgrave, 2016.
108 Ibid., p. 120.
109 Ibid.
110 Hakim Abderrezak, *Ex-Centric Migrations*, p. 25.
111 Sellman, 'A Global Postcolonial', p. 754.
112 Edward W. Said, *The World, the Text, and the Critic*, Cambridge, MA: Harvard University Press, 1983.
113 Theodor W. Adorno, 'Cultural Criticism and Society', *Prisms*, trans. Samuel and Shierry Weber, Cambridge, MA: MIT Press, 1983 [1967], pp. 17–34, p. 31.
114 Rebecca Solnit, 'The Ideology of Isolation', *Call Them by Their True Names: American Crises (and Essays)*, London: Granta, 2018, pp. 43–50, 49.
115 F. Scott Fitzgerald, *The Great Gatsby*, Harmondsworth: Penguin, 1976 [1926], p. 170.

Bibliography

Abderrezak, H., *Ex-Centric Migrations: Europe and the Maghreb in Mediterranean Cinema, Literature, and Music*, Bloomington, IN: Indiana University Press, 2016.
Agier, M., *Borderlands: Towards an Anthropology of the Cosmopolitan Condition*, Cambridge: Polity, 2016.

Adorno, T.W., 'Cultural Criticism and Society', *Prisms*, trans. Samuel and Sherry Weber, Cambridge, MA: MIT Press, 1983 [1967], pp. 17–34.
Ali, T., *The Extreme Centre: A Second Warning*, London: Verso, 2018.
Arendt, H., *The Origins of Totalitarianism*, New York: Harcourt, 1994 [1951].
Arrighi, G., 'Lineages of Empire', in Gopal Balakrishnan (ed), *Debating 'Empire'*, London: Verso, 2003, pp. 29–42.
Arrighi, G., *Adam Smith in Beijing: Lineages of the Twenty-First Century*, London: Verso, 2007.
Ball, A., 'Kafka at Bank Check-point: De-normalizing the Palestinian Encounter before the Law', *Journal of Postcolonial Writing*, 50:1 (2014), 75–87.
Bekers, E., Bowers, M.A. and Heff, S., 'Imaginary Europes, Phantoms of the Past, Conceptions of the Future?', *Journal of Postcolonial Writing*, 51:2 (2015), 127–131.
Bello, W., *Dark Victory: The United States, Structural Adjustment and Global Poverty*, London: Pluto Press, 1994.
Bernard, A., 'No Way Through: Approaching the West Bank Checkpoint', *Journal of Postcolonial Writing*, 50:1 (2014), 88–102.
Bourdieu, P., *Firing Back: Against the Tyranny of the Market 2*, trans. Loïc Wacquant, New York: New Press, 2003.
Brister, R., 'Sounding the Occupation: Joe Sacco's Palestine and the Uses of Graphic Narratives for (Post) Colonial Critique', *ariel: A Review of International English Literature*, 45:1 (2014), 103–129.
Butler, J., *Notes Toward a Performative Theory of Assembly*, Cambridge, MA: Harvard University Press, 2015.
Césaire, A., *Discourse on Colonialism*, trans. by Joan Pinkham, London: Monthly Review Press, 1972 [1950].
Chalk, B.T., '"Sensible of Being Étrangers": Plots and Identity Papers in *Banjo*', *Twentieth Century Literature*, 55:3 (2009), 357–377.
Chamayou, G. *Drone Theory*, trans. Janet Lloyd, Harmondsworth: Penguin, 2015.
Cockburn, A., *Kill Chain: Drones and the Rise of High-Tech Assassins*, London: Verso, 2016.
Crary, J., *24/7: Late Capitalism and the Ends of Sleep*, London: Verso, 2014.
Deckard, S., 'Cacao and Cascadura: Energetic Consumption and Production in World-ecological Literature', *Journal of Postcolonial Writing*, 53:3 (2017), 342–354.
Delisle, G., *Jerusalem: Chronicles from the Holy City*. London: Jonathan Cape, 2012.
Denning, M., *Noise Uprising: The Audiopolitics of a World Musical Revolution*, London: Verso, 2015.
Dickens, C., *Great Expectations*, ed. Charlotte Mitchell, Harmondsworth: Penguin, 1996 [1861].
Dickinson, K., *Arab Cinema Travels: Syria, Palestine, Dubai and Beyond*. London: BFI/Bloomsbury, 2016.
Edwards, B.H., *The Practice of Diaspora: Literature, Translation, and the Rise of Black Internationalism*, Cambridge, MA: Harvard University Press, 2003.
Emery, M. L., 'Caribbean Modernism: Plantation to Planetary', in Mark Wollaeger and Matt Eatough (eds), *The Oxford Handbook of Global Modernisms*, Oxford: Oxford University Press, 2012, pp. 48–77.

Fanon, F., *The Wretched of the Earth*, trans. Constance Farrington, Harmondsworth: Penguin, 1990 [1961].

Farnsworth, F., '"What I Saw for Myself": Collating Polyphonic Voices in Joe Sacco's Palestine Narratives', *Cambridge Journal of Postcolonial Literary Inquiry*, 6:2 (2019), 199–219.

Fitzgerald, F.S., *The Great Gatsby*, Harmondsworth: Penguin, 1976 [1926].

Flassbeck. H. and Lapavitsas, C., *Against the Troika: Crisis and Austerity in the Eurozone*, London: Verso, 2015.

Gerrits, A., *Nationalism in Europe since 1945*, New York: Palgrave, 2016.

Gilroy, P., *After Empire: Melancholia or Convivial Culture?* London: Routledge, 2004.

Gordimer, N., *The Pickup*, London: Bloomsbury, 2001.

Gordimer, N., *Life Times: Stories 1952–2007*, London: Bloomsbury, 2010.

Gowan, P., *The Global Gamble: Washington's Faustian Bid for World Dominance*, London: Verso, 1999.

Greenfield, A., *Radical Technologies: The Design of Everyday Life*, London: Verso, 2018.

Hamid, M. et al., 'The turmoil of today's world: Leading writers respond to the refugee crisis', *The Guardian*, 12 September 2015. Available at: www.theguardian.com/books/2015/sep/12/the-turmoil-of-todays-world-leading-writers-respond-to-the-refugee-crisis (accessed 23 August 2019).

Hamid, M., *Exit West*, St Ives: Hamish Hamilton, 2017.

Hardt, M. and Negri, A., *Empire*, Cambridge, MA: Harvard University Press, 2000.

Jameson, F., *The Antinomies of Realism*, London: Verso, 2015.

Jones, R., *Violent Borders: Refugees and the Right to Move*, London: Verso, 2016.

Kouvelakis, S., 'Borderland: Greece and the EU's Southern Question', *New Left Review II*, 110 (2018), 5–33.

Lapavitsas, C., *The Left Case Against the EU*, Cambridge: Polity, 2019.

Lazarus, N., 'The Fetish of "the West" in Postcolonial Theory', in Crystal Bartolovich and Neil Lazarus (eds), *Marxism, Modernity, and Postcolonial Studies*, Cambridge: Cambridge University Press, 2002, pp. 43–64.

Lazarus, N., 'Spectres Haunting: Postcommunism and Postcolonialism', *Journal of Postcolonial Writing*, 48:2 (2012), 117–129.

Lindqvist, S., *"Exterminate all the Brutes": One Man's Odyssey into the Heart of Darkness and the Origins of the European Genocide*, trans. Joan Tate, New York: The New Press, 1996.

Mason, P., *Why It's Still Kicking off Everywhere: The New Global Revolutions*, Second Edition, London: Verso, 2013.

Mason, P., *Postcapitalism: A Guide to Our Future*, London: Allen Lane, 2015.

McKay, C., *Banjo: A Story without a Plot*, New York: Harvest, 1970.

Mo, T., *Pure*, London: Turnaround Books, 2012.

Moore, J.W., *Capitalism in the Web of Life: Ecology and the Accumulation of Capital*, London: Verso, 2015.

Mouffe, C., *For a Left Populism*, London: Verso, 2018.

Olusoga, D. and Erichsen, C.W., *The Kaiser's Holocaust: Germany's Forgotten Genocide*, London: Faber & Faber, 2010.

Panitch, L. and Gindin, S., *The Making of Global Capitalism: The Political Economy of American Empire*, London: Verso, 2012.

Rose, J., *Proust Among the Nations: From Dreyfus to the Middle East*, Chicago, IL: Chicago University Press, 2011.

Sacco, J., *Palestine*. London: Jonathan Cape, 2003.

Said, E.W., *The World, the Text, and the Critic*, Cambridge, MA: Harvard University Press, 1983.

Scott, D., *Conscripts of Modernity: The Tragedy of Colonial Enlightenment*, Durham, NC: Duke University Press, 2004.

Sellman, J., 'A Global Postcolonial: Contemporary Arabic Literature of Migration to Europe', *Journal of Postcolonial Writing*, 54:6 (2018), 751–765.

Shamsie, K., *Home Fire*, London: Bloomsbury, 2018.

Shaw, K., 'BrexLit', *Brexit and Literature: Critical and Cultural Responses*, ed. Robert Eaglestone, London: Routledge, 2018, pp. 15–30.

Sheller, M., *Mobility Justice: The Politics of Movement in an Age of Extremes*, London: Verso, 2018.

Smith, A., 'Migrancy, Hybridity, and Postcolonial Literary Studies', in Neil Lazarus (ed), *The Cambridge Companion to Postcolonial Literary Studies*, Cambridge: Cambridge University Press, 2004, pp. 241–261.

Solnit, R., 'The Ideology of Isolation', *Call Them by Their True Names: American Crises (and Essays)*, London: Granta, 2018, pp. 43–50.

Spencer, R. 'The Politics of Imperial Nostalgia', in Graham Huggan and Ian Law (eds), *Racism, Postcolonialism, Europe*, Liverpool: Liverpool University Press, 2009, pp. 176–196.

Steiner, G., *Language and Silence: Essays 1958–1966*, London: Faber & Faber, 1985.

Streeck, W., 'Why the Euro Divides Europe', *How Will Capitalism End? Essays on a Failing System*, London: Verso, 2016, pp. 165–183.

Tait, T., 'Some will need to be killed', *London Review of Books*, 16 November 2017. Available at: www.lrb.co.uk/v39/n22/theo-tait/some-will-need-to-be-killed (accessed 23 August 2019).

Thorn, H., *Anti-Apartheid and the Emergence of a Global Civil Society*, Basingstoke: Palgrave, 2006.

Varoufakis, Y., *And the Weak Suffer What They Must? Europe, Austerity and the Threat to Global Stability*, London: Vintage, 2016.

Wallerstein, I., *The Decline of American Power: The U.S. in a Chaotic World*, New York: New Press, 2003.

Winder, R., *Bloody Foreigners: The Story of Immigration to Britain*, London: Abacus, 2004.

Wright, E. O., 'Participatory Economics: A Sympathetic Critique', in Robin Hahnel and Erik Olin Wright, *Alternatives to Capitalism: Proposals for a Democratic Economy*, London: Verso, 2016, pp. 17–47.

Films

Divine Intervention: A Chronicle of Love and Pain. Dir. Elia Suleiman, 2003.
Four Lions. Dir. Christopher Morris, 2010.

Websites

'Trump calls some unauthorized immigrants "animals", in rant'. Available at: www.nytimes.com/2018/05/16/us/politics/trump-undocumented-immigrants-animals.html (accessed 23 August 2019).

'Highest levels of world's most toxic chemicals found in African free-range eggs: European E-waste dumping a contributor', 24 April 2019. Available at: www.ban.org/news/2019/4/24/rotten-eggs-e-waste-from-europe-poisons-ghanas-food-chain (accessed 23 August 2019).

3

RECONCILIATORY PRACTICES

In this chapter, we look at how reconciliatory practices have sought inspiration from local geographies and from specific social and cultural practices in order to ensure that attempts at lasting collaboration are drawn from within. Reconciliation is understood in this chapter as both a structural and political process but also as an attempt to voice, in narratives of all kinds, a desire for connection. These attempts are not always successful and we are mindful of historical contexts in which a national conversation on colonialism has not been fully aired or debated. Practices of reconciliation ordinarily look to remove shame, address perceived past injustices and encourage a conciliatory approach to the future. We have found, however, that oftentimes, the very terms of reconciliatory attempts ignore or pay scant attention to the specificity of perceived wrongs that coalesce around the ownership (legal or informal) and use of land, and the extent to which this binds communities to place. Narratives such as Alan Duff's *Once Were Warriors* (and Lee Tamahori's subsequent film), J.M. Coetzee's *Disgrace*, Romesh Gunesekera's *The Match* and Achmat Dangor's *Bitter Fruit* illustrate ways in which locality, and the knowledge – or lack of knowledge – of one's surroundings fully informs the extent to which compromise is permissible. This idea of reconciliation has for too long in literary studies operated as an unquestioned but favourable outcome for the postcolonial process. This chapter looks closely at the requirements for such outcomes, pointing out the frequent complexities and limitations of knowledge itself.

In the texts and films that we examine here, reconciliation works across conceptual frameworks. In some instances, it is very present as a mode of interaction working within a certain logic, often within a political framework, following certain expectations that are often preconceived. In other contexts, reconciliation as an idea or a mode of interaction emerges as an unforeseen opportunity that coalesces around certain events or arises from the very locations within which tensions exist. It is useful to understand reconciliatory practices here, therefore, as a certain type of work or labour, one that is not always willingly undertaken and one that does not always result in a beneficial outcome but that nevertheless has the capacity to expose the limitations of reconciliation. It seems to us that there is a tension here in the postcolonial context – to be seen to be participating in reconciliatory practices is to be part of a shared future that may unwittingly seek to underplay or undermine a certain understanding of the past. Though this is examined in more detail in the next chapter, it is worth considering here the extent to which the spaces of formal reconciliation – courtrooms, formal and informal hearings, and commissions, are not the only arenas in which this kind of work is undertaken. Here, we expand the potential that different locations, such as the home, the bar, the university, the street, and a cricket match, all have to provide the motivation and indeed the tools for various forms of reconciliatory practices to take place. Paying attention to these moments can help us to expand the reach and possibility of the work of reconciliation across gender, class, age and ethnic identities. These moments can also provide us with the tools needed to recognise the very moments that make up the longer projects of reconciliatory practices.

The term 'reconciliation' is most often used in the context of the various commissions that have justifiably been set up over the past decades in order to formally address what the former South African minister for justice, Dullah Omar, has called 'a necessary exercise to enable countries [in this case South Africa] to come to terms with their past on a morally acceptable basis and to advance the cause of reconciliation'. Understanding the exercise as advancing a cause suggests the longevity of such an exercise and indeed makes it clear that the work will be ongoing – in our understanding, this further suggests that this ongoing work will have to take place *outside* the confines of formal political frameworks and institutions. Commissions of this sort that have taken place in East Timor, Liberia, Korea, Canada and elsewhere have sought to bureaucratise and place structures around such exercises in order to remain publicly accountable and also to ensure a certain form of legitimacy. As Kevin Avruch and Beatriz Vejarano note, 'they function in a wide variety of socio-political settings with varying levels of support (international, governmental, and popular) resources and constraints, and with varying degrees of success'.[1]

They also have a function beyond this – to serve as repositories of history and as archives of suffering. Beyond the often-limited abilities that they may have to prosecute or perform other forms of reparative justice, truth and reconciliation commissions are generally understood to be most influential in their legacies. These commissions, however, have their own genesis, in particular legal, social and political frameworks, and operate within a specific, often nationalist,[2] mandate in each case. 'A great deal of controversy', argue Avruch and Vejarano,

> not to mention passion, that surrounds the workings and assessment of these commissions by different parties, has to do with the tension existing between the two poles of [the] continuum: [vengeance

and forgiveness] the putative primordial human impulse to wreak vengeance or to offer forgiveness, for terrible wrongs done. The tension has to do as well with arguments about whether notions of justice and 'truth' are related necessarily or merely contingently.[3]

These more abstract symptoms of formal reconciliatory methods are often what is picked up or reconfigured in informal reconciliatory practices. These moments continue to engage with the presence of these formal structures as they and we try to understand how and why they can often appear inadequate to the complicated everyday task of continued negotiations.

In his article 'Novel Truths: Literature and Truth Commissions', Paul Gready explores what he calls the 'unique truth practices and repertoire available to the novel as a genre, as distinct from other genres such as the human rights report'.[4] Novels, Gready argues have 'engaged with the speaking truth to reconciliation paradigm, but have also shone a light on issues such as the enduring appeal of revenge and retribution'.[5] These 'truth' practices we take to mean the various nuanced ways in which novels explore the truth both conceptually and as a revelatory motif, employed to either expose or conceal actions.

In J.M. Coetzee's *Disgrace*, we see how certain forms or attempts to build connections can constitute a life's work and an exhausting one at that. Taking into full account what has often been described as David Lurie's exploitative relationship with his younger student Melanie Isaacs, his refusal to however come out in public and repent his actions firmly places the tension of formal reconciliatory practices at the forefront. When asked by a member of the hearing panel that has been brought together to investigate the charge of sexual harassment whether he has consulted anyone such as 'a priest, for instance, or a counsellor', Lurie's curt 'I am beyond the reach of counselling'[6] somewhat thwarts the expectation that all human actions have their counterpart in some institutional context that can repair perceived failings. The reconciliation required here by the panel is not between Melanie and David but indeed between David's idea of himself as 'no longer a fifty-year old divorcé at a loose end'[7] but a desirable and desiring individual, and the broader structural understanding of him as belonging to what a member of the panel, Farodia Rassool, terms 'the long history of exploitation of which this [hearing] is a part'.[8] This, it seems, is one step too far for David. Asked whether his admission of guilt represents his 'sincere feelings', Lurie refuses to be put in what he sees as the impossible position of 'demonstrating their sincerity'.[9] 'Rejecting the efficacy or authenticity of confession in the public sphere' argues Jane Poyner, 'Lurie is propelled into a journey of self-discovery and personal atonement which ultimately is revealed to be morally bankrupt'.[10] The issue of moral bankruptcy can be revisited later. What is interesting here is that Poyner points to Lurie's journey as an action that he needs to undertake at the end of which he might find a better version of himself. This indicates the extent to which the individual, and his actions in this context, seem to somehow be taken as a general failing of the moment; 'the long history of exploitation' that Rasool gestures towards. This cannot however be contained in one individual and one individual's sacrifice will not atone for the wrongdoings of centuries. Here, it seems that Coetzee is well in tune with the very limits of formal reconciliatory practices. As Avruch and Vejarano point out, 'it is precisely in trying to apply what may be therapeutically effective at the interpersonal level to the collective level that reconciliation often seems to lose clarity and become more ambiguous as an approach to peacebuilding'.[11]

In other words, attempting to apply the framework of collective blame, as the informal hearing into Lurie's actions does, cannot encompass or accommodate the context of individual desires and actions. The two actions seem to run parallel, as we later see in the novel. Lurie's daughter Lucy's attempt to, what Poyner has described as, 'find her sense of place and to accept collective responsibility for white oppression'[12] stalls her own expression of private pain. Although silence and suffering are here discussed as occurring in interiority, the novel can however access other manifestations of these. Certain moments act in ways that problematise any progressive form of collective reconciliation and instead show the process to be evolving simultaneously at the public and private level. Though characters may *say* certain things, what *happens* to them and how they inhabit their experiences exposes the price of such lofty ideals. As Gready notes 'redistribution and reparation' in *Disgrace*, 'and even penance and a dreadful rite of passage required to remain and belong, are conducted through hate, rape and robbery'.[13] In this context, the labour of reconciliation is the bringing together of internal and silent pain with the expectations of an outwardly morally demanding society that is itself operating in the context of intuitionalist reparatory reconciliatory practices. 'You tell what happened to you, I tell what happened to me',[14] Lucy tells David, appealing to not only her right to narrativise the experience in whichever way she can but also to separate what parts of the story will be held up to inquiry and public scrutiny and what parts will not. As Lurie intuitively guesses, 'Lucy must work her own way back from the darkness to the light',[15] thus endorsing the fact that regardless of her decision to tell a particular version of her story, the work that she needs to do to reconcile herself to her experience and her actions is hers alone to undertake and will take time.

Lurie's observation that Lucy lies about the *duration* of the attack also reflects the subjectivity of the experience of truth-telling itself. The overarching expectation in institutionalised reconciliatory practices is that somehow the containment of victimhood and accountability can surpass urges to seek retributive justice. In this framework, as Gready notes, commissions such as the South African Truth and Reconciliation Commission (TRC) counted 'among its most important innovations [...] an individualized amnesty provision, in which amnesty for specific acts was made conditional on full disclosure and political motive'.[16]

Disgrace itself upends any belief that such a practice, however carefully conceptualised, can be contained in any way, but also reveals the impossibility of anticipating the form that this subjective justice will take. Ranging from violence to others and violence to oneself, imagining new forms of existence that holds this suffering within it seems to mock the notion of containing the wrongs of the past in a report or in a process, regardless of how well intentioned this structure may be. Rosemary Jolly argues in 'Desiring Good(s) in the Face of Marginalized Subjects: South Africa's Truth and Reconciliation Commission in a Global Context',[17] that it is also possible to see the TRC as 'the locus of a ritual of reconciliation that does not depend on closure, one that can invoke the past in the name of the future' and she calls on the concept of the process as 'ritual' to be invoked as a tool that works as a 'surplus', moving us 'beyond the mechanics of secular and legal concepts of violation, testimony, proof, confession, judgment, punishment [and] financial compensation'.[18] For Jolly, an understanding of ritual and a 'focus on the form of ritual, rather than its content'[19] has the power to perhaps reify reconciliation as a practice that is, however, in perpetual motion.

It is interesting to see however the ways in which the form of ritual can sometimes directly contradict the requirements of a forward-looking movement that seeks to somehow understand the past. Achmat Dangor's 2001 novel *Bitter Fruit* has rightly been read as an attempt to, in Ronit Frenkel's words, '[illustrate] the ambiguity inherent in the various ways we synthesize that past as individuals and as society as a whole'.[20] The novel, as Poyner argues, is interested in how 'responsibility on the national-political plane' can co-exist alongside 'the sphere of personal responsibility',[21] especially when the characters are both victims but also now involved in the formal machinery of reconciliation. As Gready notes, '*Bitter Fruit* is one of a number of South African novels that examine violence that is folded into intimate, interpersonal, everyday relationships. If relationships are damaged, marked by betrayal, then the past enters the present as "poisonous knowledge"'.[22] Although it is crucial to read *Bitter Fruit* in light of these interpretations, it is also productive to read the ways in which some of the characters cannot reconcile themselves at all to this new post-apartheid reality, regardless of the potential that it holds.

Their struggle is not with the anxious anticipation that some form of retribution will come out of formal reconciliatory practices, nor is it with the violent past and how it might be addressed and processed in future. Rather, Dangor is radical in his willingness to give voice to the struggle to reconcile with what appears to be a new reality. Though not unique in finding ways to declare disappointment with the new South Africa, some of Dangor's characters actively feel loss at the end of the struggle and often do not recognise themselves in this new landscape, even as the political structures work to make the sacrifices of the struggle apparent. In inviting perpetrators to confess their participation in acts of violence and in persuading victims to relive their pain, the formal reconciliation practices risk erasing complex subjectivities and experiences. On the other hand, we do see in *Bitter Fruit* the advantages of a public system that does allow for some form of witnessing, though this itself functions to close down other forms of suffering. A trail of disappointments is evident in the memories of those who ostensibly have the most to gain from a reconciled post-apartheid nation.

The protagonist Silas and his brother-in-law Alec both seem unable to come to terms with their new condition. Here, survival and the law have entirely different connotations and register something exciting and dangerous. Speaking directly of the pre-apartheid era, Alec remembers that,

> [B]ack then everyone recognised that the need to survive was paramount, so that breaking the law, dealing in stolen goods, running fah-fee or owning a shebeen were all acts of survival, and every occupation had its own dignity. And survival in those days – if you were black – meant having to accommodate forces more powerful than yourself. Now moral zealots were running the world. [...] Law and order, it's the joke that whites sold us.[23]

Alec's contemptuous rants are, however, echoed in how others talk about how 'the days of the MK hero are gone' (68)[24] and how the truth and reconciliation work has swallowed up the ideals and idols of the struggle itself. Characters involved in the militant and ideological aspect of the anti-apartheid struggle are portrayed in *Bitter Fruit* as having nowhere to go now that the past has been temporarily compartmentalised in order to assess its damage. In this context, certain actions of the past have also been politicised in order to fit into a reconciliatory framework: in other words, some experiences and not others come to stand in for a varied and complex relationship with the past. Silas, in particular, is often driven to contemplate a past that in many ways he preferred:

> Silas drove through the early-morning traffic, thinking about how things had changed. Now the lanes were clogged with people like him, black and white [...] but ten years ago [...] [e]verywhere, there would have been buses and Kombi-taxis ferrying black people to their jobs – domestics, power-station workers, railway clerks, hospital orderlies, policemen coming on duty. Around the Johannesburg central station, the takeaway cafés would have been busy selling pap and steak, roasted mielies, the kind of fast food that nevertheless sustained workers all day. Ja, in many ways *it was great back then, a simpler, more wholesome life.*[25]

Though it is doubtlessly controversial to wish for this time back and though there is a heady mix here of nostalgia and partial memory at play, here Silas nevertheless insists on how, for him, 'life in the city was strangely normal then, given how abnormal the whole country was'.[26] Silas's day job consists of trying to reconcile the exact role and remit of the TRC and determine the extent to which it can equitably investigate excesses of violence committed during apartheid from all sides. This inevitably puts those strongly associated with the liberation struggle on the defensive as they insist on the necessity of their actions and are not willing to publicly denounce them. It seems inevitable that in a post-independence context, the narrative of the liberation struggle will be disputed. In many ways, the perceived necessity of certain actions associated with the liberation struggle, such as those described by Alec as well as other more violent ones, does not sit comfortably with the commitment of a formal reconciliation practice to adjudicate on the basis of law. This inevitably is where the difficulty of reconciliation truly lies: to have to somehow reconcile the fact that actions borne out of a particular volatile context where often these actions were undertaken in the name of survival may now come to be seen as somehow obstructing the course of justice. For some participants in the anti-apartheid struggle, the expectation that one form of futurity requires the extinguishing of a no-longer-palatable past, simply cannot be accommodated. For those who can only look forward 'don't understand us' laments Silas, 'what we struggled for and why'.[27] Incredibly, although the past is where his wife was sexually assaulted and raped by a white security policeman, it is here that Silas's mind returns to contentment as he

> thinks of the past, increasingly summoning up happier times, epochs of greater clarity, times without this ambiguity he sees everywhere. In his home, in his office, in the country, in the grand scheme of things, in the religions of the God and in the godlessness of politics, there is a growing area of grey, shadowy morality.[28]

It becomes clear in *Bitter Fruit* how any formal reconciliation process requires that certain parameters be established. These parameters often require personal silences or, indeed, a reactivating of suffering for the good of the collective. In *Bitter Fruit*, some of the silences revolve around the feeling of purpose that threatens to evaporate in the quagmire of official practices that take characters away from the streets, from the difficult but often purposeful liberatory practices and the thrill that this can bring. Silas is now a spin doctor, trying to keep the peace between competing narratives of the ANC and TRC and the gulf between the commission and government. This is not his only fight, however, as he and others struggle to reconcile the purpose of the new condition that they find themselves in because, as Silas says 'after all, he is only a township bushie'.[29] It seems that these old categories have much to teach the more hard and fast rules of a results-driven commission.

In a very different context, Alan Duff's *Once Were Warriors* (1990)[30] and Lee Tamahori's film of the book (1994) look to explore characters' reconciliation with an imported image of themselves that is at once generative and destructive. Not borne out of any formal reconciliatory context, Duff's protagonists nevertheless seek to formulate legitimate ways of being in a world that bears few secure coordinates. Duff's novel was controversial at the time of its publication for ostensibly not providing the world with a positive Maori image and, indeed, the success of the film, made in 1994, came as a surprise in this context. Indeed it was difficult to teach this text without commenting on this aspect. As Corinn Columpar argues, this controversy 'made [the film], prior to its release, a cause for disquietude on the part of many'.[31] Yet it seemed that, as the film's director Lee Tamahori stated, the crowds turned out to watch it as, even though 'it happens to be a bleak vision [it] is our vision'.[32]

This is a statement that deserves to be taken seriously as it suggests a reckoning with the spectrum of experiences available to any given community. Rather than only viewing the film as a 'narrative of relentless violence',[33] or chastising the film and book for not pairing this violence 'with representation of the historical conditions that have produced such violence',[34] an issue that Columpar herself deems potentially impossible to achieve equitably, we want to suggest that the characters themselves are on journeys of reconciliation with what it means to be a contemporary Maori subject. Certainly, there is horrific violence in the film, towards women and men and amongst men. There are also multiple forms of abuse enacted in both the book and the film. An understanding of the social context of the narrative cannot, however, fully and unproblematically accommodate a historical context narrativised in such a way that would permit us to draw a straight line between the past and the present where injustices committed in the past unwittingly represent pretexts or justification for contemporary actions.

Viewing the narrative's setting, rather than reading the action as intermittent acts of violence threaded together loosely, allows us to look at how characters position themselves in relation to their everyday experience and understand or interpret the role of the past in that experience. This labour of reconciliation is difficult and is often avoided, and for good reason. Often an uncritiqued and celebrated heritage does not, or cannot, provide an immediately useful legacy for communities who live, work and socialise in tough social conditions. The title itself alerts us to the tension: *Once Were Warriors* – how then to carry an idea of one's history and bring it to the present: in other words, how to *reconcile* this idealism with a struggling and stratified community? What is remarkable in the narrative is the extent to which the legacy can be both revered *and* repelled. What seems most evident to us in this revisiting of *Once Were Warriors* are these performances of reverence and repulsion that Duff and Tamahori seem keen to emphasise and the overwhelming expectation that characters embody these experiences. One of the achievements of the novel is to experiment with *how* characters think about and understand their present lives in relation to a particular version of the past. Here, the form that *thoughts* take is as important as the content as these meanderings often do not have any logical end and neither do they have a static conceptual thread. Take here, for instance, Beth, the wife and mother in the narrative, thinking about her relationship to the white New Zealanders,

> They're like strangers – they are strangers to most Maori I know. May as well be from another country the contact the two races have. Oh but I can't blame em half the time when you see all the crime, or so damn much of it, is committed by us. Hell, I dunno, must be something in the Maori make-up makes us wilder. Basically we're good. We share things. We'd give our shirt off our back to another [...] And we have this [...] Beth thinking hard, trying to match up instinctive understanding with a suitable word – passion. We got passion, us Maoris. Or maybe it's style. But not like the Negro style you see on the TV of being swank, hip, cool, moving with their black rhythmic grooving, not that kind, but a cross between that and the less showy whites.[35]

This engagement or negotiation is one that occurs quite frequently in the text and in different ways in the film. Surprisingly, rather than look closely at what such a layered thought process can reveal, criticism often leans towards the conclusion that the Maori in the book are presented by Duff as 'the "empty vessels" [...] non-traditional indigenous people living lives stripped of meaning through lack of contact with traditional culture'.[36] 'The book's hope', writes Treagus, 'comes from reconnection with *Maoritanga*, traditional way of life and its values'.[37] It is not at all clear how this conclusion is reached as both novel and film articulate and present so many reasons why this trajectory is neither *desirable* nor frequently *feasible* for all the characters depicted. Though we can see and indeed sympathise with the urge to provide solutions that might free characters and communities from pain and subjugation in all its forms (gendered, social, sexual and racial), Duff and Tamahori produce fully fledged and flawed characters who have intricate inner lives and complex public lives. As Columpar notes,

> Maori people have for centuries been involved in an on-going engagement – the nature of which has ranged from resistance to cooperation, separatism to integration, assimilation to nativism – with a dominant culture that diverges from their own and a variety

of settler communities, including those of the colonizing nation as well as subsequent immigrant populations.[38]

This engagement includes ongoing attempts to reconcile how to live in the present while also negotiating these wide-ranging social realities. It's also not clear how we, or the characters, can separate definitively what the effects of the 'dominant culture' are as they remain implicated within it in their daily lives through the various institutions that govern civil society (such as the police, the educational system, the welfare state, etc.).

As Beth's inner dialogue above shows, what is she in her role as Maori? What does it mean to her to be designated as Maori and in relation to what exactly? Though there is much value to retrieving and re-centring elements of traditional culture that can work alongside the reclamation of positive identities – and the book and film do this as well – it is not, nor should it be, the entire story. The struggle of certain individuals is borne not necessarily out of their estrangement with an originary culture that holds all the answers, but rather out of their inability or unwillingness to only ascribe generic positive features to those origins. Thus, Beth wonders whether there might be something 'wild' about the Maori, or something extreme that is akin to 'passion'. Though these may well be internalised stereotypes, they nevertheless give shape to everyday experience:

> it's a big problem being a Maori in this world [...] and we used to war all the time, us Maoris. Against each other. True. It's true, honest to God audience. Hated each other. Tribe against tribe. Savages. We were savages. But warriors, eh. It's very important to remember that [...] But we – our men anyway – are clinging onto this toughness thing, like it's all we got, while the rest of the world's leaving us behind.[39]

These thoughts bring to life the unstructured form that comes with thinking about questions as fundamental as how an understanding of inherited pasts is performed or inhabited in the present. Duff describes these negotiations in Beth's mind as 'message-like wordings appearing in Beth's brain, her half-enlightened, half-befuddled mind'.[40]

It seems worth considering that some of the tensions here reside precisely in this idealised past. Reconciling a life that comes with many difficulties but also with many pleasures, with an inherited legacy that cannot easily be accessed, brings new strains to lived experiences. Whatever Beth might think, her husband's Jake's interior life is populated with African-American icons: *they* provide the blueprint for his role and reputation as Jake the Muss, and his love of Sugar Ray Leonard and Muhammad Ali is evident and their presence is sometimes more real to him than the Maori myths. Pondering on the name of a street, Taniwha Street 'after the water monster from Maori myth', Jake asks himself, 'so what does a taniwha look like? he'd challenge a believer. And so far he'd never had a satisfactory reply'.[41] It's clear that, like Beth, he moves through spaces aware of this alternative and much more ethereal world, whose power and potential, however, he is not entirely convinced of. He is clear on how he may have ended up the man that he is. Though he understands how dominant his violent reactions are, 'it never occurred to [him] that there might be something wrong with his outlook, perhaps his mind. It couldn't: damn near every man he mixed (drank) with thought the same. He was sure they did.'[42] Upon reflection, it seems clear that the conditions that have arisen as a result of difficult socio-economic realities and limited labour and educational opportunities, not to mention long-standing ethnic and racial structural inequalities, *nevertheless* themselves form the conditions for a reality that then produces its own internal logic and modes of participation. Duff is masterful at revealing the pull that this can engender between, on the one hand, pride in this other ancestral heritage, and disgust (and anger) at its perceived uselessness in the face of intransigent social conditions. A particularly memorable scene in the book sees Jake mesmerised by what he sees as a microcosm of his community at the bar he frequents with his friends. While listening to the beautiful singing of his wife's friend Mavis, he recalls Dame Kiri Te Kanawa, the famous Maori opera singer renowned for performing at Prince Charles and Diana's wedding as he moves further and further into the bar and is warmly greeted by his fans and friends:

> I cried that day to see a Maori – a *Maori* – singing for royalty in front of the whole world. Cried. Only thing, I didn't like that damn dress she wore, made her look like she'd bought it from the Sally Op Shop, eh. And people laughing at that and saying it was the Maori coming out in their Kiri, her lack of taste in a Pakeha world with all their headstart years of so-fist-i-cay-shun. [...] Oh, kia ora! Jake being greeted in Maori, the language of his physical appearance, his actual ethnic existence, and yet they could be speaking Chink-language for what it mattered [...] made him uncomfortable if they spoke it to him, so Jake always replied in emphatic English... [though he goes on to claim how he loves it when these older men] did their imitation of his imitation [Mohammed] Ali shuffle.[43]

This insight into Jake's thought process animates this seemingly endless and almost daily negotiation of the various social and cultural identities that circulate simultaneously. The book, and more specifically the film, work hard to also attempt a bifurcation that works in visual ways to present us with what at first glance seem like two separate choices – to either embrace and seek guidance and solace in what stands in for cultural heritage or to seek community and belonging in very different social organisations that, however, when looked at closely, do not wholly reject this heritage. What emerges, rather, is the realisation that the provenance or origin of actions that seem to be underpinned by individual and social choices cannot always remain tethered to their supposed primary function. For example, when the older son in the family Nig joins the local gang, is initiated by them and gets a tattoo on his face, it might be desirable to read this as a refusal of a particular idea of being a Maori warrior. Treagus argues that '*Once Were Warriors* refuses an essentialist version of being Maori. There is no return to the lost past but instead a strong, brave commitment to the urban present, of which Nig, wearing his stylised *moko* of contemporary design, is part'.[44] Although an admirable and seductive reading of the events, the book and film do also contend with those who push a version of the 'lost past' and give voice to those who resent this, as the examples above have shown.

The younger son Boogie (Mark) is placed into social welfare custody due to his low level involvement in petty crime. Initially resistant to the methods used at the young offenders home, the welfare officer, who is also a Maori preacher, tries to convince him that pride in oneself as Maori can be generated through the recounting and appropriation of warrior prowess. When Boogie claims he hates the home and all it stands for, the preacher reminds him that he does not need to *like it*. Nevertheless, in an ahistorical and decontextualised manner he recounts a glorious past where the Maori taiaha[45] revealed its potential against the British Bayonet. Visually effective, the scene nevertheless belies that one form of (controlled) anger can be used to diffuse another. These are not unproblematic connections, though seen in conjunction with Duff's use of Jake's interior monologue in the book, we can begin to see the complexity that this duality generates.

Ancestry is understood as a complex negotiation by Jake as his childhood memories do not revolve around the warrior myth. In fact, his understanding of this family's past which, when disclosed, comes as a shock to Beth and their children[46] is situated in another more humiliating and powerful myth: that Jake's family were not part of the dominant warrior communities at all but rather, due to the ancient legacy of having become prisoners in battle, existed in a more servile position, in a context of what Jake calls 'slaves'.[47]

> Five hundred years, that's what they used to tell us Heke kids. Five hundred years of the slave curse bein on our heads [...] as for the kids related to the chief: if you went within a hundred fuckin yards ofem they'd be throwin stones, yelling and screaming at us to get away, go home [...] Bullying us. Picking on us. Hitting us.[48]

Though the novel does not set this past up in order to excuse Jake's behaviour, the revelation, as understood by Jake does however consciously introduce another level of complexity to any argument that would seek to unproblematically transpose or adapt an idealistic notion of heritage that itself has been modified to suit the contemporary period. Here, we see that Jake is unable to fully align himself with the ways in which Maoris in the present seem to collaborate in some form of collective dream of the past. Beth, shocked to think that perhaps she has somehow missed this detail, proclaims how 'to read the newspapers, on the TV every damn day, you'd think we're descended from a packa angels, and it's the Pakeha who's the devil'.[49]

This is not to take away from the very real social and political realities that produce and maintain unequal structures in the very material existence of a large portion of the Maori community as represented in *Once Were Warriors*. Work opportunities seem scarce, pay is poor and the police disproportionately target Maori children while offering little support to homeless young adults. The women in the community seem to have little opportunity to either work outside the home or, indeed, access the resources required to be fully involved in family life. It is spurious and disingenuous to understand the singing, partying and violence only as escapism, however. These actions arise from, and are part of, the complex set of circumstances that result in community formation. That this community does not somehow uphold an idealised vision of people honouring their past does not mean that there is not a continuous and often painful process of reconciliation within the various versions of it. Sometimes an unexpected comfort, sometimes a painful memory, this heritage requires constant negotiation in the present.

Our next example of a complicated process and practice of reconciliation is the game of cricket. 'There's really something very strange about people who like cricket', according to Robert McLiam Wilson – so strange, in fact, that the Ulster novelist goes on to describe the 'tiny solace' that he, a resident of Paris, had taken a few days after the deadly terrorist attacks in that city in November 2015 by watching, of all things, cricket, specifically the satellite coverage of the Australian opening batsman David Warner's mammoth innings of 253 in the second Test match against New Zealand in Perth. Warner's feat, batting for the duration of the first day of the match at a characteristically high strike rate of ninety odd, brought home to McLiam Wilson the disconcerting, though for him instructive and reassuring, contrast between overpowering grief and the 'extraordinary happiness that this bright but wistful sport can bring' (though not, presumably, to many Parisians). Cricket also reveals productive tensions between the pressing urgency of the political present and the game's 'mournful nostalgia', between the event's tragedy and cricket's comedy (its frivolity and gaiety but also its oft-noted concern with ideas of justice), between the perpetrators' murderous chauvinism and the distinguishing inclusiveness of this 'nonsensical pursuit', and between the cricket follower's fondness for the varied humanity of cricket players and the unsmiling militancy of the attackers.[50]

McLiam Wilson's discussion introduces us to cricket's exemplary capacity for a kind of fragile and qualified reconciliation of the divisions and hierarchies inflicted by British imperialist violence. This odd pastime or, as we'll characterise it, following C.L.R. James, this versatile form of cultural expression, retains much of its historical ability to mean radically different things to radically different audiences. Cricket, like any other form of aesthetic or cultural practice, does not stand still; it moves or rather is taken from place to place and in the course of these movements, it accrues new dimensions, uses and meanings. Cricket after all is an intrinsically diverse game, with its seemingly infinite dramatic permutations, its multiple formats, the assorted territories in which it is played with distinctive styles and approaches dependent on their different climates, soils and subsoils, as well as, most significantly, the various ideologies and aspirations of the people who play and watch. As it travels, cricket, again like any other form of cultural or aesthetic activity, speaks eloquently of the experiences and hopes of participants and audiences. This often extremely elongated game still gives powerful voice to its rural and pre-industrial origins, for example, just as its defining 'gentlemanly' code of moral conduct and obedience to the umpire recalls its role in exporting an image of colonial masculinity and social order during the era of high imperialism. But then the opportunity the game afforded in Britain's colonies for colonised subjects to compete openly on more or less equal terms with their civilisational 'superiors' made cricket into an expression of social equality and even anti-colonial revolt. Cricket's mobility is nothing other, ultimately, than its proven capacity not just to move across territories and thereby find new audiences and constituencies but also, by virtue of its status as an intensely meaningful aesthetic practice, to articulate a kind of imaginative movement into a utopian space of political transformation.

Our aim is to show that Romesh Gunesekera's cricket novel *The Match* brings to light something that its protagonist and narrator does not fully see.[51] The novel permits and encourages its readers to appreciate what Alexis Tadié has called 'the essential worldliness of cricket, its ability to be appropriated and reinvented' in ways that challenge the legacies and continuities of empire.[52] The 'match' in the novel's title refers both to a one-off fixture arranged towards the start of the text between a motley band of Australian and Sri Lankan expats in the unlikely setting of a reclaimed swamp in early 1970s Manila and, in what is effectively the novel's denouement, a one-day international in 2002 between Sri Lanka and India at The Oval in central London. Cricket is acknowledged by Gunesekera's novel to be the postcolonial sport *par excellence*, one that by virtue of its colonial history and even its very structure has become, as it were, a world game, a cultural practice that has travelled and continues to travel, to develop and acquire new significance and a variety of both political and aesthetic meanings. Moreover, cricket's aesthetic significance in *The Match* is inseparable from something that Gunesekera's protagonist only partly sees, what we shall call cricket's utopian and reconciliatory dimension or, put differently, in the words of

Hans van den Broek, cricketer and narrator of Joseph O'Neill's *Netherland*, cricket's capacity to 'imagin[e] an environment of justice'.[53]

What *The Match* emphasises is not just the variety of meanings successively attached to the game by crowds and other critics, meanings that could scarcely be further from the orthodox or conventional view of the game as a nostalgic bastion of 'Englishness' and empire. For what cricket eventually signifies in the novel is something like an extra- or post-national inclusiveness. Anthony Bateman reminds us that for cricket's shrewdest expositor, the polymathic Trinidadian Marxist C.L.R. James, 'the relatively unmediated experience of the crowd was positively constitutive of cricket's meaning as a cultural form'.[54] It is above all this 'radically democratic reformulation of the aesthetic of cricket',[55] this worldly and unceasing process of interpretation and reinterpretation, one that revises and rejects the conventional association of cricket solely with the past, with empire and with nationalism, that potentially makes cricket, according to James and as seen in *The Match*, a harbinger of what Raymond Williams calls emergent values and even emergent political structures and forms of human subjectivity.[56]

Cricket is at once a game and, according to James, a *bona fide* aesthetic practice. What is more, cricket, James goes on to argue in *Beyond a Boundary*, because of the peculiarities of its structure, is a 'dramatic spectacle'[57] unlike any other sport, even baseball, the game that it most closely resembles.[58] As is well known, James's aim is to present cricket not just as popular entertainment but as a form of art, no less than opera, ballet and especially classical Greek theatre are forms of art.

> Once every year for four days the tens of thousands of Athenian citizens sat in the open air on the stone seats at the side of the Acropolis and from sunrise to sunset watched the plays of the competing dramatists. All that we have to correspond is a Test match.
> (*BB*, 158)

This is neither burlesque nor mock-heroic; James is deadly serious. Test cricket in particular, James argues, is a prolonged theatrical performance that unfolds over several days and a series of discrete acts (sessions and innings) and episodes (deliveries). In a Test match, engrossing interplay takes place between representative individuals who typify forces greater than themselves, both the team – the fortunes of which can rest on each moment of concentrated antagonism between batsman and bowler – and the respective communities whose values and aspirations are invested in the 'national' side. Cricket is also, as James says, a visual art (*BB*, 199), a game that at the highest levels requires very high and varied degrees of specialised technical skill, and that, therefore, allows for the public display of what all cricketers, James included, call 'style' (*BB*, 206). Cricket is, of course, a team game. But its episodic structure, its series of discrete, succinct and repeated instalments of competition between individual players (batsman, bowler and, more often than not, fielder), means that, as cricket's second shrewdest expositor, the American Marxist Mike Marqusee, has pointed out, cricket 'allows diverse personalities to flourish'.[59] The game is long enough and the skills it requires are varied enough for different personalities to be expressed there. The distinctive personalities and styles of individual players are key reasons for the game's vernacular appeal, in addition to being, James maintains, sources of pleasure for crowds whose knowledge of the game means that they are continually reading and responding to specific aesthetic and dramatic actions.[60]

Yet, to interpret and to understand a player or a match or even a particular shot or delivery, as opposed to merely enjoying a game of cricket, or more precisely to enjoying the game in its fullest sense, is for James to trace the historical and political circumstances that have shaped representative events and performances on the field of play. The style of Garfield Sobers, for example, the great Barbadian all-rounder and captain of the West Indies Test team in the late 1960s and early 1970s, however *sui generis* it appeared to be, could only be accounted for by combining the most meticulous scrutiny of Sobers' technique with a broader awareness of the historical developments that allowed Sobers' approach to be honed and fulfilled. The cricketer – and especially the *West Indian* cricketer – is, for James, an artist in the public sphere, his technique, his accomplishments and his very manner contingent on, and expressive of, the mindset of an engaged and insistent public. The grace, daring, imagination and confidence of that style, James argues, are not things inborn but rather products of and, indeed, catalysts for the creative self-assertion of a newly independent people.

> Garfield Sobers I see not as a fortuitous combination of atoms which by chance have coalesced into a superb public performer. He being what he is (and I being what I am), for me his command of the rising ball in the drive, his close fielding and his hurling himself into his fast bowling are a living embodiment of centuries of a tortured history.[61]

Sobers' accomplishments must be viewed historically not as inborn talents or, in the familiar though backhanded (in fact, racist) compliment used in the past about Caribbean cricketers, endowments of 'nature'. Identifiable social and political developments, from 'the rise in the financial position of the coloured middle class and the high fees paid to players by the English leagues' (*BB*, 10) to the establishment of political sovereignty and therefore the arrival of West Indians as agents of their own destinies, allowed for the training and fulfilment of Sobers' exceptional aptitude.

James is adamant on this point. When Sobers drove the rising ball off the back foot, he was not exhibiting some inborn knack, let alone showcasing some facet of his race, but expressing his inheritance of a long tradition of creative adaptation to the matting (as opposed to turf) wickets used up to that point in the Caribbean. James recalls the similarly accomplished 'back play' of H.B.G. Austin around the time of the First World War. Austin was a white man, like George Challenor who was 'the originator of West Indian batting' (C, 250). We could recall James's dismay, in an article on 'Cricket and Race', at the description in a *Washington Post* article of the baseball player Willie Mays as 'a black athlete' who 'ran black, swung black, and caught black'. Mays, according to the *Post*, articulated 'possibilities of uninhibited expression' in his play. But so too, James insists, returning the focus to cricket, did W.G. Grace and Victor Trumper, who were white. In the 1960s, Frank Worrell's West Indians 'tried to restore to cricket what it had lost' by playing creatively and imaginatively, but 'they were not expressing a blackness', James insists. What I believe James is getting at is that each of these players articulated and represented an alternative to the conformism and alienation of the human personality by capitalist social relations, relations that had, of course, been a particularly grievous burden for black men and women to bear but resistance to which was a matter of universal concern. West Indian cricketers did not represent national or cultural, let alone racial, self-aggrandisement. Rather, they represented the emergence of a potentially democratic politics and culture, and they anticipated new and more creative and well-rounded forms of human subjectivity.[62]

So, when James the journalist describes the Guyanese batsman Rohan Kanhai batting for a scratch team of West Indian players against an England XI at the end of the 1963 season, his trained eye is on Kanhai's aesthetic expression or performance of human freedom. In his clever manipulation of the bowlers and his inventive boundary-hitting, Kanhai was 'a West Indian proving to himself that henceforth he was following no established pattern but would create his own' (C, 169). 'At that moment, Edgbaston in 1964, the West Indian could strike from his feet the dust of centuries [...] He was free as few West Indians have been free' (C, 171). The deeds of this cricketer are images of freedom and self-sovereignty, which have a particular meaning and significance in the Caribbean context of course. But they are also a kind of general augury of a dis-alienated existence. Kanhai furnishes for the crowd images and examples of achieved creative expression. And because those images and examples are made available for the scrutiny, criticism and edification of large masses of people, the whole world of cricket-playing and cricket-watching actively anticipates, indeed constitutes, a kind of rehearsal for a genuinely democratic and postcolonial existence.

James's reading of Caribbean cricket effectively reminds us of something that Fredric Jameson has repeatedly argued, which is that the historicist interpretation of cultural texts requires the critic to adopt a particular, identifiably Marxist concept or understanding of history. History is conceptualised by Jameson in *The Political Unconscious* (1981) as the history of resistance and struggle, an arena in which different classes, values and visions of social and economic organisation fight it out: 'History is what hurts'.[63] Jameson therefore exhorts the cultural critic to employ what he calls a Marxist 'negative hermeneutic' (*PU*, 291), the practical work of reading and interpreting texts as expressions of what James calls 'centuries of a tortured history', at the same time as employing a Marxist 'positive hermeneutic' (*PU*, 292) that views the cultural text in question as engaged in a process of resistance to dominant structures and ideologies and even in a more or less explicit rehearsal of emergent structures, practices and values. The critic is thus called upon to undertake a decipherment of what Jameson calls 'the Utopian impulses' of 'cultural texts' (*PU*, 296). This is exactly what James does with cricket. He traces the complex and mediated connections between aesthetic form and historical struggle or, put differently, between the audacity with which Sobers drives the 'rising ball' and a people's self-possessed defiance of centuries of transportation, enslavement and belittlement. Indeed, the significance of the game's finest all-rounder is even greater than that. For what Sobers' comprehensive proficiency at all aspects of the game represents for James is nothing less than an augury of a form of subjectivity that has transcended impairment, alienation and specialisation: 'the division of the human personality, which is the greatest curse of our time' (*BB*, 195). Sobers himself may or may not be such a subject, but that form of advanced subjectivity is what his style represents.

James always provides evidence for his judgements about players and styles for, in his own words, analysis without technical knowledge 'is mere impressionism' (*BB*, 178), though he does not and cannot presume that his readers will always agree with him. Our point here is that this democratic susceptibility to interpretation, which is perhaps nothing other than a somewhat grand way of saying that cricket watchers endlessly read and reread the game and treat it, as James does, like a cultural text, is what makes cricket an aesthetic practice par excellence. West Indians, *Beyond a Boundary* contends, creatively refashioned the culture of their colonisers, finding in cricket, a game that helped to uphold colonial authority by instilling self-discipline and team loyalty and by promulgating both an ethical code of behaviour and an ideology of social equality (both of which contrasted with the flagrant injustice and inequality of the colonial West Indies), a form of cultural expression that could instead be made over into a device of protest and self-emancipation. Social passions, as James puts it, used cricket as a medium of expression (*BB*, 54). Refashioning, or rather repurposing, its ideology, and reinventing the manner in which it was played, West Indians turned cricket into a pursuit that expressed and promulgated their political and social aspirations. *Beyond a Boundary* amounts to a radical re-reading of cricket's established political meanings and a celebration of its intrinsic diversity. Cricket has been customarily associated with a pastoral and backward-looking vision of 'Englishness' and empire in which social conflicts are imaginatively resolved by an ethos of teamwork and obedience to the rules. But cricket emerges from James's study transformed utterly into the archetypal anti-colonial aesthetic form, both a versatile practice and an extremely mobile signifier, its styles and meanings capable of being radically refashioned by players and spectators alike, in different periods and, crucially, in different places across the radically different and unevenly developed territories to which the game has travelled. Crucially, cricket thus becomes a *utopian* aesthetic practice in Jameson's sense.[64]

Gunesekera's novel narrates the early life and middle age of Sunny Fernando who, despite his name and its allusion to the weather associated with his favourite game, is a man of a decidedly sombre disposition. Growing up in Manila in the early years of the Marcos dictatorship and later drifting from student life in London to an unprofitable business selling cameras, Sunny's incessantly backward-looking life is haunted by missed opportunities, broken connections and repressed memories. Framed by the novel's epigraph from Henri Cartier-Bresson, Sunny's growing absorption in photographic technique and the novel's climactic snapshot of an incident in 'the match' in 2002 at the Oval between India and Sri Lanka, this is a novel that frames Sunny's life as a series of detailed close-ups. World events are focalised through Sunny's rather blinkered perspective, often in a free indirect style that prevents the narrative voice from glossing Sunny's thoughts with much knowledge of wider events and contexts. Just outside or on the edge of the frame of this melancholic narrative of drift and introspection are such consequential events as the onset of the Marcos dictatorship (which Sunny's father serves), the protracted civil war in Sunny's native Sri Lanka between the government and the Liberation Tigers of Tamil Eelam (LTTE), the Eastern European revolutions of 1989, the rise of China and the terrorist attacks on New York in 2001 – all of them somehow connected in a way that Sunny himself can't quite see (*M*, 249).

Worldly events take place largely offstage. Much of what we understand as 'history', in the sense of large events and the exigencies of political struggle, takes place behind Sunny's back, or on the periphery of his vision, and is experienced most clearly through culture, especially cricket. For example, the later incidents glimpsed on the television and the earlier ones, such as the student protests and jeepney strikes in pre-Martial Law Manila (*M*, 9), appear distant proceedings which, from the perspective of the Fernandos' 'swanky Makati enclave of executive households' (*M*, 13), 'could have been on another planet' (*M*, 35). The world of the young Sunny is 'far removed from the Vietnam War and the skirmishes in Mindanao, the private mercenaries, the gangsters, the New People's Army and the military roaming the Philippines' (*M*, 54). He is a young man engrossed by thoughts of his mother's death – for which he secretly blames his father. But what lies just beyond Sunny's life of introspection and bewilderment is the unfolding narrative of world history itself, of failed or arrested decolonisation, of neo- and re-colonisation, of Western support for postcolonial dictatorships and the consequent struggles and rebellions, and the confusion of socialist and terrorist counter-movements that results.

Sri Lanka, even more so than Pakistan and the 'emerging Bangladesh' (*M*, 72), becomes in the novel *the* paradigmatic example of this postcolonial history of defeat, repression and violence. Sunny is only just conscious of the incompetence and venality of the 'so-called left-wing coalition' (*M*, 64–65) that took power after independence, the 'insurgency' (*M*, 67) against Bandaranaike's administration, and the later confusing round of ceasefires, government offensives and suicide bombings. Sunny's father, Lester, moved to the Philippines in 1967 to work as a journalist, convinced that Marcos, the 'heroic champion of social justice and civil liberties', was at the vanguard of third world liberation and 'delirious at the dream of a land that might combine El Dorado with Fleet Street' (*M*, 12). Compromised by a society controlled by money, however, Lester gave up journalism 'and went into the more lucrative business of marketing and PR' (*M*, 13). To all these tumultuous events and developments, Sunny is a distant spectator, his only and extremely idiosyncratic mode of access to them being through cricket, which begins 'to fill Sunny's sense of that world between private fantasy and public communion' (*M*, 63). What cricket represents in the novel, then, is an aesthetic practice freighted, indeed frequently over-freighted, with significance, value and meaning. For the novel's readers and, eventually, for Sunny, cricket provides a means of reflecting on this grim history of defeat and failure and of envisioning substantive alternatives to it.

In the early part of the novel, set in Manila in the 1970s, Sunny's friend Robby suggests that they organise a game of cricket involving Sunny's cricket-besotted father Lester, Lester's cronies and cosmopolitan acquaintances, and a motley circle of their own expat school fellows. Cricket promises 'to transform their uprooted lives' (*M*, 16), both to give them a temporary purpose, due to the demands of practice and preparation, and to bring together lives otherwise alienated by deracination and political compromise. Lester's Australian associate Martin Thompson recalls the first ever one-day international between Australia and England, which replaced the rained-off third Test in Melbourne in 1971. The very idea of a one-day international puzzles Lester, but from it emerges a proposal to challenge a visiting government delegation from Happy Valley, Hong Kong, to a match, 'single innings each, limited overs' (*M*, 65). The match itself, in which Sunny's scratch team of émigrés, adepts and flabby seniors successfully chases down a relatively low target off the last ball, is certainly no pastoral affair. It takes place on 'reclaimed swampland' with 'few trees and hardly any birds' (*M*, 70), most of the fauna having been annihilated, as Martin observes, by the Japanese invasion during the Second World War (*M*, 71). Tina, the young woman with whom Sunny is infatuated and the ablest batter of them all with her supple 'textbook strokes' (*M*, 48), secures victory. What this first match denotes, therefore, is a kind of egalitarian inclusiveness – since victory is secured by a female player and in spite of Sunny's nerviness and the ineptitude of Lester and Robby – even though that value is asserted both against the faux inclusiveness of English cricket and its pastoral delusions *and* in the face of, as Lester acknowledges, the growing crescendo of off-stage violence in 'the rest of the damn world' (*M*, 72).

This Makati XI has played its first and last match. Martial Law is declared in 1972 and Sunny leaves to study engineering in London. And there, too, history continues just outside the range of Sunny's newly acquired Voigtländer camera. 'Sunny ignored all of it', IRA bombing campaigns, three-day weeks, wildcat strikes and especially postcolonial traumas, taking his cue instead 'from those around him for whom Ceylon was only ever a cup of tea, and Manila a type of envelope' (*M*, 80). Back home, his estranged father distances himself from his friends, attending corporate functions where he speaks 'only to praise Marcos's New Society' (*M*, 82). Neither London, nor Liverpool – whose waterfront 'was once Britain's industrial anchorage' (*M*, 89) and where Sunny travels to stay with the family of his friend Ranil – prompts Sunny to think of the connections that make up the larger narrative of colonial, neo-colonial and potentially postcolonial world history. Only his private memories and fantasies of cricket allow him to do that,

> imagining the sea route from the mouth of the Mersey to Manila, a merchant ship carrying a cargo of cricket paraphernalia for the Makati XI, circling the globe and drawing his disjointed life back together, healing rifts, smoothing the furrows of anxiety, the knot in his head.
>
> (*M*, 91)

This crisis of alienation and 'hollowness' (*M*, 109) that slowly consumes Sunny is thus emblematic of a larger global crisis of postcolonial defeat and trauma. Cricket in the novel represents something like equality and inclusiveness or reconciliation, an aesthetic principle to set against the lasting inequalities of colonial power and against the reinvigorated certainties of national and ethnic belonging. But in England, especially under the Thatcher governments of the 1980s, cricket is, as Sunny tells Robby, 'a very exclusive game' (*M*, 119). Sunny cannot get into a team, not even the team that he naively imagines his workmates play in on 'all their summer weekends in some green and pleasant country field' (*M*, 118). For 'England ran on eccentric notions of privilege' (*M*, 119); 'Makati-style' class divisions, government repression and 'voguish' xenophobia prevail there too (*M*, 146). It is only by returning to Sri Lanka to visit his father's friend Hector that Sunny starts to make some sense of his past and of his future. Hector tells him about how Sunny's mother and father first met on the famous evening that Donald Bradman visited Ceylon, the great batsman stopping over with his Australian side on the way to becoming 'Invincibles' in England in 1948 (*M*, 143). According to Hector, Sunny's father, whom Sunny now sees as just a Marcos crony, 'wanted the world, you know, to find the world' (*M*, 144). Worldliness here recalls Said's capacious definition, encompassing both the lonely Sunny's desire for companionship ('You see, Sunny, you find only part of the world in yourself' (*M*, 144)) and the original universalist aspirations of anti-colonial liberation, something like Lester's idealistic dreams of comprehensive political change that, though they may have been dashed upon the rocks of neo-colonial tyranny, Sunny will henceforth resolve to bring back into focus with his camera.

The photographer Sunny is at first 'obsessed by death, loss, things coming apart' (*M*, 145). Yet, he is briefly made conscious of the connectedness of different lives and situations by the 'sickening' television reports of the anti-Tamil pogrom of 1983 in Colombo. 'This was a part of him destroying itself. There are no boundaries in our lives, he thought' (*M*, 153). Distanced from his wife Clara, burying his head in his darkroom (*M*, 155) and hardly ever reading a newspaper (*M*, 168), Sunny is insensible to the sweeping away of Marcos and Mrs Gandhi, to Tiananmen Square, Bucharest, the Velvet Revolution and the Gulf War. Nothing has 'weight' (*M*, 173) for him except the minutiae of photography. But what Sunny eventually realises is that photography, indeed art in general, which therefore includes cricket, provides access to the actual, not in the complacent way that Clara's no-nonsense father Eric tells him, because there 'is a great deal to be learnt outside fiction' (*M*, 162), but because the 'great deal to be learnt' can, in fact, be acquired *through* fiction and other such cultural practices. And photography will capture for Sunny an image not of the past, on which he morbidly dwells, but of a present that alludes to, and helps create, a future – both his own and that of the postcolonial world of which he is a representative citizen, with his directionlessness, his disenchantment and his 'uncertainties of belonging, race and class' (*M*, 182).

'"Look at the world every way you can, Sunny", he would croon. "There's a lot of world out there to see"' (*M*, 24). There is an element of cliché in Hector's crooning counsel of course, as there is in the novel's description of the 'place of healing' that 'Sunny had been seeking all his life' (*M*, 183) and especially in the outlook of the eclectic spiritual group that the elderly Hector joins, which aims to 'create an energy centre for world peace on an island of fractured dreams' (*M*, 191). What Sunny admires about photography is its implicit avoidance of cliché, the way it appears to capture an instantaneous moment or experience in time, an experience that is unmediated by hackneyed or formulaic words and that is in many ways irreducibly subjective, contingent and singular (*M*, 185). Photography and cricket, and ultimately a photograph of a game of cricket, furnish less trite and more empowering visions of futurity. It is cricket, ultimately, in this meandering novel bookended by two multiply meaningful matches, that represents (though it does not, and of course cannot, provide) an alternative to the personal and collective traumas of postcolonial history. Lester dreams of spreading the game beyond its traditional territories and meanings.

> 'No, Hector. This is not colonial claptrap,' Lester continued. 'You see how golf has been transformed internationally. Cricket might well become an All-Asian game, you know. But we need it to grow in South-East Asia, the Far East. Maybe if it flourished in the Philippines, like in Australia, India, Pakistan and Ceylon, the rest of the region might take it up. Imagine Laos, Thailand, Indonesia all hitting the Brits for a six. A true game of the South'.
>
> (M, 43)

Rudolf Navaratnam even fantasises about spreading the game to China, the country whose rise, Hector later tells Sunny, because of the wholesale corruption of the ideals of the LTTE, is now his 'only hope' (M, 203). 'Transformed internationally', this imagined game of the Global South may hit the Brits for six but the political hope that it embodies, for Sunny and at an earlier time for his father, has precious little to do with aggressive nationalism. The news of suicide bombings and Sri Lankan government offensives makes Sunny immune to the patriotic euphoria that greeted the Sri Lankan team's victory in the 1996 World Cup. 'The country was jubilant and the cricketers became national heroes. But did that make a real difference?' (M, 235).

Cricket in the novel provides political meaning that is significant and even utopian but never trite or nationalistic. Sunny is 'hooked' on the first Test match between England and Sri Lanka in May 2002. Following Hector's advice, he attends the second day's play at Lord's with his old Leica camera. But what he finds there is 'a world away from those games Sunny had passed in the middle-distant countryside, where the beer was warm and the mayflies snored and matchstick figures played an indistinct game' (M, 262). Sunny expects 'sunlit oaks, a blue sky, a pavilion from the colonial era with picket teeth and gin rims' (M, 258). Far from these nostalgic, Orwell-inspired (and John Major-resuscitated) clichés of a game that embodies an unchanging set of pastoral, national and colonial values, Sunny finds a thrillingly complex and unpredictable phenomenon. This is a contradictory sub-culture of eccentrically attired 'aficionados' (M, 259), of enthusiasts like Sunny who conspicuously fail what his boss Freddy calls 'the Norman Wisdom test' (M, 259) (a satire of Norman Tebbit's notorious 'cricket test' of national loyalty), of 'solidarity' and 'festive laughter' (M, 260), of the incongruous city-centre 'green lung' (M, 262) of the playing area, of solicitous security guards and electric scoreboards, of good-natured and inebriated supporters cheering for their own side *and* the opposition, of a largely white and English crowd standing to applaud the Sri Lankan opener Marvan Atapattu's sizeable innings of 185 and later to bay bloodthirstily for Sri Lankan wickets.[65]

A Test match is a changeable and ambiguous event that is, by turns, 'carnival' and 'execution' (M, 273). Sunny is enthralled by the 'peculiar' 'thrill' of the match (M, 272), the rapt focus and distracted daydreaming that this fluctuating occasion engenders, the creative freedom it affords the performers, its shifting temporal rhythms, as well as its whims, quirks and permissiveness, not to mention its potential to flout expectations, transgress boundaries and provoke reflection. But what really shocks him out of his characteristically past-besotted melancholia is a chance meeting during the lunch interval with Tina, the Makati XI's star batter, and her husband, the XI's oafish Australian fast bowler Steve. Tina is evidently insecure and unhappy, a 'free spirit' now hopelessly 'entangled' in a life of inanity and privilege, and so Sunny decides not to meet them as agreed after the stumps are drawn.

Sunny watches the end of the Test on television, though it peters out into a tedious draw, and he journeys to the final day of the third Test at Old Trafford, where England pull off an unlikely win. The novel ends with Sunny attending the one-day international between Sri Lanka and India at the Oval. He again takes his camera because 'Sunny wanted to photograph hope embedded in love. Or love embedded in hope. Something promising despite the true nature of the world' (M, 293). But in addition to the memorable image that Sunny finally captures, an event with which the novel concludes, the scene at the Oval provides a series of memorable images and examples of the diverse and often contradictory experiences that crowds bring to and derive from the game. A one-day international in the subcontinent, Marqusee observes in his account of the 1996 World Cup, can be many things at once: 'a popular festival, a global media event, an elite social occasion, a political platform, a gladiatorial contest, an aesthetic delight and a nationalist jamboree'.[66] This game between two Asian teams on an English ground encapsulates these multiple, paradoxical and finally utopian meanings, as well as the integral role played by spectators in actively constructing those multiple meanings. The crowd, 'predominantly South Asian this time' (M, 297), is extremely ebullient and noisy:

> This was cricket at full decibel. A game where every ball was a missile and the field an arena of gladiators. Sunny realized he had known nothing about real One-day cricket. Nothing. These fans had not come to watch but to participate: the players were not kings but servants of the crowd. They existed only to please the crowd. Do their bidding or be hauled off.
>
> (M, 297)

Members of this heterogeneous multitude of Indian and Sri Lankan supporters admonish the players for incompetence and slow play, start up 'anti-colonial, anti-white and anti-Pakistani' chants (M, 299), argue over those chants, cheer en masse for the struggling Sri Lankan team and tease two good-natured and intoxicated 'old codgers', one of whom turns out to have lived in India for several decades and whose name, Hutton, that of one of Yorkshire's and England's greatest ever batsmen – Len Hutton – prompts the exultant and chauvinism-defying chant of 'Hutton is an Indian'. The Sri Lankan followers chat and sing in Tamil and Sinhala (*M*, 305). The crowd is at all times and in countless and contradictory ways responding to the game by fashioning various interpretations, outlooks and affiliations. More often than not, they are improvised affiliations that momentarily transcend the national allegiances of individual spectators, who not only cheer for each other's team but exchange pakoras, genial mockery and gentle reproofs for wayward behaviour.

'There is not one, but many cricket publics', as Marqusee has pointed out, 'and among them an endless tussle takes place over the meaning and ownership of the game' (*ABE*, 17). One thing that distinguishes the gladiatorial Oval crowd is its diversity. Another word for diversity in this context might simply be the game's impressively democratic quality, which is usually trammelled and frustrated by social hierarchies and commercial imperatives. Marqusee worries that cricket crowds are being stripped of their 'collective creativity' (*ABE*, 115): atomised, regulated, distracted and their responses increasingly choreographed by everything from the intrusive music that greets every boundary and every dismissal in limited-overs games and the big screens that ceaselessly flash up ads and exhortations to the lamentable spectacle of dancing cheerleaders, flamethrowers and other imitative, misplaced gimmicks. 'Only in the democratic domain, where cricket and its meanings are shared and shaped by multitudes', Marqusee argues, 'can there arise a force strong enough to override the manipulations of the elite' (*ABE*, 292).

The crowd at the Oval helps to open out cricket's meanings to the, as yet unwritten, democratic future craved by James and Marqusee. This climactic match was itself a forgettable and one-sided contest, India chasing down a modest target of 202 with four wickets and twenty-eight balls to spare: 'Sri Lanka, demoralised after losing the Tests 2-0, barely showed up', as cricket's 'bible' *Wisden* informs us.[67] But what this otherwise uneventful and forgettable match means in a deeper sense, for Sunny though more specifically for the novel's readers, is something far more auspicious. Besides the momentary transcendence of national affiliations in the crowd and the crowd's unruly energy and democratic inclusiveness, there is a kind of epiphany for Sunny. He rushes to the front of the stand to take a photograph of a prostrate pigeon hit by the ball in the outfield, a 'dove of peace' whose unfortunate fate briefly hushes the raucous crowd and whose body is retrieved and tenderly cradled by the nearest fielder, 'a pair of clasped hands pray[ing] to a dying bird' (*M*, 304).

> There was something significant happening here, he knew, no matter what the outcome of the game would be. Perhaps it was the power to silence that comes with death, however small the life, and our need to overcome it. To find some brief moment of care. Hope. The tender possibility of renewal. This man, this game, this bird was salvation. The timing was perfect. Anything seemed possible: peace, love, joy, life everlasting [...] It was all in the frame. Sunny saw it all.
>
> (*M*, 304)

It is cricket, or more precisely this unusual and seemingly innocuous but extremely meaningful incident, that places events and possibilities finally 'in' rather than outside of Sunny's 'frame'. Gunesekera is not W.G. Sebald; there is no enigmatic *photo trouvée* standing in for Sunny's fictional snapshot, which we therefore do not see. Marqusee describes the task of describing and explaining a game that is so open-ended, inclusive, multiform and, to use his useful word, 'polysemous' (*ABE*, 8) – a game that he therefore sees as 'a rich realm of human possibility' (*M*, 256) – as like 'trying to take a snapshot of a creature for ever on the wing' (*M*, 257). In this case, alas, Sunny snaps a creature that is no longer on the wing! Yet the dazed bird, in addition to the tender solicitations of Sri Lanka's cover-point fielder, is also an image of cricket's capacity for rejuvenation. *Wisden*'s report of an otherwise unremarkable match tells us that one Tendulkar 'square cut hit an unsuspecting pigeon, which was carried off the field by Jayawardene; it later recovered'.[68] By the end of the novel, 'some divisions, at least, were close to healing' (*M*, 306), those between Sunny and his wife and son, if not yet the infinitely more painful divisions of Sri Lanka's 'suicidal war' (*M*, 306) and the larger postcolonial conflicts and ruptures that Sri Lanka exemplifies and for which in this novel both Sri Lanka and the Philippines partly stand.

What we want to suggest then, is that cricket emerges from Gunesekera's novel as a game that is *still* capable of carrying alternative or subversive and democratic meanings quite different to those conventionally or, as it were, officially ascribed to the game, even to the limited-overs game. For nostalgists and other conservatives, the popularity of shorter forms of the game, principally Twenty20 cricket as well as 50-over one-day internationals, spells the definitive demise of the longer forms of first-class and Test cricket, with their leisurely pre-industrial rhythms and allegiances, gentlemanly codes and greater scope for complex and elongated dramatic action.[69] The truth is that short-form cricket's considerable democratic potential, by which we mean its sheer mobility, the diverse ways in which it is played and watched, is being held back by the crass commodification imposed by the game's administrators, broadcasters and sponsors. If fans watching the Australian 'Big Bash' or the Indian Premier League are really lucky, a batsman will be run out, bowled or stumped, at which point the bails will start to flash!

But these tournaments' big crowds cannot be put down to this kind of flashy marketing. All cricket tournaments for the last 20 years have been marketed in exactly the same way, even in England's deservedly unloved 'Bash'-like 'Blast'. In truth, the large crowds in India and Australia are more likely to be a result of the fact that cricket has a ready-made public, albeit one often prevented from watching matches by paywalls and exorbitant ticket prices. There are important lessons here about the game's essentially democratic, which is not to say market-friendly, appeal.

What *The Match* shows is that even the limited-overs version of the game is sufficiently 'polysemous' to allow for different, imaginative as well as subversive and utopian forms of cultural expression, particularly on the part of the crowds and spectators who attend the match with which the novel concludes. Not only crowds but also cricketers endlessly reshape the medium so that, as James puts it, cricket 'can give new satisfactions to new people' (*BB*, 222). We should acknowledge the imaginativeness and ingenuity of limited-overs cricket. Even James, a connoisseur and in his youth a practitioner of strictly orthodox stroke play, reminisces about Wilton St Hill lofting the ball over mid-off for boundaries in an intercolonial match with strokes that he had obviously invented on the spot. James suggests that the invention of shots and other spontaneous attempts to counteract unexpected stratagems from the opposing team, thus showcasing a player's virtuosity and ingenuity, 'is where a future for big cricket lies' (*BB*, 87). Who could deny that the invention of new shots, such as Kevin Pietersen's 'switch hit' or Tillakaratne Dilshan's 'Dilscoop' or 'ramp shot' or Natalie Sciver's 'Natmeg' (a never-before-imagined but relatively low-risk clip through the legs behind square), affords new opportunities for inventiveness, enjoyment and interpretative engagement? The same goes for the development of new bowling strategies such as the use of greater and more frequent variations during a bowler's spell or even in the course of a single six-ball over or the unforeseen usefulness of slow bowlers in Twenty20, in addition to the often breathtaking ingenuity and agility of fielders required to effect improbable run outs, to prevent good shots from going for four and to catch the ball on, or even frequently over, the boundary rope.

'No longer an instrument for socializing black and brown men into the public etiquette of empire, [cricket] is now an instrument for mobilizing national sentiment in the service of transnational spectacles and commoditization', as Arjun Appadurai claims.[70] But the view that cricket is now almost wholly commodified, given over to the meanings and priorities of neoliberal elites, is belied by the fact that, like any work of art, cricket can always be performed and experienced differently. Cricket attracts and produces worldly citizens, not just chauvinistic consumers. The belief that cricket has now been definitively neoliberalised, as it were, is consistent with what is still the general tenor of English writing about cricket, elegy being its natural mode, as Bateman suggests.[71] What *The Match* succeeds in demonstrating, by contrast, is cricket's openness to the future and its enduring capacity to develop new forms and meanings.

The opening chapters of Marqusee's *Anyone But England: Cricket and the National Malaise* (1994) are the closest anyone has come to writing a Marxist history of cricket and a comprehensive critique of its dominant ideology. Marqusee reminds us, first, of the ways in which the cricketing myths of civility and equality on the field of play have frequently masked the imperial violence that took place in the territories to which cricket was exported – violence that was abetted, indeed impelled, by many of the modern game's founders. Marqusee also looks at how the enduring image of cricket as a game rooted in an idealised English – and as Bateman reminds us, specifically *Southern* English (*ABE*, 76) – rural past has served the similarly ideological purpose of disguising class conflicts on the domestic front too; in a great deal of cricket writing, the game is constructed ideologically as a symbol 'not just of social harmony, but of social hierarchy' (*ABE*, 29), as well as of order, law and 'manliness' (*ABE*, 46).[72] The Victorian middle classes made of cricket, in James's words, a 'moral discipline' (*BB*, 166) and therefore a crucial aspect of their culture. The game's success 'in the most diverse places and among people living lives which were poles removed from that whence it originally came' signifies, however, as James argues, 'that it contained elements of universality that went beyond the bounds of the originating nation' (*BB*, 166).

Cricket, in James's view, travelled across the globe and then took root in certain locales, though it did so not in the fortuitous way that airborne seeds travel and take root. In reality, the game served an important ideological function in the service of imperialist domination. Cricket then bore some 'strange fruit' in the colonies (*BB*, 42), as James puts it, precisely because it helped to articulate and catalyse the struggle against imperialist domination. James expects a lot of cricket; the game has been complicit in exploitation and, what is more, it has expressed and communicated alternatives to exploitation, and not only imperialist exploitation, for the diversity and creativity that the game encourages has succeeded in outlining substantive alternatives to the wholesale alienation and impairment of the human personality by consumerism and alienating wage-labour. Cricket, for James, is a democratic and anti-colonial practice, in essence though not always in fact. There are significant exceptions to this rule, or rather instances of where cricket fails to live up to its democratic ideals that not even James acknowledges.[73] Neil Lazarus has argued that 'the validity of James's examination of West Indies cricket as a socially expressive practice consists in its *method*'.[74] Cricket is an aesthetic practice, best and most instructively analysed with the aid of a method that, while it attends closely and competently to the game's distinctive technical features, also recognises that matches, performances and styles are the end products of larger social and political developments, in particular struggles over social and political power. Moreover, the meanings that critics and spectators give to the game are multiple. They also evolve and are transformed in the course of cricket's responses to those larger developments and in the course of cricket's travels from one territory to another.

Conclusion

In all these texts reconciliation is shown to be a taxing process that is not imposed from without but rather emerges tentatively, as we have said, from within, that is, from particular geographies, practices and contexts. Reconciliation is a word (and goal) that is as frustratingly nebulous as it is politically essential. Addressing injustice and pursuing reconciliation are protracted and ongoing tasks, often partial or even complete failures that cannot ever be mapped out in advance. In Gunesekera's *The Match*, the entire history and future of the postcolonial world, with its partial triumphs but also its setbacks and wrong turns, its potential for democratic renewal and the transcendence of the nation-statist legacy of empire, is illuminated by the aesthetic spectacle furnished by the quirky but durably meaningful game of cricket. Sunny finally peers beyond his fixation with his own disappointments and away from his backward-looking preoccupation with lost opportunities. He starts to think through the complex possibilities of global communication and even reconciliation as well as democratic rejuvenation represented by the perennially mobile and protean art form of cricket. These possibilities are incarnated in *The Match* via very fleeting but striking images of an ebullient and unpredictable cricket crowd alternately asserting and abandoning national allegiances, of snapshots of hope, popular involvement and solidarity.

In *Bitter Fruit*, as Ana Miller observes, Silas's wife Lydia 'refuses to allow her experience to be subsumed into institutional frameworks that deal with the past in superficial and problematic ways'. If her husband, the government functionary, deals with the past by 'managing' it and thus repressing his own trauma, Lydia uses silence 'as an act of resistance against the appropriation of her personal trauma' of rape.[75] The whole novel is composed in free indirect style; the main narrative voice very subtly absorbs the idioms and perspectives of its characters, never allowing any external or purportedly omniscient moral commentary to impose itself on the judgements, decisions and actions of its wounded protagonists. So, it is extremely impressive that Lydia declines the opportunity to testify before the Truth and Reconciliation Commission: 'Nothing in her life would have changed because of a public confession of pain suffered. Because nothing could be undone, you could not withdraw a rape, it was an irrevocable act, like murder'.[76]

How can such traumas be exorcised, the incalculable acts of casual or premeditated viciousness and degradation, let alone the structurally embedded and excruciatingly-difficult-to-shift violence of entire social and economic systems? Certainly not, surely, by mealy-mouthed official apologies, commissions and government amnesties or even by the 'radical restructuring' of those larger systems that Benita Parry recommends in the South African context.[77] For, as Lydia soberly insists, the violence that has been done 'could not be withdrawn, not by an act of remorse or vengeance, not even by justice'.[78]

'*Justice*', muses the introspective Magistrate in Coetzee's endlessly suggestive anti-colonial allegory *Waiting for the Barbarians*: 'once that word is uttered, where will it all end?'[79] The end is not prescribed, let alone pictured in that novel or in any of the texts and films we have discussed in this chapter. Reconciliation is understood more as a process than a goal, one involving countless unofficial acts of remembrance and reckoning, as well as public procedures of documentation and confrontation. It has political, cultural, social and economic dimensions. And reconciliation is an extemporaneous and unfinished task. When Lurie in *Disgrace* tries to imagine an alternative to the manifold violences he is learning to confront, in effect to picture what 'grace' might look like, he is at a loss. Problematically, he links the violence of apartheid to what he sees as the retributive sexual violence suffered by his daughter Lucy; she apparently sees the attack differently. How, the novel wonders, can various forms of injustice be conceptualised and understood? What, moreover, does justice even look like? Lucy is reading *The Mystery of Edwin Drood*, Charles Dickens' unfinished novel, an indication perhaps that the acts of conciliation, contrition and restructuring that these works contemplate and tentatively undertake are part of an uncompleted, perhaps even in some sense, given the magnitude of the injustices that have been done and cannot be undone, an uncompletable task.

Notes

1 Kevin Avruch and Beatriz Vejarano, 'Truth and Reconciliation Commissions: A Review Essay and Annotated Bibliography', in *OJPCR: The Online Journal of Peace and Conflict Resolution*, 4:2 (2002), 37–76, 38.
2 Ibid., p. 37. Avruch and Verjano point out that most commissions take place in the contexts of transitional governments.
3 Avruch and Vejarano, 'Truth and Reconciliation Commissions', p. 39.
4 Paul Gready, 'Novel Truths: Literature and Truth Commissions', in *Comparative Literature Studies*, 46:1 (2009), 156–176, 156.
5 Ibid., p. 157.
6 J.M. Coetzee, *Disgrace*, London: Vintage, 2000, p. 49.
7 Ibid., p. 52.
8 Ibid., p. 53.
9 Ibid., p. 55.
10 Jane Poyner, 'Writing Under Pressure: A Post-apartheid Canon?', in *Journal of Postcolonial Writing*, 44:2 (2008), 103–114, 109.
11 Avruch and Vejarano, 'Truth and Reconciliation Commissions', p. 41.

12 Poyner, 'Writing Under Pressure', p. 109.
13 Gready, 'Novel Truths', p. 168.
14 Ibid., p. 98.
15 Ibid., p. 107.
16 Ibid., p. 158. Gready also reminds us of other important innovations, such as the 'four-fold definition of truth' encompassing 'factual or forensic truth', 'personal and narrative truth', 'social or "dialogue" truth' and 'healing and restorative truth'.
17 Rosemary Jolly, 'Desiring Good(s) in the Face of Marginalized Subjects: South Africa's Truth and Reconciliation Commission in a Global Context', in *South Atlantic Quarterly*, 100:3 (2001), 693–715.
18 Ibid., p. 710.
19 Ibid., p. 711.
20 Ronit Frinkel, 'Performing Race, Reconsidering History: Achmat Dangor's Recent Fiction', in *Research in African Literatures*, 39:1 (2008), 149–165, 163.
21 Poyner, 'Writing Under Pressure', p. 111.
22 Gready, 'Novel Truths', p. 170.
23 Achmat Dangor, *Bitter Fruit*, London: Atlantic Books, 2001, p. 85.
24 Ibid., p. 68. MK here refers to the armed wing of the African National Congress, Umkhonto we Sizwe.
25 Dangor, *Bitter Fruit*, p. 97, emphasis added.
26 Ibid., p. 98.
27 Ibid., p. 108.
28 Ibid., pp. 164–165.
29 Ibid., p. 165.
30 Alan Duff, *Once Were Warriors*, New York: Vintage, 1995.
31 Corinn Columpar, '"Taking Care of Her Green Stone Wall": The Experience of Space in Once Were Warriors', in *Quarterly Review of Film and Video*, 24:5 (2007), 463–474, 463.
32 Ibid., p. 463. Originally quoted in Robert Sklar, 'Social Realism with Style', in *Cineaste*, 21:3 (1995), 25–27.
33 Ibid., p. 464.
34 Ibid. Citing the work of Leonie Pihama, 'Repositioning Maori Representation: Contextualising Once Were Warriors', in Jonathan Dennis and Jan Bieringa (eds), *Film in Aotearoa New Zealand*, Wellington: Victoria University Press, 1996, pp. 191–193, p. 191.
35 Duff, *Once Were Warriors*, p. 43.
36 Mandy Treagus, 'Representing Pacific Tattoos: Issues in Postcolonial Critical Practice', in *Journal of Postcolonial Writing*, 44:2 (2008), 183–192, 187 (citing Athol Chase, 'Empty Vessels and Loud Noises: Views about Aboriginality Today', in *Social Alternatives*, 2:2 (1981), 23–27, 24).
37 Treagus, 'Representing Pacific Tattoos', p. 187.
38 Columpar, '"Taking Care of Her Green Stone Wall"', p. 466.
39 Duff, *Once Were Warriors*, pp. 47–48.
40 Ibid., p. 48.
41 Ibid., p. 57.
42 Ibid., p. 51.
43 Ibid., p. 64.

44 Treagus, 'Representing Pacific Tattoos', p. 189.
45 A long hand-weapon traditionally made of wood or whalebone.
46 Duff, *Once Were Warriors*, p. 102.
47 Ibid., p. 103.
48 Ibid.
49 Ibid.
50 'The solace of an Australian summer – when cricket brought hope and light', 19 November 2015. Warner's subsequent career has been more chequered of course. Perhaps nothing illustrates the fallible humanity of cricketers or the durability of cricket's ethos/myth of 'fair play' than the extremely anguished public and media response to the illegal use of sandpaper to alter the condition of the ball in the third Test match against South Africa in Cape Town in 2018, allegedly at the behest of Warner, then Australia's vice-captain. The player responsible plus Warner, the captain, the coach and eventually the Chairman of Cricket Australia subsequently lost their positions.
51 Romesh Gunesekera, *The Match*, London: Bloomsbury, 2006. Subsequent references will be given in the main text after *M*.
52 Alexis Tadié, 'The Fictions of (English) Cricket: From Nations to Diaspora', in *International Journal of the History of Sport*, 27:4 (2010), 690–711, 692.
53 Joseph O'Neill, *Netherland*, London: Fourth Estate, 2008, p. 116.
54 Anthony Bateman, *Cricket, Literature and Culture: Symbolising the Nation, Destabilising Empire*, Farnham: Ashgate, 2009, p. 167.
55 Ibid., p. 194.
56 We are borrowing this concept from Raymond Williams in order to describe how cricket often succeeds in articulating 'new meanings and values, new practices, new relationships and kinds of relationship', *Marxism and Literature*, Oxford: Oxford University Press, 1977, p. 123. Though these meanings and so on may only be materialised in tentative and incomplete ways in the present, they would actually prevail and become dominant, to use another of Williams' terms, in a genuinely postcolonial and even post-capitalist form of social and economic organisation. Could one even call cricket a 'residual' cultural practice, in Williams' terms, a remnant from the past that points the way to a different kind of future?
57 C.L.R. James, *Beyond a Boundary*, London: Serpent's Tail, 1984 [1963], p. 196. Subsequent references will be given in the main text after *BB*.
58 Its distinctively dramatic structure does not mean, of course, that cricket alone among sports should be considered a form of art. Roland Barthes' celebrated reading of the Tour de France as a kind of epic, for example, presents the race as an aesthetic spectacle in which all kinds of (often contradictory) desires and aspirations are invested. Since the Tour is primarily a struggle – not just against other riders but against physical and natural limits and above all, in the mountains, against gravity – there is something heroic and even positively blasphemous in riders' feats, Barthes contends. The Tour, he acknowledges, is also a commercial enterprise through and through, as well as a nationalist myth and a reactionary fantasy that furnishes images of feudal hierarchy in the fealty owed by *domestiques* to their team leaders. A versatile and ambiguous myth, The Tour is 'a generator of ideological alibis' as much as it is, crucially, also a Promethean myth that anticipates individuals' liberation from their domination at the hands

of society and nature. *Mythologies*, trans. Richard Howard and Annette Lavers, New York: Hill and Wang, 2012 [1957], pp. 126–130. The Uruguayan writer Eduardo Galeano waxes lyrical about the importation and elaboration of football in South America. The origins of the Brazilian national team's imaginative tactics and techniques, as well as an alternative to the win-at-all-costs mentality of the football business and football jingoism, are to be found in the 1910s and 1920s in the rule-breaking panache of the Brazilian game's first mixed-race superstar, 'O Tigre' Artur Friedenreich, who 'brought to the solemn stadium of the whites the irreverence of brown boys who entertained themselves fighting over a rag ball in the slums'. Eduardo Galeano, *Football in Sun and Shadow*, trans. Mark Fried, London: Fourth Estate, 1997, p. 39.

59 Mike Marqusee, *Anyone But England: Cricket and the National Malaise*, London: Verso, 1994, p. 49. Subsequent references are given in the main text after *ABE*.

60 By construing the playing and watching of cricket as aesthetic endeavours, James is defying a tradition of Marxist criticism that sees all sport as serving an ideological purpose, as, in Theodor Adorno's words, a way of training participants 'into modes of behaviour which [...] are required of them by the work process' and, for Trotsky, a diversion of revolutionary 'passions' and attributes 'along artificial channels'. Theodor Adorno, 'Free Time', in Jay Bernstein (ed), *The Culture Industry: Selected Essays on Mass Culture*, London: Routledge, 1991, pp. 162–170, p. 168; Trotsky quoted in Jonathan Dart, 'In Defence of Sport', in Michael Lavalette (ed), *Capitalism and Sport: Politics, Protest, People and Play*, London: Bookmarks, 2013, pp. 30–36, p. 30. As Andrew Smith has argued, James provides a materialist reading of culture that discards conventional distinctions between high and low or 'intellectual' and 'popular' while insisting on the need to make critical and evaluative judgements about cultural creativity, 'The Window and the Wardrobe: C.L.R. James and the Critical Reading of Sport and Literature', *Journal of Postcolonial Writing*, 52:3 (2016), 262–273.

61 C.L.R. James, *Cricket*, ed. Anna Grimshaw, London: Allison & Busby, 1989, p. 232. Subsequent references will be given in the main text after *C*.

62 As Dave Renton's study of James's work shows, this militant advocacy of democracy is its common denominator, from James's advocacy of anti-colonial liberation, his critique of the wrong turns made by postcolonial regimes in Ghana, Trinidad and elsewhere, his insistence on the democratic relationship between cricket crowds and the game's forms and meanings, and his claim in Trotskyist debates about the fate of the Soviet Union that democracy, not planning or state ownership, is the hallmark of socialism. Dave Renton, *C.L.R. James: Cricket's Philosopher King*, London: Haus Books, 2007.

63 Fredric Jameson, *The Political Unconscious: Narrative as a Socially Symbolic Act*, London: Routledge, 1981, p. 102. Subsequent references will be given in the main text after *PU*.

64 We wonder if James himself sometimes fell short of this insight into the democratic openness of cricketers, games and styles to multiple different readings. James, for example, put the cautious play of English and Australian sides in the post-war period down to what he calls the 'Welfare State of mind'. This is a surprising phrase from a Leftist like James, though by depicting post-war English cricketers as plodding functionaries of a bureaucratic system, James reveals his

recognisably Trotskyist suspicion of a Western capitalist system that had unexpectedly gained a new lease of life and legitimacy by effecting a series of 'state capitalist' compromises with the social democratic aspirations of organised labour leading to higher wages, better housing, educational opportunities and so on. There are other ways of reading post-war English cricket. The English game had been controlled since the mid-nineteenth century, as Marqusee shows, from the Marylebone Cricket Club and Imperial Cricket Conference at Lord's cricket ground in London by a social 'elite', drawn first from a class of landed rentiers and later from industrialists and those who had made their money in the city and wished to make themselves over into landed rentiers. The hypocritical cult of amateurism helped maintain the fiction that cricket represented a fantasy of social hierarchy and order. 'Professionals', meanwhile, were attracted to cricket largely because it enabled them to make a living (often by bowling, which is physically the hardest role in any cricket side). The whole 'professional' outlook typified most perfectly in the decades after the war by the exceptionally cautious batting of Yorkshire's Geoffrey Boycott (frequently accused of a selfish preoccupation with his batting average at the expense of his team's chances of victory) or by the extremely belligerent, high-speed bowling of Yorkshire's Fred Trueman, appear as both (or rather, for the interested onlooker, *mean* both) the dour professionalism that James bemoans *and* a forthright assertion of the rights and aspirations of a social class traditionally condemned by the English game to penury, subservience and contempt but given a new presence and power in English life and thus in English cricket by the welfare state compromise. Social class, in short, is a key determinant of the ways in which English cricket is played and watched.

65 It is still difficult to watch a game of cricket on a weekday, the improbable 'green lung' spread out before you amidst the unlovely post-industrial terrain of Old Trafford or the dilapidated redbricks of Headingley, without experiencing both the pleasure and guilt of putting to one side the clock-bound routines of wage labour. As Marqusee observes, 'you enter a world where the clock is ticking to an ancient, irregular rhythm' (*ABE*, 54). The green expanse of the cricket field is both surprising and incongruous when seen against the meticulously parcelled up properties with which it is surrounded; indeed, Marqusee reminds us that boundaries were not written into the Laws until the 1870s (*ABE*, 48). Thinking of the time and not just of the spaces in which cricket is played, the exceedingly (in some ways absurdly) protracted duration of a four- or five-day match is a standing rebuke to what the Marxist historian E.P. Thompson famously describes as the shift in our inward apprehension of time contingent upon industrial capitalism's need to discipline labour by rigidly separating work and free time and by dividing up the working day into precisely scheduled tasks. E.P. Thompson, 'Time, Work-Discipline, and Industrial Capitalism', *Past and Present*, 38 (1967), 56–97. Its incongruous and unstable spaces, in addition to the prolonged and irregular rhythms of cricket's time, are referred to by Marqusee, intriguingly, as cricket's 'under-developed features' (*ABE*, 48). They are evidence of the game's 'incomplete accommodation with the modern world' (*ABE*, 88). Cricket points a way beyond the temporal and spatial logics of capital, not least because it never quite came to terms with them in the first place.

66 Mike Marqusee, *War Minus the Shooting: A Journey Through South Asia During Cricket's World Cup*, London: Mandarin, 1997, p. 15.
67 *Wisden Cricketers' Almanack 2003*, ed. Tim de Lisle, Alton: John Wisden, Lawrence Booth, 2003, p. 532.
68 Ibid., p. 532.
69 The three- or four-day first-class game is based in the Caribbean on the different territories, in England on historic counties, in Australia and India on states and in Sri Lanka on long-established sports clubs. International five-day Test cricket, meanwhile, is based on nine countries. Test cricket was, until recently, both the most prestigious and the most lucrative form of the game as well as the form to which the lion's share of the game's resources was devoted. Now widely assumed to be on its last legs, Test cricket appears to have been superseded by its more marketable offshoot, Twenty20 cricket, as played in the enormously lucrative Indian Premier League and in the equivalent competitions in England, Bangladesh, Australia, South Africa, Pakistan, New Zealand and the Caribbean. An appreciation of the wholesale commodification of the T20 game as well as of the derivative way in which it is marketed can be gained simply by perusing the inane monikers of these interchangeable tournaments (the NatWest Blast, the KFC Big Bash, the Ram Slam T20 Challenge and even the Dream 11 Super Smash) and their interchangeable franchises (the Kolkata Knight Riders, the Guyana Amazon Warriors, etc.). The shorter TV-friendly duration of these forgettable turkey shoots, plus their fewer and simpler dramatic narratives, stale marketing gimmicks and US-style team franchises, are aimed at attracting a larger market share of spectators schooled in other kinds of sport and entertainment. As ever, cricket administrators and their armies of expensive consultants focus on marketing the game (usually patronisingly and therefore unsuccessfully) to people who don't like cricket while alienating people who already do.
70 Arjun Appadurai, *Modernity at Large: Cultural Dimensions of Globalization*, Minneapolis, MN: University of Minnesota Press, 1996, p. 42.
71 Anthony Bateman, *Cricket, Literature and Culture*, p. 61.
72 The most perfect distillation of cricket's ideology can be found in the Reverend James Pycroft's *The Cricket Field* of 1851:

> A cricket field is a sphere of wholesome discipline and good order [...] The game of cricket, philosophically considered, is a standing panegyric of the English character: none but an orderly and sensible race of people would so amuse themselves [...] The game is essentially Anglo-Saxon.
> (Quoted in Marqusee, 1994, p. 62)

The game and its ideology would subsequently be exported, of course, as Marqusee shows (p. 93), so that these images of social hierarchy and order might license and conceal not only class power at home but imperial domination abroad. Colonial subjects, too, might aspire to be members of this orderly and sensible race, though as James observes, they might only approach 'that distant ideal – to attain it was, of course, impossible' (1994, p. 30).
73 It is unquestionably true, for example, as Anima Adjepong has argued, that James is inattentive to the role of women in constructing the meanings and practices of West Indian cricket and to women's exclusion for decades from the field of

play,' "Periodically I Pondered over It": Reading the Absence/Presence of Women in *Beyond a Boundary*', in David Featherstone, Christopher Gair, Christian Høgsbjerg, and Andrew Smith (eds), *Marxism, Colonialism, and Cricket: C.L.R. James's 'Beyond a Boundary'*, Durham, NC and London: Duke University Press, 2018, pp. 123–136.
74 Neil Lazarus, *Nationalism and Cultural Practice in the Postcolonial World*, Cambridge: Cambridge University Press, 1999, p. 169, emphasis in original.
75 Ana Miller, 'The Past in the Present: Personal and Collective Trauma in Achmat Dangor's *Bitter Fruit*', *Studies in the Novel*, 40:1/2 (2008), 146–160, 148.
76 Dangor, *Bitter Fruit*, p. 156.
77 Benita Parry, *Postcolonial Studies: A Materialist Critique*, London: Routledge, 2004, p. 183.
78 Dangor, *Bitter Fruit*, p. 156.
79 J.M. Coetzee, *Waiting for the Barbarians*, London: Vintage, 2004 [1980], p. 118.

Bibliography

Adjepong, A., '"Periodically I Pondered over It": Reading the Absence/Presence of Women in *Beyond a Boundary*', in David Featherstone, Christopher Gair, Christian Høgsbjerg and Andrew Smith (eds), *Marxism, Colonialism, and Cricket: C.L.R. James's 'Beyond a Boundary'*, Durham, NC and London: Duke University Press, 2018, pp. 123–136.
Adorno, T., 'Free Time', in Jay Bernstein (ed), *The Culture Industry: Selected Essays on Mass Culture*, London: Routledge, 1991, pp. 162–170.
Appadurai, A., *Modernity at Large: Cultural Dimensions of Globalization*, Minneapolis, MN: University of Minnesota Press, 1996.
Avruch, K. and Vejarano, B., 'Truth and Reconciliation Commissions: A Review Essay and Annotated Bibliography', *OJPCR: The Online Journal of Peace and Conflict Resolution*, 4:2 (2002), 37–76.
Barthes, R., *Mythologies*, trans. Richard Howard and Annette Lavers, New York: Hill and Wang, 2012 [1957].
Bateman, A., *Cricket, Literature and Culture: Symbolising the Nation, Destabilising Empire*, Farnham: Ashgate, 2009.
Coetzee, J.M., *Disgrace*, London: Vintage, 2000.
Coetzee, J.M., *Waiting for the Barbarians*, London: Vintage, 2004 [1980].
Columpar, C., '"Taking Care of Her Green Stone Wall": The Experience of Space in Once Were Warriors', *Quarterly Review of Film and Video* 24:5 (2007), 463–474.
Dangor, A., *Bitter Fruit*, London: Atlantic Books, 2001.
Duff, A., *Once Were Warriors*, New York: Vintage, 1995.
Frinkel, R., 'Performing Race, Reconsidering History: Achmat Dangor's Recent Fiction', *Research in African Literatures* (2008), 39:1, pp. 149–165.
Galeano, E., *Football in Sun and Shadow*, trans. Mark Fried, London: Fourth Estate, 1997.
Gready, P., 'Novel Truths: Literature and Truth Commissions', *Comparative Literature Studies*, 46:1 (2009), 156–176.
Gunesekera, R., *The Match*, London: Bloomsbury, 2006.
James, C.L.R., *Beyond a Boundary*, London: Serpent's Tail, 1984 [1963].

James, C.L.R., *Cricket*, ed. Anna Grimshaw, London: Allison & Busby, 1989.
Jameson, F., *The Political Unconscious: Narrative as a Socially Symbolic Act*, London: Routledge, 1981.
Jolly, R., 'Desiring Good(s) in the Face of Marginalized Subjects: South Africa's Truth and Reconciliation Commission in a Global Context', *South Atlantic Quarterly*, 100:3 (2001), 693–715.
Lazarus, N., *Nationalism and Cultural Practice in the Postcolonial World*, Cambridge: Cambridge University Press, 1999.
Marqusee, M., *Anyone But England: Cricket and the National Malaise*, London: Verso, 1994.
Marqusee, M., *War Minus the Shooting: A Journey Through South Asia During Cricket's World Cup*, London: Mandarin, 1997.
Miller, A., 'The Past in the Present: Personal and Collective Trauma in Achmat Dangor's *Bitter Fruit*', *Studies in the Novel*, 40:1/2 (2008), 146–160.
O'Neill, J., *Netherland*, London: Fourth Estate, 2008.
Parry, B., *Postcolonial Studies: A Materialist Critique*, London: Routledge, 2004.
Pihama, L., 'Repositioning Maori Representation: Contextualising *Once Were Warriors*', in Jonathan Dennis and Jan Bieringa (eds), *Film in Aotearoa New Zealand*, Wellington: Victoria University Press, 1996, pp. 191–193.
Poyner, J., 'Writing Under Pressure: A Post-apartheid Canon?', *Journal of Postcolonial Writing*, 44:2 (2008), 103–114.
Renton. D., *C.L.R. James: Cricket's Philosopher King*, London: Haus Books, 2007.
Sklar, R., 'Social Realism with Style', *Cineaste*, 21:3 (1995), 25–27.
Smith, A., 'C.L.R. James and the Critical Reading of Sport and Literature', *Journal of Postcolonial Writing*, 52:3 (2016), 262–273.
Tadié, A., 'The Fictions of (English) Cricket: From Nations to Diaspora', *International Journal of the History of Sport*, 27:4 (2010), 690–711.
Thompson, E.P., 'Time, Work-Discipline, and Industrial Capitalism', *Past and Present*, 38 (1967), 56–97.
Treagus, M., 'Representing Pacific Tattoos: Issues in Postcolonial Critical Practice', *Journal of Postcolonial Writing*, 44:2 (2008), 183–192.
Williams, R., *Marxism and Literature*, Oxford: Oxford University Press, 1977.
Wisden Cricketers' Almanack 2003, ed. Tim de Lisle, Alton: John Wisden, Lawrence Booth, 2003.

Websites

'The solace of an Australian summer – when cricket brought hope and light', 19 November 2015. Available at: www.theguardian.com/sport/2015/nov/20/the-solace-of-an-australian-summer-when-cricket-brought-hope-and-light.

Films

Once Were Warriors, dir. Lee Tamahori, 1994.

4

MEMORY AND THE PAST

The fourth and final chapter is on memory and the many ways in which postcolonial texts imagine and reimagine the past. What this chapter seeks to do is think through the ways in which openings to different futures are frequently made possible by critical explorations and representations of assorted pasts. Traumatic memories of dispossession as well as invigorating recollections of resistance and struggle are variously accentuated, suppressed, expurgated and disputed in texts. How, we want to ask, do these imaginings and reimaginings of the past inform strategies and prospects of liberation in the present and future? How is the past memorialised, registered, invented, distorted, shaped and then shaped again in and by stories and images – in short, constructed and made use of in the course of ongoing struggles over the legacies and actualities of colonialism? We look in this chapter at Derek Walcott's last poetry collection *White Egrets* in order to pose questions about how the poet and his poems are recalling but also inventing traditions and lineages as part of a perennially conflicted attitude to empire's legacies and an ambiguous understanding of time. Eavan Boland's poetry imaginatively reconstructs a past for Irish women characterised by hardship and fortitude that inspires empowering perspectives on liberation in the present. David Lean's *Lawrence of Arabia*, Richard Attenborough's *Gandhi*, Rolf de Heer and Peter Djigirr's *Ten Canoes*, Nikita Lalwani's *Gifted* and Assia Djebar's *Fantasia* are all, we hope to show, compulsively preoccupied with various pasts to the precise extent that they are involved in fashioning and contesting various kinds of future. They reach into the past only to discover exhilarating but sometimes also disquieting possibilities.

The first thing we need to do is register postcolonial theory's very reasonable and long-standing concern that the representation of somebody else's past is an act of appropriation. Indeed, Neil Lazarus has gone so far as to accuse the field of a 'blanket repudiation of representation itself' as an ethically and politically dubious endeavour.[1] Lazarus, we think rightly, is very sceptical about this tendency in postcolonial studies; while he acknowledges that aesthetic representation is always an ethically fraught endeavour, he also believes that aesthetic representation is also an indispensable source of knowledge (of others and of oneself). There are, of course, considerable difficulties and dangers to any act of political or aesthetic representation. To speak for the other risks speaking *over* the other, silencing her or him and thus compounding the original injustices inflicted by colonial powers who also represented the other in the stronger sense of controlling her or his destiny through violence. For Gayatri Spivak, of course, in an important categorical statement, *the subaltern cannot speak*. There is no form or language available in colonial or even nationalist historiography, in official or canonical culture, in the corporate media or indeed anywhere except in their own voices and formats for individuals and groups excluded from hegemonic power (especially 'the subaltern as female' who for Spivak 'is even more deeply in shadow'[2]) to make known their distinctive experiences and aspirations.

There is by now a sizeable sub-genre of critical responses to Spivak's alternately celebrated and notorious statement. Critics have asked facetiously whether the subaltern can vote, the implication being that the voices and the agency of subaltern groups are constantly being exerted and registered.[3] Benita Parry thinks the reputed silence of the subaltern in Spivak's account uncomfortably resembles the mysterious taciturnity conventionally attributed to the colonised 'other' by imperialist ideologies. The attribution of silence to the subaltern, Parry contends, accidentally effaces the centuries of subaltern resistance to, for example, British rule in India:

> Thus while protesting at the obliteration of the native's subject position in the text of imperialism, Spivak in her project gives no speaking part to the colonized, effectively writing out the evidence of native agency recorded in India's two-hundred-year struggle against British conquest and the Raj.[4]

By focusing on symbolic or epistemic violence, Spivak, despite her professed and decidedly idiosyncratic Marxism, encouraged the widespread inability in postcolonial studies to conceptualise imperialist systems that were primarily economic and also political. Moreover, does the seeming absence for Spivak of a lingua franca of shared assumptions and objectives paint a decidedly unappealing vision of cultural separateness and even incommensurability? Is Spivak's own dauntingly abstruse prose style a reflection or even a performance of the difficulty and maybe the impossibility of establishing connections between speakers and audiences?[5] Spivak herself has misgivings about what she calls this 'inadvisable remark'.[6] We don't propose to adjudicate in these important theoretical controversies. But we do want to observe that their range and longevity is testament to the rawness of the nerve that Spivak's original essay touched. For postcolonial texts do incessantly return to the perils and pitfalls of representing the other's past. They also take risks and insist on representing certain voices that need to be heard even when they are well aware of the charges of inauthenticity that might come their way. They ask again and again whether, even in accentuating heroic stories of resistance or bearing witness to atrocities and injustices, stories about the past are inadvertently compounding those injustices by speaking not only about but also *for* and therefore *over* the dispossessed and, in the process, once more silencing them. Our wider point in this chapter is that postcolonial texts about the past are acutely conscious of this complexity and regularly negotiate it – that is, the ethically and politically fraught question of representation itself – in extremely distinctive and often ambivalent ways.

Representation is as difficult as it is necessary. Political institutions or texts cannot literally represent the other, in the sense of exactly reproducing her or his desires, interests, experiences and so on. But that does not mean representation is impossible or objectionable. To go down this route in postcolonial studies would be to reproduce silences where we have only just begun to learn to listen. This is certainly true of aesthetic representation. The colonised subject makes known her experiences in her own words but only in order to reach potentially sympathetic audiences whose preconceptions may be altered and swayed. Surely the point of aesthetic representation is to provide illuminating and compelling representations of unfamiliar situations as well as mind-shifting representations of apparently familiar ones? It's true that René Magritte's pipe is not actually a pipe; it is a series of marks made by oil paint on a canvas of stretched linen. The desire for exact representation and the exaggerated despair of critics who have only just realised that exact representation is impossible are perhaps both satirised in Jorge Luis Borges's very brief story 'Del rigor en la ciencia'. Borges's typically phlegmatic narrator recalls a time when 'the Art of Cartography' 'attained such perfection' that 'the Cartographers' Guilds struck a three-dimensional Map of the Empire whose size was that of the Empire, and which coincided point for point with it'.[7] This is a satire on the belief that a representation could be anything other than a second-order and inadequate, or at best approximate, rendering of the original. Unless they pursue the doomed and pointless effort of representing an object in the world exactly, like Borges's rigorous and scientific cartographers, then representations are always mediated and imprecise portrayals, which is the most obvious and therefore the least interesting thing one can say about them.

We therefore want to stress the diverse forms of amusement, instruction and provocation that postcolonial literary representations are capable of not despite but because of this indirect, approximate and mediated quality. The meticulous empire-sized map imagined by Borges, subsequent generations realise, is 'useless' and limits the potential of imaginative writing to pursue the unexpected. So what other uses might representations have? As readers and critics, we need to navigate a course between, on the one hand, the belief that representation is a straightforward endeavour because 'the facts' are transparent and, on the other, the extreme suspicion of representation as such. This is what our texts do. Representations of the past, then, are an admittedly imperfect but ultimately indispensable means of communicating this past to different audiences. They explore, paradoxically but also instructively, the necessity and the impossibility of representation, and they also produce roadmaps for how to navigate the complexity of any historical representation. What might look initially like appropriations are more like feats of imaginative solidarity, as is the case, we will argue, with Pablo Neruda's and Eavan Boland's poems.

Assia Djebar's novel *Fantasia: An Algerian Cavalcade* (*L'amour, la fantasia*) (1985) will hopefully provide an initial insight into the difficulty and the necessity of representing the past. *Fantasia* is paradigmatically Spivakian (to coin a term) in its overt and continually underlined scepticism about the capacity of the historical novel form to reach beyond geographical and historical distance to speak authoritatively about Algerian history, though paradoxically Lazarus also adduces it as an example of a literary text that performs acts of imaginative solidarity with imperialism's victims. The book charts the period between the 1830 invasion by France, 'the cavalcade of screams and carnage which will fill the ensuing decades', and the war of liberation between 1954 and 1962.[8] Not so much weaving together as loosely combining episodes from the history of Algeria's conquest with accounts by Algerian women of their service in the war of liberation and scenes from the youth of the 'half-emancipated' (*F*, 58) narrator and protagonist (Djebar herself), the novel also harps on about its own profound misgivings about the putative universality of its author's elite French education and her cosmopolitan feminist politics. Different women, the novel's tripartite structure suggests, fight in different ways for liberation, which can mean radically different things at the different individual, political and national levels. So, in a sense it is the incommensurability of these lives and the impossibility of the author speaking adequately and authoritatively about them that are the novel's main themes.

But is this a novel at all? It doesn't look like one; the English edition includes a glossary and a detailed chronology of Algerian history. The initial accounts of the conquest of Algiers, which focus on courageous resistance and murderous violence (such as the notorious 'enfumades' of the Dahra caves), are based on official colonial archives and eye-witness accounts from letters and journals by French soldiers, publicists and anonymous hangers on. The Algerian peasant women's testimonies of the independence war are apparently unedited, though of course they have been transcribed into French. *Fantasia* indubitably *is* a novel, however, since it encourages not so much acquiescence in the unimpeachable truth of its various historical revelations but something more like uncertainty or at least a kind of productive indecision about various tensions. Is there a relationship of dependency or friction between personal and national liberation? Which is more truthful, deliberated writing or immediate speech, reflective transcription or first-hand reportage, recollection or experience, history or autobiography? And if, alarmingly, 'every language is a dark depository for piled-up corpses' (F, 181), a mediation and obfuscation of more physical and often violent forms of communication, then is 'the former enemy's language' (F, 215) of French any more or less accurate a medium for writing about an especially violent history than 'the Berber of the Dahra mountains or the Arabic of the town where I was born' (F, 204)? Which gets her closer to the dramas and sufferings of the past, Djebar's French education or her Arab-Berber origins, the rigour and critical distance enabled by exile or the vigour and sympathy of partisanship? How does one connect the political urgencies of the present to the obscurity of the historical past? These are questions that the text refrains from answering, which is Roland Barthes's very definition of the literary.

The novel presents a number of different conclusions about the ways in which Algeria's past might be re-imagined in the present. A fantasia is a feat of daring horsemanship, described more than once in the novel, a celebratory display of virtuosity and triumph. It is also a contrapuntal musical form. (The third part of the novel, 'Voices from the Past', which relates the testimonies of women who took part in the liberation war, is itself divided into a 'symphony' with five movements and a coda). A hybrid and avowedly polyphonic form, *Fantasia* does not reconcile its discrepant views on the meanings of liberation and on the alternately heroic and tortured past of Algerian women. The novel is at once a merely aesthetic (albeit virtuosic), self-absorbed and un-historical performance *and* a rifle-toting declaration of triumph and liberation. It avoids a dispassionate and objective register, being openly partisan and overtly impassioned, for example, in the description of the traces of extreme suffering communicated even by the psychopathically detached reports of asphyxiated men, women and children compiled by murderous French officers:

> Pélissier, speaking on behalf of this long drawn-out agony, on behalf of fifteen hundred corpses buried beneath El-Kantara, with their flocks unceasingly bleating at death, hands me this report and I accept this palimpsest on which I now inscribe the charred passion of my ancestors.
>
> (F, 79)

Fantasia is also an inconclusive dialogue between discrepant voices by and about the past, in particular between a melancholy conviction that the passion or martyrdom of the author's ancestors happened long ago and can now only be glimpsed in sketchy and highly mediated forms and a passionately eloquent determination to record that suffering and broadcast it.

Take this equally powerful account of the aftermath of the conquest of Algiers:

Thirty-seven witnesses, possibly more, will relate the events of this month of July 1830, some fresh from their experiences, some shortly afterwards. Thirty-seven descriptions will be published, of which only three are from the viewpoint of the besieged [...] The senior officers in particular are infected by a veritable scribblomania [...] But what is the significance behind the urge of so many fighting men to relive in print this month of July 1830? Did their writings allow them to savour the seducer's triumph, the rapist's intoxication? [...] And words themselves become a decoration, flaunted by officers like the carnations they wear in their buttonholes; words will become their most effective weapons. Hordes of interpreters, geographers, ethnographers, linguists, botanists, diverse scholars and professional scribblers will swoop down on this prey. The supererogatory protuberances of their publications will form a pyramid to hide the initial violence from view.

(F, 45)

What can be heard in the idiosyncratic French of the original and in the excellent English translation that filters these incidents and experiences through yet another layer of mediation is a language warped out of true, its musicality clotted and interrupted by neologisms and prolix constructions and by formulations such as 'supererogatory protuberances' (*apophyse superfétatoire*) that are as fastidiously precise as they are jarringly unmelodic. This is violence, figured as and including sexual violence, that is seen from the victors' predatory perspective and is, therefore, obfuscated rather than elucidated by words. Captain Bosquet's letters to his mother will 'casually' mention the '"detail"' of a hacked-off foot. Such violence is hardly displayed, let alone understood, but it is registered in the snags, catches and tears that periodically afflict Djebar's otherwise lucid French. These marks at least try to amplify 'the obscenity of the torn flesh that [Bosquet] could not suppress in his description' (F, 56). The corpses of seven women 'become, in spite of the author, scrofulous excrescences on his elegant prose style' (F, 55) but they are purposeful and expressive blots on Djebar's. This is one way of refuting Spivak's contention that the subaltern is silenced by the colonial archive; here the subaltern *cannot not speak*, since the camp-following scribblers and 'chroniclers are haunted by the distant sound of half-human cries, cacophony of keening, ear-splitting hieroglyphs of a wild, collective voice' (F, 56). That is an ingeniously suggestive statement daringly composed in the very register of colonial history (with its horror at the 'half-human' and uncivilised or 'wild' subaltern) at the same time as it locates 'between the lines', in the 'obsessional unease' and 'agitation of the killers' (F, 57), echoes of the protesting, but still to us indeterminate, anger of fighting women who are not in the least bit silent and, to the attentive listener, can be heard raging and hollering in the colonial archive.

So Lazarus's own reading of *Fantasia* in the course of his critical discussion of postcolonial theory's hostility to representation can be supplemented. Lazarus is surely correct that the novel's effort to exhume and amplify the resistant voices of Algerian history nevertheless insists on the wide gap 'between "interpretation" or "adequation", on the one hand, and "how things really were", on the other'.[9] Djebar is not writing history but a novel. Yet *Fantasia* also insists, paradoxically or rather complementarily, on the urgent if impossible task of investigating 'how things really were'. Throwing in the towel by resolving *not* to represent is just as ethically and politically enfeebling, in other words, as the appropriative determination *to* represent. The truth of Algerian women's experiences can be *both* brought to light by the novelist in a tableau of intensely vivid illustrations and testimonies *and*, paradoxically, remain forever hidden by the passage of time and by the feminist novelist's historically, culturally and linguistically distanced and thus extremely dissimilar standpoint, one that may point at but not finally overcome misrepresentation and amnesia. How could one possibly understand the horror and the literally unspeakable agony of mass asphyxiation in an underground cave or even the militant hopefulness and subsequent travails of the women who took up arms as *porteuses de feu* in the Algerian Revolution? Djebar does not profess to speak for these women or encourage readers to place themselves in their shoes. Nonetheless their voices reach us across historical distances, albeit in highly mediated and partial forms, speaking of suffering, struggle and desire. *Fantasia* is impressively convinced that a novel might justifiably and productively take upon itself the task of amplifying those voices. What those voices enjoin, whether it is mourning for suffering and death, knowledge about the vital confrontations of the past or the implications and lessons of these struggles for the prospects of liberation in the present, are questions for readers to pursue.

The writing of history may be 'a form of remembrance', as the great German Marxist critic Walter Benjamin described it under the shadow of fascism, but his correspondent Max Horkheimer's retort is also true: '"Past injustice has occurred and is completed. The slain are really slain."'[10] *Fantasia* is a novel that looks and mostly reads like testimony and that wants, in fact, to bear witness to violence and the legacy and possibility of resistance. But it also forewarns and forearms its readers against any temptation to think that the meanings of the past in the present, particularly *Fantasia*'s present of stalled decolonisation and rising religious militancy in the 1980s, are straightforwardly available and can be made into something specific and self-evident, even for the politically committed intellectual determined to resist posterity's condescension by transcribing and translating 'voices from the past'. To the contrary, those meanings must be sought out by scrupulous and self-conscious enquiry and then, since they are indeterminate and ambiguous, made available in a contrapuntal form for readers' consideration and contestation. The past that emerges in *Fantasia* is both transmitted *and* lost, palpable *and* obscure; it is a history of violence *and* courage, defeat *and* triumph; and these narratives of liberation, moreover, are personal *and* collective. The past is never dead and it's not even past, as William Faulkner famously put it. That's because, as Benjamin recognised, contests over the past are also contests in the present over the possibility of the future and, in particular in this case, over the shape and objectives of contemporary projects for liberation.

The problem, as Benita Parry sees it, of Spivak's endlessly deconstructive critical practice is that its fixation with dismantling Eurocentric representations of the non-European world leaves it oblivious to the frequent paradoxes and nuances in those same Eurocentric representations as well as curiously inattentive to non-European voices.[11] There's nothing wrong with dismantlement, in other words, but its larger purpose ought to be to erect something better in place of the imperialist structures and knowledges that critical practice has discredited. Spivak, by the way, appreciates this point. The 'inadvisable' and now disowned remark that the subaltern cannot speak was occasioned by her being 'unnerved' at the failure of a late Bengali woman, Bhuvaneswari Baduri, to communicate her experiences even to her own family. Bhuvaneswari rewrote the practice of 'sati-suicide' 'in an interventionist way', Spivak argues, by killing herself after failing to carry out a political assassination for an Indian nationalist group. The practice of 'sati-suicide', of course, was, as Spivak shows, invoked as an example of barbarous tradition by the British colonial authorities in India. By suppressing it, they might paint themselves as benevolent protectors and emissaries of a more humane civilisation: 'white men are saving brown women from brown men', in Spivak's memorable phrase. Spivak's claim is that by killing herself Bhuvaneswari radically rewrote or reclaimed this practice in order to express not her obedience to tradition or to authority but something much more rebellious. Being careful to wait until she was menstruating, lest her family mistakenly believe that the suicide was the result of an illicit love affair, she nonetheless failed to get her message across because her family recalled the incident in precisely these terms. Spivak is able to put the record straight because 'I know of Bhuvaneswari's life and death through family connections', she informs us disarmingly at the start of her influential article's penultimate paragraph. So, while Bhuvaneswari cannot speak to or through her own family, she can, it seems, speak to and through Gayatri Spivak. Spivak poses here, inadvertently presumably, as an insider who is in the know, a conduit or medium for the dead girl who has tragically extinguished her own voice but who miraculously speaks through the postcolonial theorist. Spivak then has the temerity to tell us that the subaltern cannot speak at all! To show how the subaltern cannot speak even to her own family, Spivak speaks for her.

It's possible to draw two conclusions from this interesting little slip. The first is that the subaltern never speaks, not even to Gayatri Spivak, who has accidentally forgotten her own lesson, so the unfortunate Bhuvaneswari is doomed to eternal silence. The second and more auspicious and enabling conclusion is that Spivak has unintentionally disproved her own worst fears; the subaltern does speak, but incompletely and only if we listen very carefully, seek out her words and possess the humility required not to believe she speaks through us and that we are her mouthpiece. In this case, she speaks insofar as we know with some certainty that Bhuvaneswari did not kill herself because she had a secret lover; but her voice remains intriguingly silent or at least ambiguous because, frustratingly but perhaps inevitably, we can't say definitively why the uncommitted political assassination prompted her to take her own life. Communication, in short, is difficult and incomplete but not impossible, which is precisely why the initial remark was so inadvisable. It is also why imaginative literary representations are called for.

Our point is Parry's: that Spivak's kind of deconstructive practice ties us up in knots and leads us up dead ends unless it is supplemented, as Spivak now says unequivocally that it should be, by a stress not on the inevitable failure of communication but on the difficulties as well as the immense possibilities of communication.

> Deconstruction cannot found a political program of any kind [...] Deconstruction teaches us to look at these limits and questions. It is a corrective and a critical movement [...] Politically, all this does is not allow for fundamentalisms and totalitarianisms of various kinds, however seemingly benevolent. *But it cannot be foundational.* If one wanted to *found* a political project on deconstruction, it would be something like wishy-washy pluralism on the one hand, or a kind of irresponsible hedonism on the other.[12]

Representation and communication are impossible and necessary, we are suggesting, or rather they are impossible and *therefore* they are necessary; the second claim follows from the first. Only by acknowledging how obscure and opaque the other's experience can be, how heaped over the past is by misrepresentation and forgetfulness and how easy it is to fall into received ideological ways of interpreting the lives of others and their histories, is it possible, ultimately, to represent and communicate. In so doing, critics and readers thereby contribute to the foundation, to use Spivak's word, of an ethical and political programme for overcoming imperialism.

Postcolonial texts' attitude to this vexed question of how to represent violence suffered by others in the past runs a broad gamut. At one end is the South African novelist J.M. Coetzee's narrators' and protagonists' anguished self-consciousness about their inability to ventriloquise the dispossessed. In *Foe*, his intricate retelling/adaptation of Defoe's *Robinson Crusoe*, Coetzee's Susan Barton is determined to teach Friday, whose tongue has been severed, to read and write and thus relate his experience of violence and servitude.

She ends up convinced by the cryptic symbols he draws that she is ethically and perhaps literally incapable of grasping Friday's tale. The novel is of course fully conscious of and determined to think through this predicament.

> The story of Friday's tongue is a story unable to be told, or unable to be told by me. That is to say, many stories can be told of Friday's tongue, but the true story is buried within Friday, who is mute. The true story will not be heard till by art we have found a means of giving voice to Friday.[13]

This is a typically rich and enigmatic formulation. It holds out the possibility that Friday's true story might be told, just not by the relatively privileged English narrator whose language, experiences and world view are too dissimilar to those of her mutilated factotum, whose 'foe' she must therefore inevitably remain. But this impossibility will not stop other stories being told about Friday, not least because Susan is determined to enlist Daniel Defoe's help to find the right words to tell her tale of shipwreck and rescue. Art will give 'a' voice to Friday but will find it much harder to articulate *the* voice of Friday, a task that is as ethically and aesthetically imperative as it is, finally, unfeasible since he has been silenced by the brutality of colonial power.

As always in Coetzee's work, we need to give due weight to what Derek Attridge has identified as each new novel's seeming determination to surprise as well as provoke and even nettle his readers, whether it is with *Foe*-like metafictional games or the distanced introspection of his memoirs, with the flagrantly problematic and unlikeable and even reactionary narrative viewpoints of *Disgrace* or *Slow Man*, by stretching the boundaries of the novel form itself in the inflammatory philosophical essays of *Elizabeth Costello* and *Diary of a Bad Year* or by unsettling our own established images of Coetzee's work's apparent commitment to an ascetic utopia of social equality and animal rights in *The Childhood of Jesus*, where the dreamlike world of manual work, dignified hospitableness, communal recreation and flavourless tomato pasta is less appealingly utopian than plain boring. Coetzee likes to surprise, disoblige and provoke his readers, something which is also true of *Foe*'s apparently textbook postmodern commitment to the belief that Friday's 'is a story unable to be told', except by Friday.

Foe does not necessarily renounce all representation of the other as authoritarian, which is how Spivak herself reads it.[14] The first two sentences in the above quotation are pretty unequivocal. The novelist and his protagonists can tell stories about Friday but they cannot tell Friday's 'true' story. The third sentence sounds a similar note of scepticism about the authoritarian desire to 'give' Friday a voice. But it also holds out the prospect that 'art' might allow Friday's true story to be 'heard', which implies spoken dialogue rather than written testimony. And who is the collective 'we' that will give Friday a voice? Might it include Friday himself as well as listeners from other cultures and audiences? Could 'art' name some language or form of Friday's own devising or at least a language and form that he has been taught but, Caliban-like, that he has managed to adapt and in which he might narrate his experiences, curse his oppressors and even shame and sway his former masters? In what complex philosophical sense is the 'truth' of Friday's story being defined here? We wonder if this knotty formulation of Coetzee's actually acknowledges the possibility that representation of Friday's emblematic story of violent dispossession, silencing and forced labour *is* possible after all? The whole of Coetzee's oeuvre, after all, is an effort to extend the scope of what his protagonist in *Elizabeth Costello* calls the 'sympathetic imagination'.[15]

Another exemplary response to what we are characterising as the political and aesthetic question of representation is the end of the impassioned second canto of Pablo Neruda's epic account of Latin American history, the *Canto General* of 1950. This is another text mentioned by Lazarus in the course of his discussion of what he sees as postcolonial theory's aversion to representation. We want to provide a slightly more substantial reading of it, in order to show how Neruda endeavours to provoke a kind of imaginative solidarity with imperialism's victims. The Chilean communist implores those done to death by colonial violence in the Americas to speak loudly and combatively through his voice.

> Rise up to be born with me, my brother.
> Give me your hand from the deep
> zone of your disseminated sorrow.
> You'll not return from the bottom of the rocks.
> You'll not return from subterranean time.
> Your stiff voice will not return.
> Your drilled eyes will not return.
> Behold me from the depths of the earth,
> laborer, weaver, silent herdsman:
> tamer of the tutelary guanacos:
> mason of the defied scaffold:
> bearer of the Andean tears:
> jeweller with your fingers crushed:
> tiller trembling in the seed:
> potter spilt in your clay:
> bring to the cup of this new life, brothers,
> all your timeless buried sorrows ...
>
> I've come to speak through your dead mouths.
> Throughout the earth join all
> the silent scattered lips
> and from the depths speak to me all night long ...[16]

The classic formulation of this idea is by the Czech novelist Milan Kundera: 'The struggle of man against power is the struggle of memory against forgetting'.[17] Yet few literary texts, least of all Kundera's metafictional ruminations or even Neruda's unflinchingly militant declarations of partisanship with the dead, could be unconscious of how difficult it is to wage that struggle and how vulnerable to failure. For example, the force of Neruda's militant confidence that he can ventriloquise the sorrows and dreams of the dead ('Speak through my words and my blood') is in inverse proportion to his equally firm conviction that their words and presence have been irretrievably lost ('You'll not return from subterranean time'). 'Speak through my words and my blood' and 'I've come to speak through your dead mouths' are more like desperate invocations, incantations aimed unsuccessfully at summoning the dead or declarations of intent that are predestined to fail since 'Your stiff voice will not return'. The rhetoric of comradeship with the dead is itself limiting, since it is in fact a rhetoric of fraternity ('Rise up to be born with me, my brother') and is in any case tied to an explicitly (albeit affectingly) Christian idiom of resurrection and redemption. We would add, however, that the intensity and the sheer affective power of the poet's solidarity with the dead is actually intensified by his tacit and at times overt acknowledgement that, to quote Horkheimer once more, the slain are really slain and cannot be brought back to life. These repetitious lamentations are symptoms of grief. Poetry, for the *Canto General*, is an admittedly arduous and contrived but also daring and powerful effort to 'join all/ the silent scattered lips' in cries of protest and hope. That, ultimately, is what the tradition of the oppressed (to invoke one more time Benjamin's important reflections on history) or 'subterranean time' (to use Neruda's) entails: not a hopeless attempt to correct historical violence or an authoritarian desire to speak for its victims but a desire to speak with them, to be spoken *to* and try to 'disseminate' their sorrows. In so doing, poetry turns our consciousness of past injustice into a kind of politicised grief, one that is acutely aware that these injustices have not ceased. The perpetrator, Neruda's mutilated interlocutors clearly indicate, is a system of forced and exploited labour. The silence of history's victims only intensifies our helpless solidarity with them and redoubles our desire to best the exploitative system that murdered them.

The Irish poet Eavan Boland seeks to achieve something similar, albeit in more compact forms and in a much more muted register, in her explorations of the historically neglected and marginalised lives of Irish women. 'That the Science of Cartography is Limited' begins the sequence 'Writing in a Time of Violence' from her 1994 collection *In a Time of Violence*. The title, theme and organisation of this sequence obviously recalls W.B. Yeats's 'Meditations in Time of Civil War' from his important 1928 collection *The Tower*. Interestingly, Boland is honouring a national (as well as a nationalist) poetic tradition that her poetry and critical writings otherwise accuse of occluding the voices of Irish women by elevating them to mute symbols of purity and beauty. Boland, however, strives less to bury that tradition than to praise it, or at least to integrate her work into it, by boldly and almost hubristically (or perhaps acquiescently) likening herself and her undertaking to the celebrated achievement of this massively influential yet minatory figure that looms over all subsequent Irish verse. Yeats's 'Meditations' famously strives to find 'befitting emblems of adversity' to make sense of the fratricidal violence of the Civil War, just as poems about force, sacrifice and revenge like 'The Grauballe Man', 'Punishment' and 'Strange Fruit' in the Northern Irish poet Seamus Heaney's equally celebrated 1975 collection *North* located not 'satisfactory verbal icons' but conflicted 'images and symbols adequate to our predicament'[18] of colonial occupation and sectarian warfare. Boland's work does something comparable, which is one reason why we think Boland is so anxious to signal her conflicted inheritance of a tradition of which she is otherwise so sceptical. It is the generative tensions and frictions in these poems about the past that we wish to explore.

In 'That the Science of Cartography is Limited', the obscure and hitherto unnoticed image of the unfinished famine road that the poet and her lover find in a wood on the borders of Connacht is every bit as ambiguous as Yeats's and Heaney's multiply meaningful emblems of conflict.

Look down you said: this was once a famine road.[19]

Assuming that Boland's partner is male, he proceeds (to speak anachronistically) to 'mansplain' how in

1847, when the crop had failed twice,
Relief Committees gave
the starving Irish such roads to build.

Where they died, the road ended
and ends still and when I take down
the map of this island, it is never so
I can say here is
the masterful, the apt rendering of
the spherical as flat, nor
an ingenious design which persuades a curve
into a plane, but to tell myself again that

the line which says woodland and cries hunger
and gives out among sweet pine and cypress,
and finds no horizon

will not be there.

The poem briefly adopts the apparently masterly and fussily pedagogical tone of the poet's anonymous partner, giving the exact date and other details of the 'ordeal' of the starving souls whose deaths were, of course, the most grievous instance of English colonial misrule. But this is a mode that the poem quickly rejects. 'That the Science of Cartography is Limited', its slightly awkward and wordy title, sounds like a fragment of a sentence, the beginning of which may have read either 'It is the case...' or 'It is not true...'; the poem frames it, however, as an unambiguous proposition. Time or the past cannot be represented in the spatial form of a map or a text, the poem sets out to 'prove'. This is a category error in fact, just as the first stanza states that 'this shading of/ forest cannot show the fragrance of balsam': a drawing cannot represent a fragrance. Ireland's tortured past, the poem tells us, cannot be minutely and comprehensively mapped, just as the three-dimensional sphere cannot be made flat in the way that, say, the Flemish cartographer Gerardus Mercator's sixteenth-century map notoriously misrepresents the globe by persuading a curve into a plane and thus exaggerating the size of Europe and North America.

Yet the science of cartography is limited 'not simply' by the technical impossibility of rendering time as space. The poem sets itself the science-like task, paradoxically, of 'proving' that particular science's limitations. It does so by highlighting the additional ethical reason for cartography's finite scope. The 'we' that drove to the borders of Connacht becomes the insistent 'I' of the second half of the poem; 'I' responds to her lover's peremptory instruction to 'look down' by deciding assertively to 'take down/ the map of this island' 'to tell myself again that' it does not include the road in the woodland. To take down the map is also, of course, in some sense to reject this archetypal image of the nation or do away with it, not least because the official mapping of Ireland – like the original Ordnance Survey of the 1830s and 1840s, dramatised in Brian Friel's 1981 play *Translations* – constituted an inaccurate and extremely slanted representation and Anglicisation of Irish space. Though the map does not, the poem includes 'the line which says woodland and cries hunger', 'the line' referring here, presumably, both to the road and to the line of verse which articulates, indeed 'cries' out, the road's meaning and significance. And what the line means or says here is 'hunger' and death or, more specifically, the deaths caused by the callousness and negligence of the colonial authorities.

It is left to poetry (which is of course an art not a putative science) to draw attention to the famine road, which definitely does not mean to 'masterfully' and exhaustively document the sufferings it entailed, about which the poem says precisely nothing. The poet is drawing her readers' attention to the road, of course, but she is most insistent on telling 'myself again' of its existence and its absence from official representations. This first poem in the sequence, thus, feels more like a kind of personal manifesto or programme;

its movement from 'we' to 'I' constitutes a reminder to the poet to distrust and avoid the official accounts and representations of Irish history and open up her work, instead, to the numerous unofficial and neglected aspects and narratives. There is a kind of mourning here of course, evident in the wistful and subdued tone and the scrupulous avoidance of a pastoral mode. This distinctly unpoetic poem with its rambling enjambment, uneven stanzas and lines that stop as suddenly and prematurely as the famine road itself, refuses to make beauty out of suffering.

Nobody has explained as well as the German philosopher Jürgen Habermas how, in Walter Benjamin's work, this melancholic fixation with the 'tradition of the oppressed', with memories and stories of defiance and dispossession, aims to energise political struggles in the present.

> What Benjamin has in mind is the supremely profane insight that ethical universalism also has to take seriously the injustice that has already happened and that is seemingly irreversible; that there exists a solidarity of those born later with those who have proceeded them, with all those whose bodily or personal integrity has been violated at the hands of other human beings; and that this solidarity can only be engendered and made effective by remembering.[20]

Mourning or grief is a political state therefore, one that finds lessons about the urgent need for the lives and voices of the perennially disempowered to be amplified in the present in a defiantly inconsolable preoccupation with the past.[21] The science of cartography is, ultimately, 'limited', which means that it is not everything but it is not nothing either. The mapping of the country and its past must be supplemented by something else, the identification and (in other poems) the imaginative evocation or even occupation of other voices and lives, particularly women's lives, that have been left out or pushed to the margins. Writing and reading poems about the nation's past are acts of solidarity as well as spurs to solidarity in the present.

Yet, if we look at Boland's 'Mise Eire', from an earlier collection, it becomes possible to appreciate how difficult it can be to identify these marginalised voices without speaking for them in ways that feel like an act of appropriation. We don't wish to offer any sort of glib or ungenerous critique of this poem in which a prostitute and an emigrant are made to declare 'Mise Eire' or 'I am Ireland', though it is true that Boland's attempts to make certain kinds of Irish women into representative emblems of Irish history à la Yeats (though this time emblems not of beauty or purity but of fortitude and resilience) strike us as more like examples than critiques of Irish poetry's Romantic idealisation of female figures. Boland speaks for these women who in turn speak for the nation, but too often this method feels like putting words into their mouths. What about the gaps of time and knowledge between Boland and these women and between these women and a nationalist project that has usually neglected or exploited them? Is it imprudent, or at least unconvincing, to appoint oneself a spokeswoman for dispossessed Irish women when your qualification for writing about exile is not the coffin ships that took emigrants from famine-stricken Ireland to the United States but an unwelcoming London boarding school during your father's tenure as the Irish Ambassador? However, such poems frequently want to do something quite different as well (intentionally or not, it scarcely matters), which is to document the sheer range and diversity of historical Irish women's experiences and the difficulty of knowing anything at all about them, let alone putting words in their mouths and making them personify the nation. We want to focus on a kind of productive tension within many of Boland's poems, between the familiar desire to use women as personifications of some sort of national and even nationalist ideal (women, like Ireland, representing endurance and resistance in the face of oppression) and a more inconclusive aspect concerned more modestly with accentuating the diverse experiences and meanings of historical Irish women. This is also a tension between the desire to speak imaginatively *about* historical Irish women, and in so doing to embrace their diversity and difference and acknowledge one's own inevitable historical distance from them, and a desire to speak *for* them by appropriating them for a cause.

This is also a tension between Boland's own critical writings and her poetry. In her commentaries on her own work, she objects strongly to 'the power of nationhood to edit the reality of womanhood'. Women have been elevated in the Irish poetic tradition, she argues, somewhat unspecifically, to the status of personifications of a national ideal, in the way that the Shan Van Vocht or Poor Old Woman of Yeats's allegorical *Cathleen ni Houlihan* is transformed, like the nation, into beautiful youth by the heroic military sacrifice of young Michael Gillane.[22] Women are the passive objects of that tradition, not its subjects, Boland argues in one of numerous critical explanations of her own verse. Their 'complex feelings and aspirations' are radically 'simplified' when they become merely decorative and emblematic, 'the passive projection of a national idea'.[23] Yet Boland still wants these women to be emblematic and speak for the nation: 'Mise Eire' means 'I am Ireland'. The 'dread, makeshift example' of the emigrant Irish, in the poem of that title, famously read by Boland's friend Mary Robinson at her inauguration as the Republic's president in 1990, is

> Patience. Fortitude. Long suffering

These are 'old songs', as the poem's final line admits, with just the right amount of ingratiating cliché for a ceremonial occasion; praising Irish women for their strength is surely fair enough, but there is a distinctly retro feel to patting them on the head for their patience and capacity to suffer. Boland is still wedded, in other words, to the dubious idea that the 'truths of womanhood' might denote 'the defeats of a nation', though in 'The Emigrant Irish' these defeats of exile and hardship sound oddly like triumphs or at least like somehow necessary preconditions of 'our power'.[24] Our task below is to show in detail how Boland's poetry frequently works against this reduction of historical women to the status of a national and nationalist emblem. Real Irish women are more intractable and opaque than that. Boland's poems are most suggestive, we contend, when, like 'That the Science of Cartography is Limited', they underscore the difficulty of making the nation's past mean only one thing and when they outline the past's sheer irretrievable difference from the present.

Boland's perennial subject is those women whose lives have not been thought fit for documentation, who as a consequence have fallen, in the words of her 1990 collection, 'outside history', that is, outside historical and literary writing's portrayals of Ireland's past. Her work is torn between a desire to find in suffering and enduring women a new metaphor for Ireland's national condition, which is ostensibly what happens in 'Mise Eire', and a scepticism about this kind of metaphorising that prompts her, instead, to imagine the diverse sufferings, desires and deeds of women who have usually been deemed unworthy of aesthetic representation. Take 'Anorexic' from 1980s *In Her Own Image*, which is a meditation on how the female body, or rather a particular female body, might best escape the various meanings and uses to which national, patriarchal and religious imaginings have subjected it. The implicit aim is to reclaim the female body from a tradition that has appropriated it as a voiceless icon, a vehicle for national imaginings of beauty, purity and rejuvenated youth. The poem begins in a very declamatory Sylvia Plath-like tone:

> Flesh is heretic.
> My body is a witch.
> I am burning it.

This first stanza separates off the speaker's scourged and reduced body from her mind and voice. These curt lines and compact three-line stanzas are similarly reduced. The diremption of mind and body into 'I' and 'it' and by the fifth stanza into 'I' and 'her' is not so easily achieved however, since the reduction of the body brings about a comparable reduction of the mind to the monomania of self-denial and of the voice to a one-note stridency of self-loathing. This paring back of language's descriptive power can be heard in the austere simplicity of these statements and their clipped not quite rhymes. Even here though, the ostensibly radical campaign to take charge of the body by reducing and escaping it is unsuccessful. For the body continues to accrete familiar and reactionary meanings. Better, it fails to shake them off. The body is overtly and conservatively defined by metaphor as a rebellious 'heretic' or 'witch' to be disciplined, which is hardly a feminist reclamation of women's bodies from their appropriation as battlegrounds and possessions by the Church. '[T]orching' 'her' (the body coded now as female) 'curves and paps and wiles' amounts to 'self denials', that is, to a denial of the very self, of what makes each self and each body distinctive (hence the plurals). We suspect that the poem's voice is merging with or rather performing a Catholic and nationalist as well as patriarchal discourse that wants to discipline the rebellious 'fevers' and 'wiles' of women's bodies and thinking selves. The speaker's attempt to control the body by depriving and punishing it ends up colluding with the very forces that always 'torch' and 'mesh' the body. The starved body becomes 'angular and holy', resembling both the mortified body of Christ and the hungry bodies of nationalist iconography, from the starved souls of the 'Great Hunger' of the 1840s to the graphic martyrdom of the Republican prisoner Bobby Sands.

The 'starved and curveless' body reduced to 'skin and bone' 'has learned her lesson' of submission, not least because it remains captured and defined by the controlling metaphor of holy sacrifice. 'Thin as a rib', this woman's body becomes *the* woman's body, an inexpressive and disciplined thing, reintegrated into these patriarchal discourses and thus reintegrated into the 'claustrophobia' of Adam's side next to the warlike 'drum' of his heart. Importantly, however, this reintegration has not yet happened; the speaker's body has not yet been 'caged' and her voice has not yet been stilled 'by the song' of Adam's breath. In the final stanza she has not forgotten

> the fall
>
> into forked dark,
> into python needs
> heaving to hips and breasts
> and lips and heat
> and sweat and fat and greed.

There is a last-ditch possibility, in other words, that the speaker will evade the fate of the obedient helpmeet Eve who is 'caged' by the metaphors that collaborating discourses of power use to 'enclose' women's bodies. She might embrace, instead, the 'python needs' of the rebellious and fallen Eve. In this final stanza, the speaker's once more clamorous voice refuses to forget 'the fall/ into forked dark', where 'dark' indicates the sheer obscurity and recalcitrance of bodies that were previously dragged into the light to be defined and controlled. Furthermore, 'forked' recalls Shakespeare's characterisation of the human animal in *King Lear* as 'a poor, bare, forked animal', a fallible and vulnerable but also intractable body 'unaccommodated' by the various discourses that would define and control it. It is not only the human body that is 'forked' or bifurcated in *Lear*, of course, but also the state, which has been hacked by a negligent king into separate pieces. The body, like the state, is disconnected and rebellious. In this striking final stanza, it rebelliously strains to evade metaphor entirely. There is even a radical suspicion of poetry itself, as there often is in Boland's terse and metrically irregular poetry, in particular of metaphors that give bodies singular meanings and turn suffering into clichéd 'old songs'. Linked not by metaphor but by the bare conjunctions of 'and', the body is figured instead as a site of multifarious 'needs' and desires' 'heaving' (a verb that connotes not retching this time but an intense and sensuous physicality) 'to hips and breasts/ and lips and heat/ and sweat and fat and greed'. The unadorned monosyllables of this final stanza (a 'heaving' or panting as well as rhythmical and breathless five lines rather than three) read like an affirmation of appetite and desire, of a voluptuous and erotic corporeality. Metaphors and adjectives cannot be avoided altogether, of course, for this body is still 'forked' and its needs are 'python'-like. But these terms portray it as defiantly unidealised, carnal and disobedient, determined not to be enclosed by the metaphors imposed by nation, religion and masculine power.

So, a woman's body, or at least this woman's body, always means something. But it may mean more than one thing and its meanings may reinforce or subvert the various powers with which women have often been identified, by which they have been disciplined and for which they have often been made to speak. We see Boland's critical account of her own poetry as contradictory, albeit productively so. She wants, she says, to speak of real historical Irish women in all their diversity and obscurity without making them into singular icons or exemplars of the nation's history. On the other hand, that's exactly what she wants to do, to unearth these women and speak for them and, by so doing, make them speak for the nation. This is a tension that a great poem like 'Mise Eire' productively encapsulates. In some ways it is the fundamental tension of all poetic and literary evocations of the past, which want imaginatively to imitate the dead while acknowledging how unfeasible and even ethically inadvisable this endeavour can actually be.

The poem's title is also the title of the arch-nationalist and Easter Rising martyr Patrick Pearse's patriotic lament from 1912:

> I am Ireland:
> I am older than the hag of Beara.
>
> Great my glory:
> I who bore brave Cúchulainn.

Pearse is speaking in the part of the familiar figure of the Poor Old Woman who personifies a suffering nation perennially betrayed by her submissive children and her 'irreconcilable enemies'. There is nothing necessarily wrong with that, we contend, since the imaginative occupation of fictional voices is in many ways what literature *is*: 'Writing forces unexpected, often unwelcome identifications, or it does nothing', as Jacqueline Rose states.[25] A large part of what makes Boland's version of Pearse's poem so intriguing is that it calls attention to both the advantages and pitfalls of this kind of imaginative occupation. Of course one might object to the kind of ventriloquisation that Pearse gives us, since the nation-personifying woman voiced by him is a stilted and totally passive figure, a mother of the mythologised heroes that Pearse aspired to be, and indeed in due course became, but not an actor in her own destiny. This kind of appropriation is presumably what Boland's speaker, in her starkly isolated and spot lit first line, declares that she 'won't go back to'. On the surface, it is the 'land of the Gulf Stream', that is, Ireland, that the speaker 'won't go back to'; she is identifying herself, as in the final stanzas and elsewhere in Boland's oeuvre, with the emigrant Irish. But the poet, too, and her reader are similarly distanced from a national past that is exemplified by these overlooked protagonists of Irish history.

The initial stanzas reject

> the songs
> that bandage up the history,
> the words
> that make a rhythm of the crime
>
> where time is time past.

The poem wants to refrain from 'displacing' the nation and its history 'into old dactyls', that quite rare and rather contrived measure (a stressed beat followed by two unstressed beats) apparently being nothing like the prosaic and metrically irregular poetry of 'Mise Eire'. 'No. I won't go back', the poet repeats: 'My roots are brutal.' 'History is what hurts', to quote Fredric Jameson's memorable dictum; it is violence, in other words, and is not to be celebrated or simplified in verse.[26] Yet, if truth be told, there are plenty of dactyls in this poem ('won't go back', 'animal', 'memory', 'garrison', 'guttural', 'passable', 'bandage up', 'palsy of', etc.), which may be accidental or may, in fact, be a sign that the poem is indeed displacing the nation's history into song, making 'a rhythm of the crime' almost in spite of itself. 'History' itself is a dactyl, the word and the thing; 'time past' is a series of stresses followed by extended periods of composure and reflection. If songs 'bandage' up history, then, this may be both a bad and a good thing, both a misleading censorship of past experiences of violence and struggle *and* a way of using poetry to reflect on and make sense of these bygone traumas and achievements.

So the poem does 'go back to it', adopting Pearse's title and intention, identifying its speaker's voice with two apparently representative historical women and tasking them with speaking for Ireland. 'I am the woman', the speaker intones, apparently unequivocally, 'who practises the quick frictions' 'in the precincts of the garrison' and 'the rictus of delight'. Or is she? Far from that woman's viewpoint and voice being appropriated here, she actually remains a mystery to us. The prostitute's 'rictus of delight' is a kind of reluctant performance, a technique for concealing her true thoughts, just as 'silk at the wrists' is part of a costume and a 'dove-strut' a sort of act or routine. 'Sloven' is clearly a pejorative and unsympathetic label, hardly something one would say about oneself. There is, thus, an air of concealment and mummery in the performance by the anonymous and supposedly archetypal 'woman' and in the poem's equally hammy performance *of* this woman. There is a powerful sense of the historical truth being hidden from view, just as 'quick frictions' euphemistically conceal the nature of this woman's trade.

'I am the woman', the poem continues, 'on board the *Mary Belle*,/ in the huddling cold, holding her half-dead baby to her'. The undoubtedly affecting image of the emigrant mother clutching her starved and frozen child is also a brazen cliché. Has the poet really achieved a state of identification with this once again anonymous woman or has she simply reached for an excessively familiar heart-tugging image from the repertoire of nationalist sentiment? This woman is said to be 'mingling the immigrant/ guttural with the vowels/ of homesickness', but we wouldn't know whether she is or not, for we do not hear her voice. The poem speaks for her, though it does so in similarly unmusical ways. Indeed, the poem assumes a position of superior insight, knowing what it says the woman does not. The woman in the gansy-coat

>   neither
> knows nor cares that
>
> a new language
> is a kind of scar
> and heals after a while
> into a passable imitation
> of what went before.

Songs 'bandage up' history, this poem suggests, which means that they both conceal its wounds and contribute to a process of healing. A scar, of course, is the mark of successful healing, although it also testifies to the existence and severity of the original injury. The 'new language' here is presumably English, the language of this poem of course (though not of its title or of Pearse's poem), the language spoken in American exile and the language that largely displaced Irish after the famine. So, it is the poem itself that constitutes 'a passable imitation/ of what went before', an approximate if inauthentic performance or openly fictional and imagined enactment of Irish history from the viewpoints of two customarily unreported or mischaracterised women. This is not a criticism of the poem or a tacit admission of failure on Boland's part. What else could this poem or indeed any poem be other than an 'imitation', albeit a 'passable' and therefore only partly convincing and moderately instructive 'imitation', of the voices of these imaginary figures?

The old language has been lost, these women's voices cannot be retrieved, the 'crimes' of history have been committed, their perpetrators have so far escaped punishment, and the women of Irish history can be summoned only in the form of a patently fictitious dumb show. But, in a sense, that is what all poetry and in particular the poetic evocation of the neglected protagonists of a censored national past amounts to: a tableau of moderately illuminating fictions. There is no use lamenting this fact, unless one believed naively that lost voices could somehow be made directly present again in a poem. Nor would we want to reprimand Boland for trying to articulate these voices, since when all is said and done, the imaginative occupation of a voice is what lyric poetry does. To suggest that Boland is appropriating these voices would be as unhelpful and ultimately wrong-headed as accusing Shakespeare of pretending to be Hamlet. Plato complained that poets lie, which of course they do, but they are also honest enough to tell us they are lying. In a sense the poet 'nothing affirms, and therefore never lieth', in Philip Sidney's celebrated words, just as Boland's 'I ams' are blatant performances and 'imitations'.[27] These are not appropriations therefore, but feats of imaginative solidarity. The impossibility of accurately representing the past or of bringing forgotten and deceased voices back to life is, in fact, what calls for Boland's poetry in the first place; the pastness of the past, so to speak, is its fundamental premise. The poet says she 'won't go back to' the past; in fact, she *can't* go back to it. Its opacity and the especially grievous obscurity of forgotten or deliberately marginalised Irish women's lives is, itself, the most important thing to appreciate about the history of empire; it is an arena of violence and censorship. The stories we tell about it and the characters we invent and perform must serve an appropriate purpose in the present, as Boland's often do: sometimes in Boland they are appointed spokeswomen for the dubious virtues of patience and endurance and sometimes they speak to us with many voices and accents about dispossession and that call for solidarity, disobedience and rebellion.

The lyric voice dramatised by the late St Lucian poet Derek Walcott's final 2010 collection *White Egrets* knowingly performs the familiar and even slightly clichéd role of the ageing maestro facing up courageously, if irascibly, to the unavoidable facts of infirmity and death. This collection is 'just the old story of a heart that won't call it quits',[28] a phrase that is itself, knowingly presumably, a cliché; it is a story both about being old and a story that is itself old, hoary and over-familiar. Notwithstanding its understandable self-absorption, the voice heard in these poems is also preoccupied with what is presented as the wider social and political malaise of the contemporary Caribbean. Mortality, illness and the brokenness of the individual and social body are the themes of this collection, on the distinct but figuratively connected levels of the personal and the political. This is a collection about lateness, in which lateness betokens irascibility, anger and disenchantment but also virtuosity and at times a kind of serenity. We think the collection might be playing consciously with the critically fashionable idea that artists assume a distinctive mode or style in the last phase of their work.[29] What is late about this collection? The poet, alas. But also the social and political world that is illuminated and exposed by the poem's extended metaphor of lateness. Exploring the frustrated political aspirations of the postcolonial West Indies, the persistently uneven economic development of 'too much tourist and too lickle employment',[30] the triumph of political independence alongside the humiliating servility of service-sector work, this is a very critical work that looks outwards frowningly at the wider social world as well as inwards sorrowfully at memory and bodily discomfort.

Walcott's late style or mode, of discontent and criticality, is a kind of intentional performance; his is an extremely self-conscious lateness. The poet assumes the guises of canonical figures of virtuosic or restless old age, from Shakespeare's Lear and Prospero to Don Quixote and W.B. Yeats. Walcott's lateness is, if not quite premeditated, then certainly not involuntary or merely serendipitous either. The best way to characterise Walcott's lateness would be to say that the inescapable experience of old age, with its attendant frailties and restrictions and its acute consciousness of mortality, is transmuted in these poems, in a calculating and resourceful way, into a series of metaphors for the senescence and mortality of something else, which we will call capitalist modernity in its neo-colonial mode. Moreover, the opportunities of old age, which might include a capacity for contemplation and creative reflection, an awareness of longer-term historical developments and continuities, as well as an intense appreciation of beauty and transience, enable Walcott in this volume to explore alternatives to neo-colonialism. Those alternatives take shape in visions of free and creative forms of labour and a celebration of the local and the vernacular.

Enrique Dussel argues that modernity has served historically as an ideology that has masked European colonial domination. Modernity is the thoroughly contradictory planetary culture of the world-system that first came into being with Spain's incorporation and administration of Amerindia and with the consequent constitution of Europe as the 'centre' and the rest of the globe as its 'periphery'. 'Modern' European values, technologies and political institutions, indeed capitalism itself, have all developed their distinctive character as a result of this global genesis. Free labour, for example, increasingly became a crucial aspect of the core's ideological self-image and, therefore, of its claim to be modern. But Europe's definitive competitive advantage over the Islamic, Indian and Chinese worlds in fact came about as a result of its ability to use *forced* labour: to produce value (in

Marx's sense) from the toil of vast numbers of indigenous peoples in the Americas and from millions of plantation slaves of African provenance.[31] To talk about modernity, then, is not just to talk about Europe's image of itself as the origin and exemplar of what it means to be modern, but to think about how that narrow and self-serving, as well as extremely durable, conception of modernity came about in response to a process of 'modernisation' that was, to put it mildly, much more complex and uneven. Capitalist modernity, in short, is a profoundly contentious and contradictory, not to mention catastrophic and crisis-prone, phenomenon, one that is limited (as Dussel puts it) and that, since its inception, *always has been limited* and is in fact *constitutively limited* by 'the impossibility of the subsumption of the populations, economies, nations, and cultures that [modernity] has been attacking since its origin and has excluded from its horizon and cornered into poverty'.[32]

All of Walcott's work registers the weight and appeal of a European aesthetic tradition that it perceives and even partly constructs from the oblique angle of a formerly colonised subject. What is so intriguing and challenging about *White Egrets* is that it combines both a militant disavowal of a colonial or, more accurately, neo-colonial system in the Caribbean on the Dussel-like grounds that it has inflicted forms of exploitative labour with a conscious and even enthusiastic indebtedness to the modes and forms of European aesthetic tradition. The poet rails against new forms of colonial domination and their impoverishing effects. But he does so in the guise of a figure who is acutely and forcefully conscious of his own mortality, a role that is plainly modelled on canonical exemplars of late style like Keats, Shakespeare's Lear and especially Yeats. The tension between resisting and embracing European forebears is evident at the minutest level of the collection's form; this numbered sequence of poems of varying lengths is composed in rhyming quatrains but the quatrains do not constitute stanzas and nor are these poems, which often end abruptly or else continue unexpectedly, invariably divisible by four. Orthodox rhyme schemes give way to more complex patterns of para- and internal rhyme or even to contrived and tinny rhymes, such as 'Arethusa' with 'lose her' and 'Siracusa',[33] that find equally forceful ways of accentuating the potentially constraining nature of the form that the volume has chosen for itself. These faintly or creatively or stiltedly rhyming 'quatrains' are at once a departure from a freely adopted and patently admired tradition and an insistent reminder that the tradition in question is itself hardly proscriptive or unilinear since the quatrain is by no means a uniquely or even predominantly European form. This collection encloses itself in a tradition that is constraining and oppressive but also unexpectedly capacious, flexible and susceptible to creative innovation. This is a point about poetic form but also about what that form represents, which is modernity itself, revealed by this collection to be a radically contradictory global (as opposed to narrowly European) phenomenon.

So, *White Egrets* dramatises the imminent demise of two things. The first is the life of the poet who is fixated with memory and with the physical effects of ageing. Old age also gives the poet the opportunity to assume a part, very knowingly, often earnestly and sometimes sardonically, that he has inherited from poetic tradition. The second thing that is coming to an end, therefore, is not so much that tradition but its identity and authority. It is European modernity itself, the durable belief and practice of cleanly dividing 'Europe' as centre from its colonial 'peripheries', that is placed on borrowed time. What Dussel's analysis reveals is that the idea of 'Europe' has always been a kind of sleight of hand, the cultural or ideological product of the careful exclusion and forgetting of the dependency of European wealth and cultural prestige *from the outset* on the expropriation of the wealth and cultural integrity of other peoples. What Walcott's volume does is occupy that tradition, not just to herald its demise but, in so doing, to open it out to the other experiences and voices it previously occluded. Walcott's is not a submission to European modernity but an appropriation of it. These poems foretell the end of empire and the imminent, or at least potential, emergence of empire's successor, a quite different social, economic and cultural order based not on control or hierarchy but in some non-prescriptive and post-nationalist way on ideals of freedom and creativity.

At the end of the first poem, 'A sable blackbird twitters in the limes',[34] echoing the gathering swallows twittering in the last line of Keats's 'Ode To Autumn', another familiar exemplar of lateness. Walcott's is an allusive and rather self-aggrandising affiliation with a certain canonical tradition that meditates on mortality and endings. The blatant archaism of 'sable' tells us as much, as does the mourning garb of this recurring image. The poem's ekphrastic subjects, the 'life-sized terra-cotta warriors' of Qin Shi Huang to which the poet's 'rigid' 'chessmen' are likened, are still serving their dead 'emperor, his clan, his nation'. Time might have come to a disarming standstill in that 'astonishing excavation' but it continues to pass in the poet's garden. There, the 'changing light/ on the lawn outside where bannered breakers toss/ and the palms gust with music that is time's' are ominous signs of time's relentless passage. This is a source of fear for the ageing and immobile poet as he seeks to kill time by playing chess. But the shifting patterns of light as well as the palms and breakers, St Lucia's trees and its seas being perennial signifiers of place in this collection, are also sources of creative inspiration. They generate sound and 'music', the art of the Muse and, therefore, also poetry. We read this opening poem not only as a frankly paradoxical meditation on the grandeur and obsolescence of empire but also as a reflection on how the 'vows' and 'voice' of these 'breathlessly erect' guardians of a bygone empire, which is thus paradoxically both dead and alive, endow the ageing poet with a voice and purpose of his own. He sings both of an empire 'that has lost its voice' while remaining 'erect' and of something else, an outlook or set of attachments that emerges much more cryptically in the course of these poems but is perhaps alluded to in the poet's acceptance of time's uncertainties as well as in his description of the 'excavation' as 'astonishing'.

What the poet finds so wonderful and surprising about the terracotta warriors is their sheer meaningfulness.[35] Not only the chessmen and the ubiquitous white egrets but, in fact, everything that the infirm poet sees through his window is immediately transformed into metaphor. To be astonished is certainly not the same thing as being dumbfounded or deprived of speech. Astonishment is more like being rendered motionless and rapt, not like the 'rigid' and 'odourlessly strict' warriors but more like the immobile yet intensely vigilant poet confined here, in another recurring image, to a restricted but absorbing view of some 'lawn'. The astonishing but modest phenomena of natural growth and change, the geographically specific minutiae of his island that reveal themselves to the watchful invalid, are at the level of metaphor the exact opposites of empire's grandiose delusions of permanence and universality. Walcott is echoing themes of Yeats here and is even restaging the whole mise-en-scène from Yeats's 'An Acre of Grass', the incapacitated versifier in his garden resisting the temptations of serenity or defeat and, instead, invoking exemplars of angry old age. Among Walcott's many costumes, therefore, is that of the post-nationalist Yeats in old age.[36] It is not only the breakers and birds of St Lucia that astonish the poet in the course of the collection but also the sunflowers of Urbino, the Sicilian light and the 'blazing country/ in eastern Pennsylvania' that inspires a 'love for what is not your land' in 'Pastoral'.[37]

Time is both resisted and accepted in these poems. Many of them are dedicated to deceased companions and friends. They are elegies, poised somewhere between acts of mourning that reconcile the poet to the fact of death and fits of melancholia that refuse to accept loss or be appeased by glib consolations and epitaphs. Time entails mortality, of course. But it also betokens renewal. These poems therefore oscillate between two moods or modes, equanimity and indignation, acceptance and resistance. We must not overlook the fact that this is irreducibly the poet's predicament, that of nearing the end of one's life, tormented by illness and debility, filled with regrets but also with last-ditch plans, memories of pleasure and feelings of pride in accomplishment. But it would be a mistake to take all this at face value. For even the poet's life is transmuted into metaphor. The poet is constructing and performing a part or voice that threatens, at first, to accept 'the drumming world that dampens your tired eyes', to accept even 'the quiet ravages of diabetes' 'with level sentences' and the 'sculpted settlement' of ornate verse forms. The sequence entitled 'White Egrets' withstands that temptation. The poet anticipates 'that peace/ beyond desires and beyond regrets,/ at which I may arrive eventually', though evidently not yet. In the third poem of the sequence, a storm lashes the trees in the poet's garden: 'light cracks and thunder groans' like the blowing winds and cracking cheeks of

Lear's 'cataracts and hurricanoes'.[38] '"Who'll house the shivering hawk, and the/ impeccable egret and the cloud-coloured heron,/ and the parrots who panic at the false fire of dawn?"' In Shakespeare's play, of course, it is the 'houseless heads and unfed sides' of the 'Poor naked wretches' 'That bide the pelting of this pitiless storm' that alert Lear for the first time to the sheer bodiliness and mortality that even a king shares with his fellow humans. Lear resolves to embrace a kind of obligation to, or even solidarity with, his fellow beings: 'Take physic, pomp;/ Expose thyself to feel what wretches feel'.[39] Walcott, meanwhile, pities the houseless birds. The allusion to Lear is an act of self-aggrandisement, of course, but this is also an imaginative feat of compassion. The shivering hawk and the panicking parrots are symbols of imperilled nature, while the multiply meaningful and 'impeccable egret' is, as ever, an image of survival and renewal.

The egret is a 'mythical conceit',[40] an extended and highly polysemic metaphor. Egrets seemingly invite their own transmutation into images and figures or 'egret-emblems', to use Walcott's Yeatsian term, every bit as cryptic but also prolifically evocative as the Irish poet's swans: 'These birds keep modelling for Audubon',[41] the nineteenth-century American ornithologist and water-colourist. They repeatedly beseech decipherment, variously betokening ancientness and death, creative ingenuity and discrimination, angelic or 'seraphic' immortality. Yet their 'indifference' to the poet leaves them uncaptured by these various imposed meanings. They return 'like memory, like prayer' so that time and again in this collection 'an egret astonishes the page'.[42] The egret's meanings are multiple and often contradictory: they 'stalk through the rain/ as if nothing mortal can affect them'[43] and they are 'sepulchral', large and sinister creatures '"like something out of Bosch"'[44] at once immortal and deathly, emissaries from heaven and denizens of hell. What they denote, therefore, is not one single thing but the poet's capacity to transform all things into lively metaphors or, put differently, the poet's capacity to be astonished again and again by phenomena that escape secure definition. Watching and describing egrets is a task that resembles prayer in the same sense that poetry's task, in the words of W.H. Auden's elegy to Yeats, is to 'Teach the free man how to praise'.[45] 'The perpetual ideal is astonishment', paradoxically, because it is definitely not the perpetual or eternal quality of the egrets that repeatedly delights the poet but their unfailing capacity to mean different things at different moments. If empire aspires to permanence and universality, then the egrets signify the transience of nature and its irreducible specificity. If empire seeks to stabilise meaning, then the egrets free meaning up and multiply it. They permit a creative freedom of description and interpretation.

Poetry itself therefore becomes a kind of anti-imperialist emblem of freedom, independence and creativity, albeit a practice that is perennially under threat. 'The Acacia Trees' remembers when it was possible to write beneath the acacias on 'the hot, empty beach' that is now being measured up 'with tapes and theodolites'.

> I watched the doomed acres
> where yet another luxury hotel will be built
> with ordinary people fenced out. The new makers
> of our history profit without guilt
> and are, in fact, prophets of a policy
> that will make the island a mall, and the breakers
> grin like waiters, like taxi drivers, these new plantations
> by the sea; a slavery without chains, with no blood spilt –
> just chain-link fences and signs, the new degradations.
> I felt such freedom under the acacias.[46]

The poem, with its strident certainties and its shocking comparison of tourist developments to slave plantations, is untypically prosaic and didactic. But it thus serves to sketch a larger historical and political context for the rest of the collection's insistence on the creative freedom that is exemplified by the practice of writing and reading metaphors. Fences and signs are the methods of the new imperialism: fences privatise sites of liberty and community while signs fix meanings and possibilities of interpretation. Tourist development 'will make the island a mall', transforming its multiplicity of unregimented existences into saleable commodities, its people into obsequious house boys and the manifold phenomena of its natural world into reified spectacles. The twin freedoms of writing and of reading, the very freedoms practised and encouraged throughout this collection and which are placed by 'The Acacia Trees' in an explicitly anti-colonial or more specifically anti-neo-colonial political context, are exemplary freedoms to see and create things anew, to praise and be astonished by (to recognise the beauty and importance of) that which is not yet pinned down or fenced off. Of course, the poet is conscious that the power of poetry is merely exemplary rather than actual. 'Poetry makes nothing happen', to quote Auden's elegy for Yeats once more. Indeed, Walcott acknowledges in parenthesis that 'blank, printless beaches are part of my trade', since writing poetry is a service occupation like waiting tables or driving a taxi and poems too hawk images of commodified nature to wealthy foreign patrons. The point is that the promise of independence and freedom is as yet unfulfilled, or rather that the duelling mindsets and structures of freedom and empire remain locked in combat.

'The Lost Empire' recalls the sudden demise of British imperialism along with imperialism's world-encircling authority and its delusions of permanence. Barely voiced here but certainly manifest in other poems about infirmity and illness is the poet's own waning strength: 'there is no greater theme than this chasm-deep surrendering of power'.[47] If there is certainly grandeur in the fluttering flags and pennons and 'the tasselled cortège' of the expiring empire, then there is a similar dignity and solemnity to the poem itself, its stately rhyme scheme, its echoes of Prospero's celebrated valedictory speech in the fourth act of *The Tempest*, and its creator's seemingly undiminished virtuosity. An air of composed gravity presides over this poem. But it is certainly true that its willed and rather archaic and ambivalent insistence on formality (its four orthodox ABAB-rhyming quatrains interrupted in the middle by an incongruously half-rhyming additional line) complements the ceremonious 'funeral pom-poms', the marching boots and rifle's volley and the mournful last post sounded by the 'sobbing bugle'. Both the political forms of empire and empire's tightly controlled poetic expressions are expiring. In the second part of this poem, what they are succeeded by is not only the emergence of a more creatively complex rhyme scheme but a veritable celebration of informality at the level of the poem's themes. A map of the Antilles 'looks as if a continent fell/ and scattered into fragments'.[48] There follows a celebration of local places, 'from Pointe du Cap/ to Moule à Chique', and a list of vernacular and multilingual names for the islands' flora: '*bois-canot, laurier cannelles,/* canoe-wood, spicy laurel, the wind-churned trees/ echo the African crests'. The stars at night are not the imperial capitals and financial centres of 'Genoa, Milan, London, Madrid, Paris' but 'far fishermen's fires' and 'crab-hunters' torches'.

> This small place produces
> nothing but beauty, the wind-warped trees, the breakers
> on the Dennery cliffs, and the wild light that loosens
> a galloping mare on the plain of Vieuxfort make us
> merely receiving vessels of each day's grace,
> light simplifies us whatever our race or gifts.
> I'm content as Kavanagh with his few acres;
> for my heart to be torn to shreds like the sea's lace,
> to see how its wings catch colour when a gull lifts.

'This small place produces nothing but beauty' is both a prideful boast that everything produced in St Lucia is beautiful and a disappointed admission that the island is at a competitive disadvantage in the cutthroat world of late capitalism since beauty is all that it produces. Yet, *The Tempest* is perhaps not the only Caribbean inter-text present in this poem for we might also pick up an allusion to the celebrated *Cahier d'un retour au pays natal* of Aimé Césaire, the '*maître*' to whom 'Elegy' is dedicated,[49] and Césaire's excited 'Hurrah for those who never invented anything'. The 'wind-churned trees/ echo the African crests' is a reminder of the island's African rather than British provenance but also of the violent dispossession of the middle passage. 'This small place', like the similarly 'small place' of Jamaica Kincaid's Antigua, has actually produced a very great deal over the years, not least through slavery the wealth that enabled the industrial take-off of the West. That it now produces nothing but beauty is cause for regret, since the 'slavery without chains' that is tourism is by far the island's leading source of foreign exchange earnings. Yet, beauty is productive in another and much more auspicious sense. The poetic labour undertaken in this second part of the poem is nothing like the formal arrangements of the first part. What is described here is more like an ad hoc, albeit somewhat idealised, list of striking scenes from island life. The poet does not impose meaning but describes all witnesses or readers of these scenes as 'merely receiving vessels of each day's grace'.

The production of beauty, either through composition or perception, augurs an alternative form of creative or free labour. Nature is a source of astonishment, not something to be controlled and commodified. The fishermen and crab hunters are examples of forms of non-alienated labour in sustainable symbiosis with nature. Poetry itself is a form of labour that does not marshal its images or control their interpretation but simply makes those intensely resonant images available for contemplation. The 'us' who are 'receiving vessels of each day's grace' are the same inclusive 'us' who, for the poet's painterly eye, are 'simplified' by light 'whatever our race or gifts'. The names of its places and fauna are testament to the island's diverse sites of origin therefore, an effect redoubled by the perhaps surprising reference to the celebrated insularity of Patrick Kavanagh. The poem ends, ultimately, with a Césaire-like vision of post-imperial inclusivity, a 'rendezvous de la conquête' where all races and identities may converge and where it is the creative freedom of poetry itself that exemplifies a wholesale alternative to the dying age of empire. The poem is certainly, in the mode of the Irish poet, a celebration of the vernacular and of the beauty and significance of the seemingly commonplace, a vindication of *this* 'small place' as opposed to the space-devouring expansionism of empire. But it is also a hugely auspicious announcement that what makes this place, St Lucia, significant is its capacity to call forth a kind of creative practice. Composition and interpretation are forms of freedom. A breaker resembles lacework, which is not so much because everything is a work of art but because everything can be transformed into metaphor and, thus, made into a work of art. Why? Because poetry is an exemplary form of free and creative (rather than forced) labour.

Most narratives about the production of art in old age are personal and redemptive ones. Even where late works are seen to be angry and discontented rather than serene or consoling, they are still presented as crowning accomplishments of an artistic career. Where the artist might be expected to settle down or to encounter creative incapacity, late works are often presented by contrast as a sort of surprising burst of exemplary creative effort. These are the stories we tell ourselves about late style. In a sense, it is also the story that Walcott tells himself and his readers. But another story emerges in the course of this collection, one in which the life of the artist is transformed into a metaphor for something else entirely. These poems sound the Yeatsian theme of the rise and fall of civilisations and empires. Neither the ordering of time nor time's methodical arrangement by narrative are its dominant themes but time as the medium of change, creativity and mortality. Walcott's *White Egrets* is, in part, a collection of poems about the frustrations, preoccupations and opportunities of old age. But it is a collection that, while appearing to embrace the slightly clichéd figure of the ageing maestro, also uses that figure's acute awareness of the passage of time, of mortality and transience, to explore the comparable lateness and contingency of neocolonialism in the Caribbean.

Temporality, including the mortality of the poet, of the poetic tradition he ambivalently occupies and of the evanescent beauty and specificity of the island's natural world, are implicit ripostes to empire's delusions of permanence and to its continuing determination to reify and exploit the people and nature of St Lucia. Forced labour has been the underside of capitalist modernity, conceptualised from Dussel's fully global perspective, from slavery to the 'slavery without chains' of service-sector employment. But it is the creative and free labour of description and interpretation that Walcott's collection both demonstrates and enables. All of Walcott's work is unflinching in its condemnation of 'the traitors/ who, in elected office, saw the land as views/ for hotels', who exchanged freedom for dependency.[50] Furthermore, this late collection's knowing embrace of temporality and transience constitutes not just what Anthony Carrigan calls a 'counter-historicization of landscape'[51] but a veritable counter-historicisation of the Caribbean itself. The theme of *White Egrets* is not just the poet's old age but also the ways in which old age, transmuted into metaphor, illuminates the history and possible future of the Caribbean region.

Films such as David Lean's epic *Lawrence of Arabia*[52] also engage with instances of counter-historicisation and the question of how to revisit the imagined glorious imperial past while remaining attuned to the historical reality of the demise of empire. The epic has come down to us, in filmic history, as an 'instinctively' recognisable genre because we might unconsciously or consciously liken it to the 'real' – to imitating or representing an historical reality. Because it makes claims to history and to the representation of history, it commands a certain respect or gravitas that makes questioning its attempt at the real even more difficult. As Russell argues,

> The Cinematic Epic takes as its subject world historical events, the distant myths or more recent turning points of the culture. These must be treated 'epically', that is with resources of cinematic style approximating the effects of the epic in literature, great events given the largest scale of treatment; *great* as in *massive*, but also connoting grandeur and overwhelming cultural significance.[53]

Tensions arise in *Lawrence of Arabia* from the need to represent T.E. Lawrence as both exception to, but also proponent of, the structures that maintained particular types of colonial control. The film's investment in the epic nature of the story can, here, be seen as an opportunity to endow all characters with 'grandeur and overwhelming cultural significance', which to a certain extent it does. While it may seem odd to return to this film in order to locate subaltern voices, it is important to do so as representations and articulations of colonised subjects who understand themselves as beholden to others, for a version of their history is a very powerful political move. To locate these representations in epic films such as *Lawrence of Arabia* is to be attuned to the potential of popular film to contribute to this project. Although the film is primarily interested in the career and achievements of T.E. Lawrence and at times steeped in what we may call colonial nostalgia, it also offers prominent cinematic opportunities for dissenting voices from the Arab world to make themselves heard and seen. Although the context of the film is set in what Graham Dawson has called 'the establishment of that new empire in the Middle East to which Lawrence (with his conception of "our first brown dominion") has contributed',[54] the concentration on various interactions that prioritise specificity over general colonial systems of domination is intriguing. Whereas Lawrence starts out by presuming to know everything about the Arabs and to pontificate on their inability to overcome their tribal affiliations, his hard-won appreciation of their complexity presents problems for the representation of the imperial adventure overall.

In revisiting this crucial historical moment where imperial expansion was so desired and fought for, the film takes the opportunity to reflect on the means through which an unfamiliar place and peoples are made complex. In other words, returning to this particularly fraught moment of potential imperial single-mindedness, Lean prioritises representations, characters and contexts that require collaboration, integration and eventually understanding. This particular treatment of the past requires the elevation of characters that surround Lawrence and, though they may not succeed in changing him, have enough cinematic and narrative space to produce a counter-narrative. And, even as 'Lawrence comes to imagine himself as a contemporary prophet imbued with quasi-divine powers, who seeks inspiration under a thorn tree and claims to be able to "work miracles" – to lead the Arab people to their freedom',[55] Lean's choice to articulate multiple Arabs' perspective in this context is noteworthy.[56] In many ways, it is impossible to imagine a more imperial ideal than Lawrence – available to take on any mission asked of him and to sacrifice himself to achieve his objective. As Dawson notes, 'Lawrence became one of the figures registering the impact of the loss of Empire upon British masculinity' and the film 'was widely read on its release as an oppositional, anti-imperialist text'.[57] Although his closeness to the Arabs can bring the accusation of his having 'gone native' in the crudest sense, what remains most intriguing to us are the ways in which the various dialogues with the Arab characters do not actually reveal a political and established anti-imperialism as much as they reveal a strong sense of local knowledge and bounded history. It's important to look at these representations as they have the ability to reform an otherwise narrow view of this episode in imperial history as represented in popular culture. For, as Dawson notes:

> To this day, [*Lawrence of Arabia*] remains amongst the most likely sources of popular knowledge about the region and its people, thus helping to reproduce Anglocentric assumptions and perspectives, and to transmit into the present the imagined relations of power from a bygone colonial era that are inscribed in them.[58]

It seems, then, that the multifaceted story of *Lawrence of Arabia* provides both an undermining of the presumed cultural and political superiority of imperial ideology at the same time as it presents an ideal for how to imagine the best aspects of British colonialism. This is unforgettably presented towards the start of the film where Lawrence and his Arab guide appear as almost invisible dots in the vast desert.

The extent of the bravery and courage required to tackle the desert is facilitated by the widescreen shot of the sand dunes and rocks and what is clear from the start of Lawrence's journey is the extent to which, at every point, he needs assistance and guidance. Armed with his military and philosophical gravitas, he nevertheless cannot wholly navigate across the unknown terrain alone. In an early discussion with Tafas his guide, Lawrence claims to be 'different' to the 'fat people' who live in Britain, 'a fat country' bloated presumably with its own pride. Tafas is curious and takes an interest in what Lawrence tells him and in his belongings, especially his gun. In response, Tafas offers up some local knowledge by telling Lawrence that the well they are drinking from belongs to the Harith and that the water tastes bad because the 'Harith are a dirty people'. Soon after, when a member of the Harith, Ali Ibn El Kharish (played here by Omar Sharif) turns up and kills Tafas for daring to use the well, we learn that Tafas was a Hazimi of the Beni Salem tribe and knew *not* to use the well. Faced with this contextual knowledge, Lawrence nevertheless retracts into generalisations. Making an argument that Tafas was his *friend*, Ali's response is efficient: 'he was nothing, the well is everything. The Hazimi may not drink at our wells, he knew that.' Although this scene and many others like it reveal Lawrence's basic ignorance of the unwritten laws that enable the Bedouin to survive in harsh conditions, it nevertheless permits other characters to articulate an epistemology that is at odds with the one presented by Lawrence, as nuanced as that may be at times. His speech to Ali is remarkable in its confidence: 'So long as Arabs fight tribe against tribe, so long will they be a little people, a silly people. Greedy, barbarous and cruel, as you are.' Later in the film, however, he is forced to confront the Arabs' heavy military losses in their support for the Allied army in the fight against the Ottoman Turks. Upon meeting the leader of the Arab army Lord Faisal, he learns that the Arabs 'are unused to explosives and machines' and that in helping the British and allied forces fight the Turks on Arab soil he has exposed them to modern warfare and its horrific consequences. Later at a meeting in Lord Faisal's tent, we have a long recitation from the Koran presented by the official reciter to Faisal's army. In the tent, Faisal, the English officers and Sherif Ali are attentive as the words are spoken 'Verily. God is forgiving, merciful.'

It is important to state how *unusual* this is. To have words from the Koran spoken in a quiet and respectful manner that nevertheless segue into a discussion about military operations performs a unique role in this film. The sense here is that of an equal partnership and the Arabs are well aware of their strategic usefulness. When Faisal asks Colonel Brighton why the navy cannot free Aqaba, a strategically important city, from the Turks, Colonel Brighton reminds him of the superiority of Turkish artillery (12-inch guns pointing at the sea) that would bring *unacceptable* British losses. Faisal's retort, however, that the British navy are 'protecting the Suez canal' shows up his *very* clear knowledge of British interests. In this way the film also references events in 1956 when the Egyptians' plan to nationalise the Suez Canal was successful and Britain found itself stranded and having to withdraw its planned military invasion to protect its interests. Discussing Suez in the film in the context of the First World War also gives Lean the opportunity to introduce the roots of long-term imperial interests in the region and reveals a context where the interest in the Arab nations was always already *strategic*. Thus, the opportunity afforded to Faisal to speak of this openly in the film undermines any moral or ethical reason provided by Britain and the allied forces in relation to fighting the last of the Ottomans.

LORD FAISAL: 'I see that the canal is an essential British interest, it is of little consequence to us'
COLONEL BRIGHTON: 'I must ask you not to speak like that sir. British and Arab interests are one and the same.'
LORD FAISAL: 'Possibly'
ALI: 'Ha! Ha!'

In his explanation for Britain's grandeur,

COLONEL BRIGHTON is adamant: 'Look, sir, Great Britain is a small country, it's much smaller than yours. Small population compared with some. It's small but it's great. And why?
ALI: 'Because it has guns!
COLONEL BRIGHTON: 'Because it has discipline!'

This justification for the success of British colonial domination is a lesson that the Arabs must absorb and seek to emulate, yet Lord Faisal knows that the British army only seeks to, as he tells Lawrence, 'put [his] men under European officers'. These crucial scenes place certain thoughts and dialogue in characters that represent Arab historical figures. They permit a voicing of complex contemporaneous political opinion to be expressed in a way that addresses the colonial past of the Middle East and moves away from the more limited approaches delineated and explicated by more closed forms of Orientalist debates. Here, certain political and religious discussions elevate the Arabs in subtle and complex ways. 'I fear the [English] hunger for Arabia', says Faisal, anticipating British plans for Arabia beyond its purpose in the struggle to dismantle the Ottoman Empire. The context of the Bedouin involvement with the allied forces in the First World War also encompasses their own desires for self-actualisation – what came to be known as the Arab revolt and their belief, to a certain extent, that aligning themselves with the allied forces would secure support for their quest for independence in the post-Ottoman world. Faisal's words articulate a general *lack of trust* in the imperial promise of support for the Arabs. Aware also of the adventure-loving fantasies that accompany and strengthen imperial ideology and colonial conquest, Faisal tells Lawrence that he thinks him 'another one of these desert-loving English [...] no Arab loves the desert. We love water and green trees. There is nothing in the desert'. This is an extraordinary conversation that undercuts any romanticism at the heart of the colonial adventure. 'Or is it that you think we are something you can play with, because we are a little people, a silly people, greedy, barbarous and cruel?' In repeating Lawrence's words back to him, Faisal speaks back the belittling and ignorant words to the heart of empire, thus challenging both Lawrence and the viewer.

This challenge brings the Arabs up to an equal standing with the allied forces and the British Army. In his moving speech to Lawrence, Faisal reminds him and us that 'in the Arab city of Cordoba were two miles of public lighting in the streets when London was a village'. His reference here to the grand Umayyad Dynasty in the eleventh century and its unrivalled development is intended to embarrass Lawrence who, instead, rises to the challenges when he beseeches Faisal to 'be great again'. While Faisal 'long[s] for the vanished gardens of Cordoba', he understands the very real and material needs required to win a war. In cinematic terms, the equal standing of the two men conversing permits a rehearsing of both the Romantic and the crude requirements needed to fulfil success and victory. The wide shots of the small contingent of men given to Lawrence and Ali by Faisal to plan a surprise attack on the Turks at Aqaba is thrilling for its inclusiveness and camaraderie and bears none of the hallmarks of a homogeneous ruthless Arab regiment.

Here, all the men are equal, united in purpose and loyalty outside of the overarching understanding of themselves as 'Arabs'. In fact, the film does not shy away from entering into these very sensitive debates over ethnic and racial identities in the region, thus giving these questions, which are fundamental to Arab history and political discourse, a very tangible presence in popular cinema. The very construct of 'Arab' and the discursive and strategic dimension of this term is firmly rehearsed in a long discussion with Audu Abu Tayi, the leader of the Howeitat. When questioning Sherif Ali and Lawrence who they are working for in their plan to take Aqaba, their answer 'for the Arabs' troubles him.

ABY TAYI: The Arabs? The Howeitat, Ageyil, Ruala, Beni Sakhr, these I know. I have even heard of the Harith. *But the Arabs? What tribe is that?* (emphasis added)
LAWRENCE: (laughs then says): They're a tribe of slaves. They serve the Turks.

In appealing to pride and the will to fight a common adversary, Lawrence calls upon a unification needed to win the fight against the Turks. This conversation, however, points to no less than one of the central motifs in contemporary Middle Eastern socio-political discourse that continually seeks to affirm unity over distinctiveness in its historiography. *Lawrence of Arabia* performs this very debate and does not shy away from asking these central questions. In so doing, it performs an important role in the popular representation of the Arab world in cinematic history, in tune with the most significant questions emerging from an engagement with that era: the purpose and premise of colonial expansion in the Middle East and the apparent desire for 'Arab unification'.

This sense of unification against a common adversary is also the central theme in Richard Attenborough's 1982 film *Gandhi*. This film required reconsideration in the context of Nikita Lalwani's 2006 novel *Gifted*,[59] set in and around a South Asian family that has settled in Wales in the 1970s. Previous considerations of the film in postcolonial contexts had tended to dismiss it as either unprocessed hagiography or, worse yet, an example of what Salman Rushdie called the 'deification' of Gandhi. Here, Attenborough's supposed inattentiveness to the nuance and complexity of the various figures involved in the drive towards independence is under scrutiny. The success of the film, which Rushdie cannot deny, nevertheless troubles him for he feels that it is a film that does not do justice to the historical complexities and perhaps plays into ideas of exoticism and mysticism harboured by the West. Rushdie appears at times amused and at other times outraged at the failure of the film to provide some sort of political context that would make clearer the religious, social and ethnic complexities surrounding the rise of Gandhi.[60]

Returning to Rushdie's article in light of the inclusion of Attenborough's *Gandhi* in *Gifted* was a tricky exercise. Rushdie's 1991 collection *Imaginary Homelands* and the article on Gandhi within it had done a great service to postcolonial studies in revealing the very dexterous ways in which one could revisit important and revered colossi of cinematic culture and convincingly deconstruct them until any achievement they may have enjoyed crumbled in a heap of anti-imperial accusations. It's not so much that one had to agree with Rushdie's argument but rather that it was impossible to pretend that he had not made it. Neil Ten Kortenaar notes that Rushdie's 'disgust at the film is out of proportion to the film's defects, large as these are. Rushdie wants the film to be more critical of Gandhi and his philosophy of non-violence than it is. Clearly it is more than the film *Gandhi* that provokes the author's ire'.[61] In fact, Gandhi the historical figure and Gandhi the fictive character both appear in Lalwani's novel. At first he appears as a 'bumpy illustration' placed in the 'left corner of the room, by the whiteboard'.[62] Mahesh, a maths lecturer sits in his office and wonders what to say to his ten-year-old daughter who, he has just found out, has been shunned by another parent and called 'coloured'. He

> [l]ooks at Gandhi, wizened and unflinching, in the corner of his room. What would they make of this back in college, cocooned as they had been in the company of ideas? Trotskyites. Gandhian Communists – they had found plenty of names for themselves back then, chewing betel, relishing the bitter stain on their lips and debating whether class war was compatible with non-violence.[63]

This comparison jars quite violently with the passive nature of Mahesh's present dilemma. The memories of his more activist days back in India seem out of step with the quieter and more pensive attitude he adopts in the present. Nevertheless, Gandhi's image watches from the poster, at times trembling from the force of a nearby train and at other times in shadow after being obscured by the 'evening light on the grass'.[64] Lalwani's insertion of Gandhi as influential in Mahesh's life contributes to our imagining of him as having once been a vibrant, committed and politicised young man – aware of and in tune with the complex political debates of his day. However, the problems of raising his children and helping his wife to acclimatise in an environment that is not consistently welcoming seem to overwhelm Mahesh. In addition to this, the novel is keen to show the various ways in which the character's memories of India intrude and take up residence.

The novel, thus, performs the difficulties of being in two (or more) places at once and therefore complicates the representation of the diasporic imaginary. In the example above, Gandhi, what he stands for and how he has been influential, follows Mahesh into his 1970s Welsh life. Though at the start of the novel we understand this to be an homage to a cultural figure who represents protest and the fight for justice and equality, a more complex attachment to the cultural icon as represented in the film *Gandhi* later appears to represent an unspoken but deeply held pride in Gandhi's specific anti-imperialist stance. In one of the most memorable scenes in the book, Mahesh takes his wife, daughter and son to see *Gandhi* at the cinema:

> 'Today we have to concentrate and focus on what is before us. Don't let your mind wander around.' His voice was affectionate. 'Look at that poster there,' he said, gesturing at a lit placard directly opposite them. 'Now, who is that on it?'
> 'Mahatma Gandhi,' said Rumi.
> 'Good. And what is this film about?'
> 'Him.'
> 'And?'
> 'Oh, and our own history.'
> 'And how is it about our own history?'
> 'Because we are Indian.'[65]

A longer discussion ensues on the significance of watching the film carefully for its representation of *partition*. Nevertheless, much of the film's import is lost on the daughter Rumi who is disappointed at the lack of songs and the absence of any love scenes. We are therefore surprised to find that at the end of the film Rumi's mother Shreene is in tears, 'weeping heavily into a cotton handkerchief' and that 'Mehesh's eyes had a swollen gleam, visible beneath the rich sheen of light superimposed on the lenses of his glasses'.[66] It is not immediately clear why the film has brought up such a powerful reaction. Notwithstanding the fact that the assassination of Gandhi is shown both at the start and the end of the film, the understanding of the film as 'history' is too broad to allow for such a tragic reaction. However, a little later in his discussion with his friend Whitefoot, we understand a little more of what the film, watched by the South Asian family in Wales, can offer. Whereas Whitefoot seems to be a mouthpiece for Rushdie's perspective, emphasising the film's reluctance to show the marginalisation of many communities, including the Muslims, Mahesh is furious at the suggestion that Jinnah, a man 'selfish beyond belief with disastrous consequences, could be placed 'in the same sentence as the Mahatma?'.[67] Whitefoot is adamant however and claims that in financing the film the Indian government had all but produced a convincing bit of 'propaganda' with 'Evil English guys beating up the natives [...]'.[68]

Mahesh, however, is not happy to let it go and reminds Whitefoot that he *was* in India at the time of the events and that the film is about his 'life'[69] and how his family suffered badly at the hands of Muslims during partition. Whitefoot is, however, adamant that Mahesh must admit the reciprocal violent treatment of the Hindus towards the Muslims[70] but Mahesh is incapable of this, embroiled as he is with his own troubled past. Lalwani's contextualisation of Mahesh's reaction to Attenborough's *Gandhi* provides an entirely new lens through which to view and appreciate the film. Rather than understanding the film to be, in Rushdie's words, a botched example of Indian history, we might consider the naivety of the film to have some purpose nevertheless. Indeed we might consider that to strive for equal representation in such a vexed and troubled context is to risk pleasing no one. The real question might be: what work does the film do in the contemporary context of diaspora? The film could be seen as undertaking this kind of questioning itself. Though it begins with the assassination and reporting of Gandhi's funeral, Western reporters turn him into a saintly figure and the film does not shy away from presenting the sheer volume of people who attended his funeral, leaving us in no doubt as to the, perhaps unfathomable, influence that Gandhi had.

The film captures a broad-based allegiance to the person who was seen to have most persistently challenged the colonial administration from his early work as a barrister in South Africa, consistently racially abused, to his committed anti-imperial protest in India. Throughout the film, the figure of Gandhi seems to be shadowed by characters who are there to test him and to almost judge whether he is real: whether it is the clergyman or the reporter or the devoted American nun. This shadowing almost seems placed in the film to prove his existence – as though without them his story could not, would not, be believed. His legacy, in other words, is one that the film maintains has been, and will always need to be, argued for. In many ways, the inclusion of the viewing of the film within *Gifted*, in quite some detail, permits a more outward expression of the excitement and love that Gandhi brings, which is perhaps impossible to articulate in the materiality of everyday life that seeks absolutes and certainty. Thus, it is the very reasons that make Rushdie rage against the film that make it permissible for Mahesh and his wife to love it. In this way, a particular understanding of their past and an organisation of it through films allows for these diaspora characters to maintain a connection with their past selves and with the struggles and painful memories of partition. That the book includes a rigorous debate into the manifold reasons to dismiss the film, and still comes down on its usefulness, belies the often-unseen needs of marginalised communities in the postcolonial context to be seen and heard. Opportunities to experience pride for one's original home is not always forthcoming in the popular culture of the adopted nation. The inclusion of Gandhi, the man and the legend, in *Gifted*, provides one such occasion.

A very different approach to representing and articulating an indigenous past comes in the form of *Ten Canoes*, the 2006 film set in the North East Arnhem Land in Australia. A collaboration between Rolf de Heer and the indigenous people of Ramingining, the film is a thrilling example of what Linda Tuhiwai Smith has called the recovery of 'epistemological foundations' by indigenous cultures.[71] Chronology and its articulation play a large part in this recovery, as do the attempts to convey multiplicity. As Smith argues,

> The idea of contested stories and multiple discourses about the past, by different communities, is closely linked to the politics of everyday indigenous life. It is very much part of the fabric of communities that value oral ways of knowing. These connected accounts are stored within genealogies, within the landscape, within weavings and carvings, even within the personal names that many people carried. The means by which these histories were stored was through their systems of knowledge. Many of these systems have since been reclassified as oral traditions rather than histories.[72]

This tension between 'tradition' and 'history' does not seem to get resolved in *Ten Canoes* and the film is all the better for this. The making of the film itself was initially contested as another attempt to exploit indigenous peoples[73] rather than an attempt at genuine collaboration – seen perhaps as the best, if not flawless way, of putting together such a complex story on film. However, *Ten Canoes* did involve intense negotiation with the Ramingining elders who, according to Therese Davis, 'forg[ed] new ground in the area of recognition of Indigenous property rights'.[74] Her article on the collaboration process is a thrilling contextual retelling of the negotiations that grew in conjunction with the imagining of the film itself. Thus, an incorporation of the very history of filmmaking that had not always been attentive to the needs of Indigenous communities is reflected in *Ten Canoes* as the film attempts to dislodge the idea that a retelling of history can only be achieved in a chronological and totalising manner.[75] In fact, Smith outlines the various components of Western historical discourses that she views as being somewhat antithetical to an indigenous decolonising agenda. Among these are the rejection of history as adhering to a narrative of development and revolving around the 'self-actualizing subject', the pretence that history 'can be told in one coherent narrative' and that it can somewhat be said to 'begin' thus often rendering what is outside its domain as 'prehistorical, belonging to the realm of myths and traditions'.[76]

Instead, *Ten Canoes* begins with disorientating aerial shots of a lush, green landscape and the sound of heavy pouring rain. We follow a river as though we were a bird and a narrator tells us the story of his people and his land so that we can *see* the story and, therefore, know it. The narration is extraordinary as we are told about the narrator's beginnings even before he was born, at the same time as we are being taken on a journey of the trees, the insects and the waters of the surroundings.

There is no story without context and the context provides the story with a home. Moments into the film, we find ourselves in the story of the narrator's elders and, moments after that, while offering advice to a younger member of the group, an elder begins to narrate yet *another* story in order to teach him, and perhaps us, to 'live the proper way'. In attempting to locate the most productive language with which to discuss this film and how it evolves, Lyn McCredden's warning provides a sensitive framework. She argues for 'moving beyond celebrating difference' as well as looking away from 'a critique which disparages the film as an overly "static" representation of Yolngu culture'.[77] The latter comment refers to the fact that the Indigenous community seems to be represented in a similar way in the deep past and in the more recent past. However, producing an awareness that the film is concerned with how to represent the layering of time requires paying attention to the cinematic techniques used to accomplish this: 'mythic time, near-past time and the film's present are all woven through the film, using colour for mythic time, a time when anything was considered possible; and black and white for the near past'.[78] Cornelis Martin Renes argues, however, that there is a disjunction here and the film fails to adequately address 'the re-imagination of the immemorial Dreamtime and the more recent past'.[79] I sympathise with Renes' concerns about the extent to which any film that relies on and operates within the particular conventions and needs of an industry, can ever truly interrogate its own boundaries and create the space for 'ethnic agency'.[80]

However, these issues serve to problematise again the ways in which films such as *Ten Canoes* cannot hope to capture the needs of all viewers and critics. The achievement of the film, however, is to forge ahead in the face of the problems designed to force its interrogation. We are invited to enter an *attempt* to represent a world view through a medium that quite simply *cannot* evoke all times at once, for no matter how versatile cinema is, it is still beholden to a certain chronology in its material set up. Scenes must follow other scenes. In other words, we have to move from one story to another and from one moment in time and space in a way that is visible. Hence the change in colour helps us with this movement, though our understanding of what, and how, we are moving through remains somewhat elusive and may capture some of the 'layering' quality mentioned above. Careful viewing and, more importantly, *listening* invites us to move differently across the film and to organise our thoughts towards it in ways that at first may seem counterintuitive. Viewing in this way reveals that the resources of the past are, in *Ten Canoes*, not merely there to provide fodder for understanding the present. The past is there to be visited, to be used and to be shared.

The second storyteller in the film insists on going back and forth into his story when it pleases him. The film shows us this backwards and forwards movement and, in so doing, embeds one story into another and shows us their connectedness and interdependence. Rather than ask what the story is about then, we might ask *what work the various stories do* and how our investment in them tells us more about our rigid understanding of time and development than it tells us about the intricacies of layering the past.

Cinematically, it is thrilling to watch a film that does not require flashback or fade-in/fade-out techniques to introduce 'the past' and that eschews many recognisable methods to move between times. Here, we have no character reminiscing, no music to guide us to a different time. Instead, the camera moves sideways at a consistent pace as the landscape shifts and the narration orients us. Using this method, we understand that the past is always in motion – it does not belong to someone's memory, it is not a character's nostalgia and it does not perform a specific narrative function. Rather, it moves, and so the possibilities and meanings attached to it seem infinite. Sometimes the stories about our ancestors are very long, the narrator tells us, and they can *take days to tell*.

This warning undermines the possibility that the film can ever hope to tell the whole story *through the medium of film* and reminds us of the impossibility of capturing the events of the past in any 'coherent' and 'assembled' manner.[81] The story told by the elder to his younger brother is consistently interrupted by the canoe-making process and, in this way, is woven into it. At times it is the elder who tells the story and at other times it is the narrator. This dissolves a rigid idea of who can narrate the past and who the past belongs to. In this case, the story seems to be available to those who need it and for those who have the capacity to tell it. In other words, it is malleable and pliable and those surrounded by the stories of the past want to tell it and those listening want to hear it. The narrator confesses that, at some point, the story will grow into a large tree, with many branches, and yet all of these stories need to be told for 'proper understanding'. Thus, the story continues to proliferate and with it, our need for it to continue. The beauty of this film, in all its complexity, is the representation of the multiple voices of indigenous characters vying for prominence. The structure of the film allows for actors to play multiple roles and to move between and across times. Though one cannot say that the Dreamtime is captured in this cinematic experiment, for who can say what that would look like, we can certainly argue for a proliferation of pasts untethered to any hierarchical structure.

Conclusion

Priyamvada Gopal's brilliant historical study *Insurgent Empire: Anticolonial Resistance and British Dissent* shows how the sustained resistance and rebellions of Britain's colonial subjects in South Asia, Africa and the Caribbean throughout the colonial era was the vital factor in eventual decolonisation.[82] Far from liberation being a benefaction deliberately bestowed by Britain after many years of tutelage, every 'concession', democratic 'reform' and (finally) formal decolonisation itself in the decades after the Second World War were, in fact, the results of decades of petitions, protests, strikes, everyday disobedience, political organisation and often armed revolt. The colonies were not tutored by a more advanced civilisation. It was Britons, some

Britons at least, particularly feminist and working-class organisations and intellectuals, who learned from their empire what freedom might mean. They acquired, in many cases, an expanded conception of liberty that was much more substantive than the largely formal freedoms of capitalist wage labour or the freedom to accumulate made possible by forced and indentured labour in the colonies. The colonial archive of public records, statistics, royal commission reports, parliamentary proceedings and so on were the result, therefore, of this consistent and militant agency of Britain's supposedly quiescent subjects. The euphemisms and evasions of the colonial archive, its 'obsessional unease', to use Djebar's phrase once more, are powerful symptoms of the resistance offered from the outset to imperialism's unremitting violence. Again, far from being silent, the subaltern couldn't not speak in that archive, since the colonial archive existed in the first place in order to look for expedient ways to fine-tune and thereby prolong the rule of an imperial system that plundered the colonies only in the face of the constant intransigence and rebelliousness of their subjects.

Something similar can be said, we believe, in relation to postcolonial texts about the past. In them, the subaltern always speaks. 'Writing does not silence the voice, but awakens it', in Djebar's formulation.[83] These texts return to bygone incidents of dispossession and rebellion, less because the agency and the voices of colonial subjects can be directly accessed there but precisely because they cannot. Postcolonial texts compulsively imagine and reimagine the past because they are cut off from it, because it cannot be made present to us and must instead be made tenuously present through the imagination, across gulfs of time and distance. The sheer opacity of this past testifies to the salient fact about colonial power: the systematic obliteration over centuries of lives and voices. Those lives and voices can now only be partially reconstructed, painstakingly and through the creative imagination. One of the main ethical and political imperatives of these texts is their desire to enact and also encourage these forays into a past from which, in fact, they and we are irretrievably detached. They are forced to reconstruct a past imaginatively and quite openly, which is certainly not an act of deception therefore, let alone an effort to appropriate the voices of silenced subjects. Postcolonial portrayals of the past are more like scrupulous attempts to generate visions of the past that, despite the past's difference and its opacity, speak eloquently about our historical and political present and future. These portrayals may sometimes be embroiled in the very structures that sought to dominate colonised subjects. They may sometimes reveal hitherto undefined attachments forged in the close relationships between colonisers and their subjects. Nevertheless, these voices too are worth listening to for their advancement of the complicated nature of revisiting the past, even when that past is still being processed and experienced.

Notes

1 Neil Lazarus, *The Postcolonial Unconscious*, Cambridge: Cambridge University Press, 2011, p. 140.
2 Gayatri Chakravorty Spivak, 'Can the Subaltern Speak?', *Marxism and the Interpretation of Culture*, ed. Cary Nelsen and Lawrence Grossberg, London: Macmillan, 1988, pp. 271–313, p. 287.
3 Leerom Medovoi, Shankar Raman and Benjamin Robinson, 'Can the Subaltern Vote?', *Socialist Review*, 20:3 (1990), 133–149.
4 Benita Parry, *Postcolonial Studies: A Materialist Critique*, London: Routledge, 2004, p. 20.
5 Terry Eagleton, *Figures of Dissent: Critical Essays on Fish, Spivak, Žižek and Others*, London: Verso, 2003, pp. 158–167.
6 Gayatri Chakravorty Spivak, *A Critique of Postcolonial Reason: Toward a History of the Vanishing Present*, Cambridge, MA: Harvard University Press, 1999, p. 308.
7 Jorge Luis Borges, 'On Exactitude in Science', *Fictions*, trans. Andrew Hurley, London: Allen Lane The Penguin Press, 1999, p. 325.
8 Assia Djebar, *Fantasia: An Algerian Cavalcade*, trans. Dorothy S. Blair, Portsmouth: Heinemann, 1993 [1985], p. 8.
9 Lazarus, *The Postcolonial Unconscious*, p. 123.
10 Walter Benjamin, *The Arcades Project*, trans. Howard Eiland and Kevin McLaughlin, ed. Rolf Tiedemann, Cambridge, MA: Harvard University Press, 2002, p. 471.
11 Benita Parry, 'Directions and Dead Ends in Postcolonial Studies', *Relocating Postcolonialism*, ed. David Theo Goldberg and Ato Quayson, Oxford: Blackwell, 2002, pp. 66–81, p. 73.
12 Gayatri Chakravorty Spivak, *The Postcolonial Critic: Interviews, Strategies, Dialogues*, ed. Sarah Harasym, New York and London: Routledge, 1990, p. 104.
13 J.M. Coetzee, *Foe*, Harmondsworth: Penguin, 1987, p. 118.
14 Gayatri Chakravorty Spivak, 'Theory in the Margin: Coetzee's *Foe* Reading Defoe's Crusoe/Roxana', in Jonathan Arac and Barbara Johnson (eds), *Consequences of Theory*, Baltimore, MD: Johns Hopkins University Press, 1991, pp. 154–180.
15 J.M. Coetzee, *Elizabeth Costello: Eight Lessons*, London: QPD, 2003, p. 80.
16 Pablo Neruda, *Canto General*, trans. Jack Schmitt, Berkeley, CA: University of California Press, 1991 [1950], pp. 41–42.
17 Milan Kundera, *The Book of Laughter and Forgetting*, trans. Aaron Asher, London: Faber & Faber, 1996 [1979], p. 4.
18 Seamus Heaney, *Preoccupations: Selected Prose, 1968–78*, London: Faber & Faber, 1980, p. 56.
19 Eavan Boland, *New Collected Poems*, Manchester: Carcanet, 2005, p. 204.
20 Jürgen Habermas, *The Philosophical Discourse of Modernity: Twelve Lectures*, trans. Frederick Lawrence, Cambridge: Polity Press, 1987 [1985], pp. 14–15.
21 The best account of how campaigns for justice in the present might be inspired by a preoccupation with injustices perpetrated in the past in a postcolonial

context is Neil Lazarus's 'Before the Dogcatcher's Van: History and Subjectivity in Francis Barker', *Textual Practice*, 15:3 (2001), 431–446.
22 W.B. Yeats, 'Cathleen ni Houlihan', *Selected Plays*, ed. Richard Allen Cave, Harmondsworth: Penguin, 1997, pp. 19–29. See Lawrence McBride, *Images, Icons and the Irish Nationalist Imagination*, Dublin: Four Courts, 1999.
23 Eavan Boland, *Object Lessons: The Life of the Woman and the Poet in Our Time*, Manchester: Carcanet, 1995, p. 136.
24 Ibid., p. 148.
25 Jacqueline Rose, *The Last Resistance*, London: Verso, 2007, p. 144.
26 Fredric Jameson, *The Political Unconscious: Narrative as a Socially Symbolic Act*, London: Routledge, 2002 [1981], p. 88.
27 Sir Philip Sidney, *An Apology for Poetry, or, The Defence of Poesy*, ed. Geoffrey Shepherd, Manchester: Manchester University Press, 1973, p. 123.
28 Derek Walcott, *White Egrets*, London: Faber & Faber, 2010, p. 47.
29 A stringent critique of the current critical preoccupation with lateness and late style can be found in Gordon McMullan and Sam Smiles, 'Introduction: Late Style and its Discontents', *Late Style and its Discontents: Essays in Art, Literature, and Music*, ed. Gordon McMullan and Sam Smiles, Oxford: Oxford University Press, 2016, pp. 1–12; and Gordon McMullan, *Shakespeare and the Idea of Late Writing: Authorship in the Proximity of Death*, Cambridge: Cambridge University Press, 2007. For McMullan and Smiles, the preoccupation with artists' late styles is a form of biographical criticism hostile to the materialist, in particular historicist and feminist, approaches that prefer to trace the connections between a work of art and its wider social and historical contexts.
30 Walcott, *White Egrets*, p. 12.
31 Enrique Dussel, 'Beyond Eurocentrism: The World-System and the Limits of Modernity', *Cultures of Globalization*, ed. Fredric Jameson and Masao Miyoshi, Durham, NC: Duke University Press, 1998, pp. 3–31, p. 12.
32 Ibid., p. 21.
33 Walcott, *White Egrets*, p. 20.
34 Ibid., p. 3.
35 An earlier version of this reading of *White Egrets*, in the context of discussions of 'late work' and 'late life creativity', can be found in Robert Spencer, 'An 'old man in the dimming world': Theodor Adorno, Derek Walcott and a defence of the idea of late style', *Creativity in Later Life: Beyond Late Style*, ed. David Amigoni and Gordon McMullan, London: Routledge, 2018, pp. 77–99.
36 See Robert Spencer, *Cosmopolitan Criticism and Postcolonial Literature*, London: Palgrave, 2011, pp. 60–103.
37 Walcott, *White Egrets*, p. 43.
38 *King Lear*, III.2.2.
39 *King Lear*, III.4.28–34.
40 Walcott, *White Egrets*, p. 8.
41 Ibid., p. 8.

42 Ibid., p. 8.
43 Ibid.
44 Ibid., p. 9.

45 W.H. Auden, 'In Memory of W.B. Yeats', *The English Auden: Poems, Essays, and Dramatic Writing, 1927–1939*, ed. Edward Mendelson, London: Faber & Faber, 1977, p. 243.
46 Walcott, *White Egrets*, p. 11.
47 Ibid., p. 37.
48 Ibid., p. 38.
49 Ibid., p. 87.
50 Derek Walcott, *Omeros*, London: Faber & Faber, 1990, p. 289.
51 Anthony Carrigan, *Postcolonial Tourism: Literature, Culture and Environment*, London: Routledge, 2011, p. 54.
52 David Lean, *Lawrence of Arabia*, 1962.
53 James Russell, *The Historical Epic and Contemporary Hollywood: From Dances with Wolves to Gladiator*, London: Continuum, 2007, p. 10, emphasis in original. Russell is quoting Bruce Babington and Peter William Evans, *Biblical Epics: Sacred Narratives in the Hollywood Cinema*, Manchester: Manchester University Press, 1993, p. 4.
54 Graham Dawson, 'A Lament for Imperial Adventure: *Lawrence of Arabia* in the Post-Colonial World', in *Kunapipi*, 18:1 (1996), 98–112, 100.
55 Ibid., p. 105.
56 It is interesting to note that *Lawrence of Arabia* does not feature in Chahine's documentary *Reel Bad Arabs* or in Jackie Reem Salloun's *Planet of the Arabs*. These are both revealing documentaries on the negative and largely stereotypical representations of Muslims and Arabs in cinema.
57 Dawson, 'A Lament for Imperial Adventure', pp. 102–103.
58 Ibid., p. 110.
59 Nikita Lalwani, *Gifted*, London: Viking Press, 2007.
60 Salman Rushdie, *Imaginary Homelands: Essays and Criticism: 1981–1991*. London: Granta, 1992.
61 Neil Ten Kortenaar, *Self, Nation, Text in Salman Rushdie's 'Midnight's Children'*, Montreal: McGill-Queen's University Press, 2005, p. 46.
62 Lalwani, *Gifted*, p. 12.
63 Ibid., p. 10.
64 Ibid., p. 11.
65 Lalwani, *Gifted*, p. 62.
66 Ibid., p. 65.
67 Ibid., p. 70.
68 Ibid., p. 71.
69 Ibid.
70 On 17 October 2019, *The Guardian* reported that 'Manchester city council urged to reject statue of 'anti-black racist' Gandhi'. The Decolonise Network at The University of Manchester had recommended this rejection based on scholarly work undertaken of Gandhi's time working in South Africa early in his career. This was countered by comments from Mission Dharampur, who gave the statue to Manchester city council, who were themselves concerned that the Decolonise Network campaign would diminish Gandhi's legacy.
71 Linda Tuhiwai Smith, *Decolonising Methodologies: Research and Indigenous Peoples*, London: Zed Books, 1999, p. 39.
72 Ibid., p. 33.

73 Therese Davis, 'Remembering our Ancestors: Cross-cultural Collaboration and the Mediation of Aboriginal Culture and History in *Ten Canoes*', in *Studies in Australasian Cinema*, 1:1 (2007), 5–14, 6.
74 Ibid., 6.
75 Tuhiwai Smith, *Decolonising Methodologies*, p. 30.
76 Ibid., pp. 30–31.
77 Lyn McCredden, '*Ten Canoes*: Engaging Difference', in *Studies in Australasian Cinema*, 6:1 (2012), 45–56, 48.
78 Ibid., p. 49.
79 Cornelius Martin Renes, 'Reel Indigeneity: *Ten Canoes* and its Chronotopical Politics of Ab/Originality', in *Continuum: Journal of Media and Cultural Studies*, (2014), 28:6, 850–861, 852.
80 Ibid., p. 860.
81 Tuhiwai Smith, *Decolonising Methodologies*, p. 31.
82 Priyamvada Gopal, *Insurgent Empire: Anticolonial Resistance and British Dissent*, London: Verso, 2019.
83 Djebar, *Fantasia*, p. 204.

Bibliography

Auden, W.H., 'In Memory of W.B. Yeats', *The English Auden: Poems, Essays, and Dramatic Writing, 1927–1939*, ed. Edward Mendelson, London: Faber & Faber, 1977.
Benjamin, W., *The Arcades Project*, trans. Howard Eiland and Kevin McLaughlin, ed. Rolf Tiedemann, Cambridge, MA: Harvard University Press, 2002.
Boland, E., *Object Lessons: The Life of the Woman and the Poet in Our Time*, Manchester: Carcanet, 1995.
Boland, E., *New Collected Poems*, Manchester: Carcanet, 2005.
Carrigan, A., *Postcolonial Tourism: Literature, Culture and Environment*, London: Routledge, 2011.
Coetzee, J.M., *Foe*, Harmondsworth: Penguin, 1987.
Coetzee, J.M., *Elizabeth Costello: Eight Lessons*, London: QPD, 2003.
Davis, T., 'Remembering our Ancestors: Cross-cultural Collaboration and the Mediation of Aboriginal Culture and History in Ten Canoes', *Studies in Australasian Cinema*, 1:1 (2007), 5–14.
Dawson, G., 'A Lament for Imperial Adventure: Lawrence of Arabia in the Post-Colonial World', *Kunapipi*, 18:1 (1996), 98–112.
Djebar, A., *Fantasia: An Algerian Cavalcade*, trans. Dorothy S. Blair, Portsmouth: Heinemann, 1993 [1985].
Dussel, E., 'Beyond Eurocentrism: The World-System and the Limits of Modernity', in Fredric Jameson and Masao Miyoshi (eds), *Cultures of Globalization*, Durham, NC: Duke University Press, 1998, pp. 3–31.
Eagleton, T., *Figures of Dissent: Critical Essays on Fish, Spivak, Žižek and Others*, London: Verso, 2003, pp. 158–167.
Gopal, P., *Insurgent Empire: Anticolonial Resistance and British Dissent*, London: Verso, 2019.

Habermas, J., *The Philosophical Discourse of Modernity: Twelve Lectures*, trans. Frederick Lawrence, Cambridge: Polity Press, 1987 [1985].
Heaney, S., *Preoccupations: Selected Prose, 1968–78*, London: Faber & Faber, 1980.
Jameson, F., *The Political Unconscious: Narrative as a Socially Symbolic Act*, London: Routledge, 2002 [1981].
Kortenaar, N.T., *Self, Nation, Text in Salman Rushdie's 'Midnight's Children'*, Montreal: McGill-Queen's University Press, 2005.
Kundera, M., *The Book of Laughter and Forgetting*, trans. Aaron Asher, London: Faber & Faber, 1996 [1979].
Lazarus, N., 'Before the Dogcatcher's Van: History and Subjectivity in Francis Barker', *Textual Practice*, 15:3 (2001), 431–446.
Lazarus, N., *The Postcolonial Unconscious*, Cambridge: Cambridge University Press, 2011.
McCredden, L., 'Ten Canoes: Engaging Difference', *Studies in Australasian Cinema*, 6:1 (2012), 45–56.
McMullan, G., *Shakespeare and the Idea of Late Writing: Authorship in the Proximity of Death*, Cambridge: Cambridge University Press, 2007.
McMullan, G. and Smiles, S., 'Introduction: Late Style and its Discontents', in Gordon McMullan and Sam Smiles (eds), *Late Style and its Discontents: Essays in Art, Literature, and Music*, Oxford: Oxford University Press, 2016, pp. 1–12.
Medovoi, L., Raman, S. and Robinson, B., 'Can the Subaltern Vote?', *Socialist Review*, 20.3 (1990), 133–149.
Neruda, P., *Canto General*, trans. Jack Schmitt, Berkeley, CA: University of California Press, 1991 [1950].
Parry, B., 'Directions and Dead Ends in Postcolonial Studies', in David Theo Goldberg and Ato Quayson (eds), *Relocating Postcolonialism*, Oxford: Blackwell, 2002, pp. 66–81.
Parry, B., *Postcolonial Studies: A Materialist Critique*, London: Routledge, 2004.
Renes, C.M., 'Reel Indigeneity: Ten Canoes and its Chronotopical Politics of Ab/Originality', *Continuum: Journal of Media and Cultural Studies*, 28:6 (2014), 850–861.
Rose, J., *The Last Resistance*, London: Verso, 2007.
Rushdie, S., *Imaginary Homelands: Essays and Criticism: 1981–1991*. London: Granta, 1992.
Russell, J., *The Historical Epic and Contemporary Hollywood: From Dances with Wolves to Gladiator*, London: Continuum, 2007.
Sidney, Sir P., *An Apology for Poetry, or, The Defence of Poesy*, ed. Geoffrey Shepherd, Manchester: Manchester University Press, 1973.
Smith, L.T., *Decolonising Methodologies: Research and Indigenous Peoples*, London: Zed Books, 1999.
Spencer, R., *Cosmopolitan Criticism and Postcolonial Literature*, London: Palgrave, 2011.
Spivak, G.C., 'Can the Subaltern Speak?', in Cary Nelsen and Lawrence Grossberg (eds), *Marxism and the Interpretation of Culture*, London: Macmillan, 1988, pp. 271–313.

Spivak, G.C. *The Postcolonial Critic: Interviews, Strategies, Dialogues*, ed. Sarah Harasym, New York and London: Routledge, 1990.

Spivak, G.C., 'Theory in the Margin: Coetzee's *Foe* Reading Defoe's Crusoe/Roxana', in Jonathan Arac and Barbara Johnson (eds), *Consequences of Theory*, Baltimore, MD: Johns Hopkins UP, 1991, pp. 154–180.

Spivak, G.C., *A Critique of Postcolonial Reason: Toward a History of the Vanishing Present*, Cambridge, MA: Harvard University Press, 1999.

Walcott, D., *Omeros*, London: Faber & Faber, 1990.

Walcott, D., *White Egrets*, London: Faber & Faber, 2010.

Yeats, W.B., Cathleen ni Houlihan', *Selected Plays*, ed. Richard Allen Cave, Harmondsworth: Penguin, 1997, pp. 19–29.

Films

Gandhi, dir. Richard Attenborough, 1982.
Lawrence of Arabia, dir. David Lean, 1962.
Ten Canoes, dir. Rolf de Heer, 2007.

CONCLUSION

We have sought to get across in these pages the sheer range and multiplicity of postcolonial literatures as well as some sense of the various critical and theoretical tools required to get to grips with them. The aim, as we explained in the Introduction, was not just to show that texts composed in contexts that were or are enduring colonial occupation and exploitation have extremely varied forms, themes and styles. That much, we hope, has become obvious; writers and other artists dramatise their situations and perspectives in an impressive variety of ways. Postcolonial culture is 'incorrigibly plural', to use Louis MacNeice's pleasing phrase. There is a hint in that adverb of the defiance of prescriptive or normative modes. MacNeice's poem insists: 'World is crazier and more of it than we think.'[1] But, as we began by saying, we also want to highlight certain common denominators that all of these writers and works share; the most obvious of these is the overbearing and persistent as well as odious fact of colonial power itself. We wanted to read postcolonial texts in order to show what makes them singular and interesting as well as provide some terms and themes to help explain what they have in common. For us, as we made clear in the Introduction, the Warwick Research Collective's book *Combined and Uneven Development: Towards a New Theory of World-Literature* has most convincingly combined a sense of the enormous variety of postcolonial writing, disclosed through sensitive close readings, with a veritably Olympian view of what makes these texts comparable and therefore categorisable. The category they use is not *postcolonial* literature but *world* literature. World literature, for WReC, is the literature of capitalist modernity. In conclusion, we want to redress this balance a little and stress the enduring importance of the 'postcolonial', a term to which we remain stubbornly attached.

WReC want to find a more rigorous way of conceptualising world literature, a term that in recent years has begun challenging 'postcolonial literature' for prominence and disciplinary prestige in the Anglo-American academy; one is now just as (if not more) likely to find courses, degree programmes, conferences, studentships and academic jobs advertised in *world* literature as in *postcolonial* literature. WReC complain that many

CONCLUSION

invocations of world literature struggle to explain convincingly what it is that the 'world' in world literature refers to. Is it 'globalisation', which is actually a pretty nebulous term, even a kind of euphemism or alibi for the much more complex and rapacious process of capitalist expansion? Or does the term simply refer to non-European and US literatures, a seemingly innocuous designation but one that erroneously implies that Europe and the US and their literatures are somehow exceptional and normative and that therefore relegates all other literatures to a subordinate and ghettoised status? WReC are understandably dissatisfied with vague categories such as 'globalisation' and 'the West'. Nor are they particularly attached to 'the world', understood abstractly as the site of an incomprehensible heterogeneity of writers and texts. They see world literature instead as that vast body of texts of all kinds that, in the last two centuries or so, has registered the homogenising and assimilative but also immensely divisive (in a phrase, combined and uneven) process of capitalist 'modernisation'.

But what even is capitalism? Marxists understand it as an intrinsically *unequal* social and economic system that separates workers from the means of production and from the products of their labour. It is, moreover, an *expansive* system that spreads its net ever more widely over the globe in conformity to the overwhelming compulsion to accumulate capital. It is also an *imperialist* system, therefore, with undemocratic and frequently authoritarian regimes presiding over the extraction and export of primary commodities, the opening up of new markets, the exploitation of cheap labour and so on. The term 'capitalism' is more and more prominent in a discipline that is increasingly willing to identify as materialist. The oppressive realities inflicted by this system are becoming for us, in Fredric Jameson's phrase, 'the absolute horizon of all reading and all interpretation'.[2] Instead of 'perpetually looking back to Western European high imperialism', postcolonial studies is now busy, to use Sharae Deckard's words, theorising 'new imperial formations and geographies' and 're-establishing capitalism as the primary horizon of its analysis'.[3] Where once students worried about 'the other' and about cultural ambivalence, now they write essays and doctoral theses on the 'world-system', 'petrofictions' and the death of neoliberalism! But we want to stress, with the late Italian political economist Giovanni Arrighi, the close relationship between 'capitalist' and 'territorialist' 'modes of rule or logics of power', the interconnections between the control and accumulation of capital and the control and expansion of territory.[4] Imperialism is entailed and even necessitated by the accumulative logic of capitalism but it is not reducible to it or identical with it. It has thus given rise to a distinctive body of texts, which we call postcolonial literature. We think a particular discipline (postcolonial studies) is required in order to examine those texts.[5]

The truth is that we are both rather attached to that term in our work as critics and as teachers. It emphasises something that the world literature approach, even one as rigorous and salutary as WReC's, is in danger of sidelining, that is, the especially grievous form of violence and exploitation that is colonialism. Nowadays, texts like those analysed in *Postcolonial Locations* are often studied under the rubric of world literatures, understood catholically but vaguely and tautologically as the literature of the world. Seeing world literature as the literature of 'the modern capitalist world-system',[6] à la WReC, is much more exact. But even this bald formulation, which has the great merit of explaining in broad terms what world literature at a deep level is about, leaves implicit something that WReC would presumably acknowledge but that we wish to make explicit, that is, the inseparability of capitalism from imperialism and of postcolonial writing from both these vital, conjoined phenomena. Imperialism is capitalism's most atrocious and exceptional manifestation. It is the specific focus of postcolonial texts, what we called in our Introduction a historical experience or project: the multifaceted and so far unfinished efforts of peoples to free themselves from colonial rule. Elleke Boehmer offers a succinct account of what postcolonial literature is and of what the discipline of postcolonial studies is for:

> Rather than simply being the writing which 'came after' empire, *postcolonial* literature is generally defined as that which critically or subversively scrutinizes the colonial relationship. It is writing that sets out in one way or another to resist colonialist perspectives. As well as a change in power, decolonization demanded – and still demands – symbolic overhaul, a reshaping of dominant meanings. Postcolonial literature performs part of that process of overhaul.[7]

That will suffice as a definition of the specific concerns of postcolonial writing and of postcolonial studies. We wish to hold fast to the insights and potentials contained in subaltern and indigenous epistemologies, to the traditions and horizons of anti-imperialist struggle and to the distinctive forms and preoccupations of postcolonial writing. We'd like to stick with postcolonial literature, seen as complementary rather than opposed to world literature since the term emphasises the greater preoccupation of some texts with the specific logics and effects of imperialist power relations.

Perhaps we can make this point about the need for a particular category to describe texts about imperialism in another way by saying that while it would obviously make sense to describe a novel like Ngũgĩ wa Thiong'o's *Devil on the Cross* (1980) as both world literature and postcolonial literature, it would make no sense whatsoever to describe, say, the oeuvre of Ian McEwan as postcolonial literature. This is not a facetious comparison we hope, for it touches on the need for a host of more precise categories or, if you like, sub-categories to accompany the necessarily more inexact and all-encompassing descriptor of 'world literature'. The great thing about categories, in other words, is that you can have more than one of them! *Devil on the Cross* narrates the fabulous or, let's say, magic realist tale (with equal emphases on magic and intense realism) of a young rural Kenyan woman, Warĩĩnga, who gains knowledge about her country's ostensible, but in fact arrested and incomplete, decolonisation under the rule of a grotesquely venal ruling class in cahoots with the nation's former rulers and, ultimately, with the archfiend of global capitalism. Written both in the lingua franca of English, but initially in Gĩkũyũ for the purposes of wide circulation among Kenya's largest language community, *Devil on the Cross* was composed during Ngũgĩ's own incarceration in Kamiti Maximum Security Prison in the last months of the Kenyatta regime, a fact which is itself graphic testament to the oppressive continuities in that country's postcolonial or rather neo-colonial history. Warĩĩnga's uncompromising conclusion as well as, hopefully for Ngũgĩ, the novel's readers', is that the expedient alliance between postcolonial Kenya's dictatorial state and the foreign bourgeoisies that have not ceased to plunder its people and resources should be overthrown by militant political and even guerrilla action. This is, therefore, a text that is about capitalist modernity in its grievous and frustratingly durable colonial or neo-colonial phase: world literature, in other words, or literature about capitalism, but also postcolonial literature, that is, literature about imperialism, to put the matter very bluntly; the second category is perhaps a kind of vital sub-category of the former.

Suffice to say, McEwan's *Saturday* (2005) is a very different kind of book. If *Devil on the Cross*'s most memorable and concluding image is of a former office secretary removing a pistol from her handbag to slay the venal 'Rich Old Man'[8] who raped her, then *Saturday*'s is of a know-it-all brain surgeon mansplaining his support for the invasion of Iraq while perched at a kitchen island in his Fitzrovia townhouse. McEwan's work is presumably world literature in a sense, whatever its restricted and even parochial focus, but surely not postcolonial literature. What do we mean by that? Well, his fiction is obviously fraught with the background of capitalist modernity in its revanchist neoliberal phase or, more specifically, with neoliberalism in the shape of its peculiarly brazen and welcome-outstaying British avatar. Particularly in earlier novels like *The Cement Garden* (1978) and *The Comfort of Strangers* (1981) rather than in the later bandwagon-jumping issue novels like *Solar* (2010), which raises some laughs about climate change, and *Machines Like Me* (2019), which looks at the implications of artificial intelligence, McEwan's fiction's defining theme is the sadistic violence that often underlies social and especially sexual relations. It is never entirely clear whether his characters' unnerving capacity for jealousy, insecurity, cruelty and domination result from (laboriously and conspicuously researched) medical conditions or from some much more deep-rooted and consequential social pathologies, themselves resulting perhaps in part from the 'class war conservatism' of Thatcherism with which McEwan's oeuvre is almost exactly contemporaneous.

CONCLUSION

It's certainly true that McEwan's one plot, in which something shocking happens to a middle-class person about a third of the way in, focuses readers' attention on class distinctions and on the apparent vulnerability of, say, *Saturday*'s sheltered milieu of kitchen islands and drives to morning squash matches to the dimly understood noises off of violence, resentment and militant protest. One of the most interesting questions about McEwan's work, perhaps the only interesting question about it, is whether this bourgeois world is being presented ironically and whether readers are, thus, being subtly encouraged to establish a critical distance from it. When Henry Perowne's daughter reads a poem by Matthew Arnold to placate the genetic-throwback Caliban figure of Baxter who has invaded their home, are we awed by the power of aesthetic experience to soothe the savage beast or appalled by a crudely stereotypical portrait of the angry prole? Are we exasperated by the novel's apparent faith in the power of the literary imagination to fend off these rude challenges to bourgeois complacency?

There are no doubt different answers to these questions. But our point, finally, is that however one answers them, the question of which category McEwan's work does *not* belong to is very clear. It demonstrates the need for precise sub-categories within the overall category of world literature, an obvious point perhaps, but one that needs restating if we are to defend and justify the specific focus of the discipline of postcolonial literary criticism. McEwan writes modern or contemporary British fiction, Booker Prize catnip, or the contemporary British grotesque, to invoke Robert Duggan's more generous verdict.[9] One might as well group such works under the general heading of 'world literature', since their subject (however one interprets their attitude to it) is clearly the nature of class relations in a highly, if unevenly and probably overly, developed state in the capitalist world-system. But one could not and obviously must not call these novels postcolonial literature since they have virtually no interest in empire, except to view it, as it were, from the wrong end of the telescope: in the distance, such as when in *Saturday* our protagonist explains his support for the US invasion of Iraq, a position which (since this is a novel) is openly debatable and delicately inflected with irony but which is clearly a matter for the novel and for McEwan's oeuvre of subordinate rather than primary importance. 'For all the discerning talk, it's the close at hand, the visible that exerts the overpowering force. And what you don't see...'[10] What we call postcolonial literature flourishes in these ellipses, that vast zone of modern history and human experience that is empire and its manifold ramifications. A writer like McEwan does not see this world and so only hints at its existence but it is clearly very different as well as much more interesting and important than the goings on of 'gentle Marylebone'.

So by *postcolonial literature* we mean those texts that are closely rather than incidentally or distantly concerned with colonial power in either its classical or contemporary manifestations. That is not to say that texts written in and about, for example, Britain, can't be described as postcolonial: *Disappearance* is one, as we tried to show, since its overwhelming focus is on the vital historical and contemporary connections between that country and its colonies and ex-colonies. Nor are we saying that texts composed on these shores don't address empire often in very explicit and intriguing and even critical ways. We're convinced, for example, by arguments in new modernist studies (or global modernisms) that the sometimes distant and confusing but also essential and often insurgent, realities of empire, particularly in the late period of British colonialism, were an important catalyst of formal and stylistic experimentation in British and Irish modernism.[11] We are thinking here of works like Virginia Woolf's *Mrs Dalloway* (1923) and *Between the Acts* (1941), Joseph Conrad's short as well as longer fiction and Katherine Mansfield's stories. Then there is D.H. Lawrence's attempt in *The Rainbow* and *Women in Love* to find new forms and ways of using language to convey the dissolution of character and established social forms in the nineteenth and the first decades of the twentieth centuries (particularly for working-class women) under the combined pressures of war, the modern state, colonialism, monopoly and the confusing but also electrifying prospect of new forms of passionate human relationship. There's Lewis Grassic Gibbon's formally and linguistically audacious portrait in his *A Scots Quair* trilogy of Scotland's towns and country in the same period, buffeted by similar processes of migration, colonial collusion and conquest, military upheaval and revolutionary class politics. But empire is not the principal focus of these texts, even when, like *Mrs Dalloway*, they seek critically to signal suggestive links between empire and the authoritarian power of the state, patriarchal norms, class hierarchies, even the depredations of psychiatry, the aftershocks of the Great War and so on. Postcolonial writing, in our view, is distinguished, in both senses of that word, by its distinctive focus on empire in all its manifestations. We would not like to see the discipline sacrifice this specific emphasis to an extremely salutary but more general and eclectic approach to world literatures.

All of the texts we have read in the preceding chapters were concerned with this uniquely heinous and exceptional form of violence and exploitation, whether they were immediately preoccupied with land and space, mobility, memory and the past or with the prospects of reconciliation. It goes without saying that there is a lot we haven't covered. Among the things we have not found space to address in depth are colonial literature, sexuality, disability and crime fiction. Another area we have not yet covered directly but which we would like to end by discussing is the crucial preoccupation of many postcolonial texts with global warming in the present and (perhaps more surprisingly but crucially, as we will try to show) in the past. For some time, this has been a key feature or common denominator of world and especially postcolonial literatures and we'd like to give some sense of the different ways in which this overwhelmingly important new reality is explored by postcolonial texts. Our point here is that it would be a mistake to demand or await or even try to write the definitive postcolonial novel about climate change. There is no need. Nobody has ever written the definitive novel about mobility or the colonisation of land either, to cite two of our examples of salient themes of postcolonial writing. That is because, in fact, these issues baulk so massively and so insistently for writers that they insinuate themselves into postcolonial texts more or less constantly and in a pleasing and instructive variety of ways. These are the two points we want to emphasise in this conclusion: postcolonial literary criticism exists to study writing about empire (which now includes writing about climate change) and, as ever, there is more than one way of writing about these questions.

We see climate change as a manifestation of imperialism. It affects us all of course, already or in due course. The disgusting wealth of Wall Street won't save New York from being inundated by the Atlantic Ocean. Reinforced basements on private islands will provide minimal shelter for billionaires from the super-hurricanes that now regularly scour the heated-up Caribbean Sea. But the warming of the world is also a colonial issue. Those who have done least to cause it and those who have benefited least from the wealth created by burning fossil fuels are suffering the most from melting glaciers, inundated coasts, arid farmland, depleted aquifers, floods, forest fires and catastrophic storms. 'We may all be in the same boat when it comes to climate change, but most of us are in steerage.'[12] Half of the world's carbon emissions are produced by the richest 10 per cent while the poorest 3.5 billion make up a mere tenth. Twenty firms are responsible for more than a third of greenhouse gas emissions since 1965, which also means, incidentally, that a sensible first step for any strategy of mitigation would be the immediate expropriation of all of them. What Joan-Martinez Alier calls the 'environmentalism of the poor'[13] now includes not just the resistance of indigenous peoples to the enclosure and exploitation of their land, or even aspirations for sustainable livelihoods but a demand for the preservation from total degradation of the natural systems on which the Earth's poorest people precariously depend.

We would like to sketch an answer to Amitav Ghosh's question about how novels and novelists might respond to our warming world. In doing so, we will keep in mind T.S. Eliot's unanswerable rebuke to the philosopher I.A. Richards' remark that poetry 'is capable of saving us': 'it is like saying that the wallpaper will save us when the walls have crumbled'.[14] Literary texts will not save us from global warming: radical political action will. But what role can we expect postcolonial texts to play in this struggle? Ghosh begins *The Great Derangement* (2016), his important study of how climate change might be made culturally and politically 'thinkable', by expressing his puzzlement that 'climate change casts a much smaller shadow within the landscape of literary fiction than it does even in the public arena'.[15]

Climate change, he argues, constitutes 'a crisis of culture, and thus of the imagination' (GD, 9), which is why he thinks 'serious fiction' has effectively pushed it away and declined to examine its implications. The novel form itself, he argues, which is a product of the era of individualism and fossil fuel consumption, is simply not set up to deal with these large-scale and even existential questions.

We think that Ghosh is demonstrably wrong about that. He claims that it's extremely hard for novelists to make contemporary weather events believable (GD, 26), even though portraying unfamiliar events and their human repercussions as well as the large-scale processes behind them is the very definition of the task of the realist novel. Ghosh's claim that until now 'the deliberately prosaic world of serious prose fiction' (GD, 26) (a formulation ripe for interrogation if ever there was one) has avoided the sheer strangeness of climate change and species extinction, is wrong on another count: postcolonial texts of all kinds, whether realist, non-realist, anti-realist, magic realist or 'irrealist', have been conspicuously drawn to the uncanny 'presence and proximity of nonhuman interlocutors' (GD, 30) as the works of Mahasweta Devi, Wole Soyinka, Zakes Mda, Ben Okri, Wilson Harris, J.M. Coetzee, Ngũgĩ wa Thiong'o, Alexis Wright, Ahmadou Kourouma, Louise Erdrich, Witi Ihamaera, Shahrnush Parsipur, Peter Carey, Chinua Achebe or indeed Ghosh himself in *The Hungry Tide*, to cite only a bare list of names almost off the tops of our heads, should make immediately and abundantly clear.[16] We believe that many of those names, plus writers like Margaret Atwood, Doris Lessing, Paolo Bacigalupi, Kim Stanley Robinson, Annie Proulx, Kathleen Jamie, Jiang Rong, W.G. Sebald, Alice Oswald and Les Murray, are constructing a burgeoning as well as a formally and generically diverse world literature of the climate crisis.

Ghosh is surely right that the scale of the political and cultural challenges posed by climate change are truly massive, as is the fully global extent of this transformation in addition to the extremely *longue durée* of the era of fossil fuel consumption that has brought us to this emergency. But there is no reason to think that novels cannot portray these things, not least because they have long been doing so, though not necessarily in the ways envisaged by Ghosh. The novel is a curiously protean and adaptable form. The eighteenth- and nineteenth-century epics of bourgeois individualism are among its greatest achievements, but it has also shown itself well suited to the depiction of collective resistance to the depredations of fossil fuel economies. It is sufficient here to cite two examples mentioned by Ghosh himself and frequently invoked elsewhere in discussions of 'petrofictions', fossil fuel literature and the 'energy humanities':[17] namely, Émile Zola's *Germinal* (1885), with its portrayal of striking miners exploiting their power to disrupt coal's extraction and distribution, as well as Abdelrahman Munif's incomparable *Cities of Salt* quintet (1984–1989), with its detailed fictional chronicle of the establishment and consolidation of the colonial oil economy in Saudi Arabia and the Gulf monarchies.[18] Suffice to say, nothing could persuade us of Ghosh's belief that global warming is in any way 'resistant to the arts' (*GD*, 73). Ghosh himself adduces enough evidence to disprove that claim.

Where is the climate change novel, Ghosh pleads? But that makes as little sense as asking, where is the novel of capitalism or the novel about patriarchy? There are numerous works about climate change but there is no climate change novel. We suspect that the misguided bagginess and undisguised evangelism of Ghosh's own attempt at writing a climate change novel, 2019's *Gun Island*, are the unfortunate result of his unfounded worries about the resistance of the arts, in this case postcolonial literature, to global warming. *Gun Island* tries to compensate for all the mistakes and omissions Ghosh wrongly attributes to 'serious fiction'. It tries to show us every effect of anthropogenic planetary heating from catastrophic cyclones to deforestation to raging fires to species extinction to climate refugees to rising sea levels exemplified by the steady sinking of Venice and the inundation of the Sundarbans, the cluster of low-lying mangrove-forested islands in the Bay of Bengal. And it wants to *do* everything, not only to describe global warming's consequences but anticipate the alternatives and foretell the solutions. *Gun Island* wants, moreover, to *be* everything, to encompass and sublate all genres in one all-seeing super-genre (the climate change novel or perhaps *the* climate change novel) that is part globe-trotting thriller, part detective yarn, part didactic trove of facts about contemporary ecocide, part giant realist chronicle and part magic realist fable. Our view is that, by trying to do too much, Ghosh's novel ends up failing to satisfy any of the expectations incited by these various genres.

As Deen, our oddly passive narrator, is sent about the planet in business class from Los Angeles to Calcutta to Venice and the Mediterranean in a breathless effort to interpret the cryptic symbols inscribed on the walls of a remote shrine, *Gun Island* resembles nothing so much as *The Da Vinci Code*, only with more dolphins and less of the professor of symbology's commitment to the chase or, for that matter, of Dan Brown's wholehearted commitment to the genre. Nor does the novel quite have the courage of its realist convictions. Deen narrowly escapes some falling masonry on his first day interviewing refugees in Venice (though he usually works as an antiquarian book seller in Brooklyn) only to discover that the apologetic culprit is the young fisherman who previously lived by the now swamped shrine in the endangered Sundarbans and who is now making a precarious living as an immigrant construction worker! The reader's willing suspension of disbelief is itself about to come crashing down under the weight of the contrivances and coincidences that result from the novelist's greedy wish to add climate refugees to his all-inclusive portrait of the warming world. Not even the novel's magic realist convictions are sustained for long. *Gun Island* intriguingly hints at the antidote to planetary apocalypse in a kind of enlarged solidarity or affection between humans and between humans and the rest of the living world. But when, in the concluding scene, the rickety craft carrying migrants in the Mediterranean is surrounded by clouds of circling birds and hosts of benevolent dolphins bent on protecting it from a rival vessel full of racist thugs they (the birds, the dolphins and the thugs) soon disappear; it's not divine intervention or some mysterious supernatural or zoomorphic agency that delivers the migrants but the more prosaic and preachy device of a big-hearted Italian naval officer.

Ghosh tries to do everything because he wrongly believes that 'serious fiction' has so far done nothing. He seems to want in *Gun Island* to detail the effects of climate change and indicate its fully global scope. But is the novel form best suited to providing information? Much of *Gun Island* reads like a series of very thorough Wikipedia entries. '"What's a fish kill?"' Deen asks Piya at one point.[19] Well Deen, take a guess! But this isn't really dialogue of course; it is a chance for the marine biologist to explain to readers the causes of oceanic dead zones and the vulnerability of Gangetic river dolphins to discharges of chemical effluents. Interesting and extremely important stuff, of course, but a novel is probably not the best way to get this info across.

We might recall here the German Marxist critic Theodor Adorno's bracing polemic, in his 1962 essay on 'Commitment', against works that are radical mainly at the level of their content. They are in danger of simplifying the complex realities they seek to make digestible in information and images, and of patronising and disempowering readers whom they interpellate as essentially passive recipients of a message.[20] The problem with providing information is that a novel can rarely provide enough. The result, inevitably, is simplification. Adorno's example is Bertolt Brecht's 1941 play *The Resistible Rise of Arturo Ui* in which Hitler's rise to power is explored via the allegory of a Chicago mobster eliminating his opponents in order to secure control of a cauliflower racket. The play, Adorno contends, flattens out the complex social and economic origins of fascism, so that fascism appears not as the product of some of the deepest and most disturbing trends in a social and economic system (colonial expansionism and racism, the steady concentration of power in the hands of the state and large monopolies, the scapegoating of Jews for Germany's defeat in the First World War and its subsequent economic collapse, and so on) but the accidental outcome of decisions taken by unscrupulous men. The play inadvertently discourages serious thought and political organisation by giving us easy answers and easy solutions. Whatever the justice of Adorno's critique of Brecht, we wonder if it is true of Ghosh's novel; it tells us things but not enough and the result is simplification. *Gun Island* bemoans inhumanity and calls for love but it barely touches on the origins of global warming in what Andreas Malm calls 'the fossil economy', a system 'of self-sustaining growth predicated on the growing consumption of fossil fuels, and therefore generating a sustained growth in emissions of carbon dioxide'.[21] Unlike Adorno, we have no particular objection to didactic texts, not least because in this study we are celebrating the diversity of forms of postcolonial writing, though half-hearted didactic writing seems to us to make over the novel form into a poor imitation of the online encyclopaedia.

Ghosh's hotchpotch of different genres fails to provide the specific kinds of satisfaction and instruction to be gained from each one. This didactic novel is not quite didactic enough to accurately explain global warming and species extinction rather than just tell us stuff about them. It isn't sufficiently magic realist to give actual voice and agency to its intriguingly sentient dolphins, who are given a frustratingly brief walk-on (or swim-on) part. Nor does it identify the mysterious supernatural agency (the almighty? the Earth itself? the Gaia hypothesis? Giacinta's dead daughter? some dolphins?) that appears to be directing Deen's expeditions. Nor is it realist enough to leave its timorous protagonist behind and really give an exhaustive picture of the fossil fuel economy and its murderous effects. Nor, finally, is *Gun Island* enough of a conspiracy thriller or a detective novel to do what Fredric Jameson finds in the most radical examples of that genre. Deen gradually tracks the prophetic peregrinations of a figure from Bengali legend, the Gun Merchant, but they don't lead him as far as the headquarters of BP and Exxon Mobil or incriminate whoever it is that's dumping untreated waste and industrial contaminants into the tributaries of the Ganges. So this detective yarn is not a medium of 'cognitive mapping' whereby a crime such as the poisoning of rivers or the inundation of the Sundarbans 'becomes the occasion for the indictment of a whole collectivity'[22] or mode of social and economic organisation. *Gun Island* withholds the different forms of pleasure and instruction provided by each of the various genres that it impatiently shuttles between.

Luckily there are, contrary to what Ghosh alleges, plenty of 'traces and portents' (*GD*, 11) of our altered world in postcolonial texts. We are convinced that one of the most important and widely studied of these texts, surely one of the greatest novels produced anywhere in the last hundred years, the Sudanese Tayeb Salih's *Season of Migration to the North* (1966), contains just such portents. From Salih's vantage in the mid-1960s in the aftermath of Sudanese independence from the British Empire, this incomparable novel generates portents in the shape of images of a scorched landscape juxtaposed with allusions to the fossil fuel economy that has distorted and retarded independence in the wider Middle East and North Africa. There is no time, alas, to linger for very long on this concise but immensely rich and inexhaustibly suggestive work, which may be read variously as an expression of the frustrations and limitations of independence, as a critique in particular of the misogynistic structures and ideologies that characterise both the departed colonial regime and the independent nation state, as a subversive rewriting of various canonical European intertexts, as a meditation on the responsibilities of political leadership and, by WReC,

CONCLUSION

as an 'irrealist' and disturbingly insightful as well as flagrantly problematic exploration of an analogy between colonial violence and 'death-driven heterosexual eroticism'.[23] We read it as a novel that uses colonialism as an image or analogy as well as an especially grievous instance of all kinds of exploitative power, of Britain over Africa, men over women, the centralised state over the newly independent nation's neglected margins and the old over the young. A very oblique aspect of the text that, as far as we know, has received no critical attention hitherto is its typically oblique depiction of the burgeoning fossil fuel economy in the wider Middle East and North Africa and the threat it poses to the democratic aspirations of independence, the living world and even the very prospects of human survival. This is a work, to invoke Ghosh's words about Steinbeck's *Grapes of Wrath*, 'that grapples with climate change avant la lettre' (*GD*, 80).

This is a large claim, but it must suffice for now to point to a crucial scene in which our protagonist and narrator, a former PhD student in Britain who now works for the education ministry in Khartoum, is returning to the capital city from a visit to his home village on a bend in the Nile. Because he is in a hurry, he chooses not to take the river steamer and then the train (both powered presumably by coal) but the lorry (powered by petroleum) through the desert. There, the heat is as intense and oppressive as all the other forms of violence chronicled in the course of the novel.

> There is no shelter from the sun which rises up into the sky with unhurried steps, its rays spilling out on the ground as though there existed an old blood feud between it and the people of the earth. There is no shelter apart from the hot shade inside the lorry – shade that is not really shade.[24]

This short chapter is an immensely evocative *mise en scène* of existential angst, petrol-powered transportation and intense heat. 'There is not a single cloud heralding hope in this hot sky which is like the lid of Hell-fire' (*SOM*, 105). In fact 'this land in which the sun has left no more killing to be done' (*SOM*, 110) (one of the narrator's numerous rash and inaccurate forecasts) curiously resembles an apocalyptic vision of Sudan's and the entire globe's infernal future: 'The sun, the desert, dessicated plants and emaciated animals' (*SOM*, 106). In a curiously concentrated and dreamlike mode, the chapter sounds most of the novel's key themes: speculations about the narrator's doppelganger Mustafa Saeed and about Mustafa's baffling and appalling chronicle of sexual abuse of British women; the Orientalist fantasies by which those women are beguiled and that Mustafa exploits; the narrator's own anguished lust for Mustafa's widow Hosna; a whole milieu of rapid, if intensely uneven, cultural and technological modernisation encapsulated by the lorries, the oddly intense craving for cigarettes of a Bedouin man in the desert and a broken down government car full of soldiers sent to arrest a woman who has killed her husband (the very 'crime' that a forcibly married Hosna will subsequently perpetrate); and the cryptic but meaningful symbols of the 'unending' road and the 'merciless' sun (SOM, 109).

> The sun is the enemy. Now it is exactly in the liver of the sky, as the Arabs say. What a fiery liver! And thus it will remain for hours without moving – or so it will seem to living creatures when even the stones groan, the trees weep, and iron cries out for help.
> (SOM, 111)

No hints are given in this scene, nor could they have been given, except with contemporary readers' retrospective knowledge, of the causal connection between fierce heat and the fossil economy.[25] In any case, *Season of Migration* never traces specific violences, whether sexual violence, colonial violence, the violence of the newly independent nation state or the violence of the narrator's emotional despair, let alone the intensifying violence of the sun, to an easily identifiable cause. The novel even leaves open the possibility that these violences are the result not of recognisable and rectifiable causes but of a 'contagion that oozes from the body of the universe' (SOM, 104). Yet the novel does discreetly equate and connect them; for example, it will later be Hosna who vainly 'cries out for help', like the anthropomorphised stones and trees and iron in this image, when she is attacked by the elderly lech Wad Rayyes.

We wish to follow up on a suggestion made by Andreas Malm that, from the standpoint of our warming world, novels from the past may increasingly be seen to furnish what he calls anticipations or (after Walter Benjamin) dialectical images that prefigure our current predicament. His examples include Ghassan Kanafani's *Men in the Sun* (1963) with its unforgettable central image of three exiled Palestinian workers perishing meekly in a broiling tank as they wait to be smuggled over the Kuwaiti border to find work in the new oil economy. Malm reads the plot and even the stark title of Kanafani's novel as an allegory and even a prophecy, whereby the oil boom pulls dispossessed workers defencelessly towards the heat and away from their temperate homeland. In Malm's reading of Conrad's novella *Typhoon* (1902), the catastrophic hurricane is not a metaphor at all but a catastrophic hurricane, and the smoke-belching steamship *Nan-Shan* that charges inexorably towards it is an image of the warming world crewed by pig-headed officers while the 'coolies' are crammed helplessly into the hold. Yet the enraged indentured labourers and Kanafani's migrant workers also allude, as Malm acknowledges, 'to a logical, as yet unrealized, possibility: that of resistance, of breaking out of the confines before it is too late'.[26] Why didn't they cry out and rebel? is the question that Kanafani's text asks of the dead workers. These images from the past show that the warming world has long been in preparation, Malm argues, but also that the fossil economy that lit the fires, which is also a colonial economy, has always been vulnerable to forms of resistance. They are also 'counter-narratives' therefore.

Season of Migration also alludes to the possibility of a change of course. When the narrator and his fellow travellers stop and rest after nightfall, the 'war' against the sun ending in temporary victory, they inaugurate a vivid tableau replete with images of rest, comradeship and coolness. They say their night prayers, roast a sheep brought by the gathering Bedouins, toast 'the good health of the Sudan' with crates of beer, and sing and dance in an inclusive circle of light formed by the headlights of numerous vehicles at 'a festival of nothingness in the heart of the desert' (*SOM*, 114). 'This is the land of poetry and the possible – and my daughter is named Hope', the narrator gushes. 'We shall put down and we shall build, and we shall humble the sun itself to our will; and somehow we shall defeat poverty' (*SOM*, 113). This utopian vision of a future reprieve from the violences that pervade the novel is swiftly dispelled almost as soon as it is conjured. So, when the motorised caravan leaves the next morning, the chapter ends by reminding us of the originary violence of the sanguinary battle that sealed the British conquest in 1898: 'We caught up the sun on the peaks of the mountains of Kerari overlooking Omdurman' (*SOM*, 115).

The sun has always been intense at such latitudes of course. But the winters in Sudan are getting warmer, rainfall patterns have altered in the last two or three decades and large areas of arable land have been lost to accelerating desertification. Humbling the sun to our will is a phrase that might recall the familiar anthropocentric desire to dominate and enslave nature. We think of Captain Ahab in *Moby Dick*, that personification of hubristic and self-defeating violence against nature: '"Talk not to me of blasphemy, man; I'd strike the sun if it insulted me."'[27] But to us, Salih's narrator's ambition sounds more like a desire to temper the heat. *Season of Migration* registers a scathing critique of a neo-colonial system that will continue to 'direct our affairs from afar' (*SOM*, 53) and of 'the new rulers of Africa, smooth of face, lupine of mouth, their hands gleaming with rings of precious stones' (*SOM*, 118). But it is also an exploration of alternative models of the conscientious revolutionary leadership that the narrator may or may not resolve to embrace at the end of the novel, and of more cooperative and egalitarian social forms. Does it also hint at alternatives to the exploitative and calamitous fossil economy? Mustafa Sa'eed may disappear in the course of the novel, overwhelmed as a perpetrator as well as a victim by the multiple violences it portrays, but his second life as a respected farmer in this isolated village also represents a kind of alternative to the prolonged violence and inequality of postcolonial Sudan.

The narrator's friend Mahjoub describes Mustafa as an 'irreparable loss' for the Agricultural Project Committee. It is Mustafa who advised the villagers on reinvesting the profits, opening a cooperative shop, lowering prices, securing supplies and bypassing the merchants and profiteers who may have conspired to kill him. 'Now, there was a man – if there is any justice in the world – who deserved to be a minister in the government' (*SOM*, 102). The narrator recalls seeing Mustafa explaining to the committee why all farmers must respect the rules by not 'opening the water to their fields before the time allocated to them [...]; especially was it incumbent on members of the Committee to set a good example, and that if they were to contravene the law they would be punished like anyone else' (*SOM*, 12). The whole novel is suffused with such incidents and images in which a kind of superficial technological modernity (the engines of lorries, cravings for cigarettes, the sound of incessantly puttering water pumps) is set against allusions to or tantalising hints of a much more substantive form of modernisation, for which the goals of 'justice in the world' and the defeat of poverty may serve as useful shorthands. *Season of Migration*'s images of intense heat are not just an expression of, to use Ghosh's phrase, 'anxiety and foreboding' about 'the earth and its atmosphere' (*GD*, 124). The novel delineates, admittedly very faintly and tentatively, an egalitarian collective life and substantive decolonisation, which the colonial fossil fuel economy has since contrived to block in North Africa and the Middle East.

Timothy Mitchell's *Carbon Democracy* and Andreas Malm's *Fossil Capital* argue that the fossil fuel economy has always been a form of class power in Britain, the 'historic homeland' of global warming as Malm calls it, and then in British and American colonies in the Middle East.[28] Malm shows that the introduction of steam power in Britain was an anti-democratic class project. Steam-powered machines didn't shirk or rebel; their introduction set the pattern for autonomous and rebellious workers to be replaced by more biddable and regimented proletarians. By replacing water with coal, British capitalism and its all-important cotton industry could burst out of the structural crisis of the 1830s and 1840s by smashing the unions and squeezing more output out of fewer workers at lower cost.[29] Yet the digging and transportation of coal, as Mitchell shows, was itself always vulnerable to slowdowns and strikes. Indeed, the wave of industrial militancy in Britain's coalfields before and after the First World War was one reason for the switch from coal to oil power. Britain therefore extended its colonial control over Iraq and the Gulf States in the 1920s. US and British power helped found the autocratic kingdom-colony of Saudi Arabia.

Britain's decisive competitive advantage in developing a fossil fuel economy came from the good luck of having giant quantities of easily extractable and transportable coal at home and its ability to call upon inexpensive inputs of labour and agricultural products from India and, later, the rest of the empire.[30] The political and military domination of India and the suppression of India's autonomous path to development coincided with the rise of coal-fired steam power. These were the reasons for the colonisation of Sudan. The invasion and occupation of Egypt in 1882 was undertaken to ensure access to the Suez Canal, while the slightly later colonisation of

CONCLUSION

Sudan ensured the stability of British Egypt by defeating the Mahdist 'revolt'. Taking possession of the Upper Nile Valley also deterred the encroachments of rival imperial powers in the region, such as Belgium and France.[31] These considerations became even more important during and just after the First World War in the context of Britain's domination of the Middle East (increasingly in alliance with the United States) and its vast oil reserves. Britain's transition from a predominantly coal-based to a predominantly oil-based fossil fuel capitalism, India's and Egypt's long struggles for independence, Britain's doomed battle to maintain control of the Suez Canal and its eventual retreat from empire, the establishment of the authoritarian petro-state of Saudi Arabia by the House of Saud in alliance with British and American power, the durable if adaptable system of colonial relationships with the Gulf monarchies,[32] are all chapters in the story of the determination of Anglo-American power to safeguard profitable conditions for capital accumulation by controlling, through essentially colonial means, the flow of fossil fuel energy from the Middle East. First, Sudan mattered because through Egypt ran the profits and resources of British India to the world's major fossil fuel-powered economy. Later, Egypt was an essential conduit for the oil pumped out by the dependent colonies and semi-colonies of Iraq, Iran and the Gulf monarchies. Then, Sudan mattered even more because its poverty made it a source of regional instability and because it became, itself, a major oil producer, albeit one increasingly inclined under al-Bashir to cut resource-for-infrastructure deals with China and whose major oil-producing region seceded in 2011 as South Sudan.

So the fossil economy, Malm and Mitchell show, has always been a capitalist as well as an imperialist economy. If steam power enabled the crushing of the trade unions in the historic homeland of global warming in the first half of the nineteenth century, then oil necessitated the crushing in the second half of the twentieth century of liberationist movements in Iraq, Iran and Egypt to nationalise the energy companies and to redistribute and reinvest the surpluses. Our point is that fictions like Salih's or Kanafani's or Munif's or even Conrad's might indicate, however obliquely, democratic alternatives to the colonial depredations of the fossil fuel economy.

Season of Migration is not *about* global warming of course. It is about, among many other things, the manifold and competing possibilities of independence. Those possibilities included substantive democratisation, the interrogation and dismantling of ingrained patriarchal ideas and structures, the overturning of the centralised colonial state, in short, a substantive process of 'modernisation' that involved not just the adoption of new technologies but ultimately the wide-ranging revision of violent and exploitative practices, structures and ideologies. One essential aspect of decolonisation, we are suggesting, was the creation of alternatives to the colonial economy of fossil fuels. Postcolonial texts might indicate ways of contemplating and even re-joining these struggles.

CONCLUSION

It is obvious that a comprehensively decarbonised world economy would need to be very radically transformed in order to defeat poverty and see 'justice in the world'. For a start, a decarbonised world economy would necessitate the expropriation of the fossil fuel corporations as well as planning and coordination between states. Massive state investment in renewable energy will be directed by large publicly owned banks with enormous lending capacity. Aaron Bastani argues that a complete global transition to renewable energy will demand the dismantling of the durable structures of colonial power. Enough solar energy hits the Earth every ninety minutes to provide current global demand for a year; Britain's stroke of luck at the start of the nineteenth century (its plentiful seams of accessible coal) might soon be repeated, this time by poor countries near the Equator able to humble the sun to their will, to use Salih's narrator's phrase. Previously poor countries may enjoy a competitive advantage in solar power. Wealthier countries will presumably have to finance the transition, perhaps via an International Bank for Energy Prosperity to administer a new 'One Planet Tax' on every tonne of CO_2 emitted in high-GDP countries 'to channel resources from affluent countries – who are overwhelmingly responsible for climate change – to poorer ones, who are set to disproportionately suffer its most adverse consequences'.[33] Suffice to say, the fossil economy has been an imperialist system. It follows that the decarbonised world economy will need to be a post-imperialist system.[34]

Ghosh declares, wrongly, as we have argued, that writers have been ignoring climate change and that the novel has not been up to the task of addressing it.

> When future generations look back upon the Great Derangement they will certainly blame the leaders and politicians of this time for their failure to address the climate crisis. But they may well hold artists and writers to be equally culpable – for the imagining of possibilities is not, after all, the job of politicians and bureaucrats.
> (GD, 135)

But the fault lies not with how postcolonial literature is written but with how Ghosh reads it. Imperialism, including 'green imperialism'[35] and now that especially atrocious form of imperialist violence that is global warming, are everywhere in postcolonial writing, as ever in a satisfying heterogeneity of forms and modes.

Of course, there is no reason to be complacent about the potential of postcolonial texts to indicate ways of escaping the death spiral of the fossil economy. Stephen Graham fears a potential 'switch from the military neoliberalism of the past two decades to a full-scale fascism organized around control of fossil fuels'.[36] William Davies argues that we have entered the post-hegemonic phase of neoliberalism, a sort of zombie neoliberalism in which the wealth-hoarding of rentiers and speculators no longer takes place under the cover of the pretence that sooner or later some of this prosperity will trickle down to the poor.[37] What Peter Fleming calls *nihi*liberalism is becoming more brazen and more violent.[38] The struggle between a sustainable economic and ecological order and the 'climate fascism' of resource wars is already underway, according to Christian Parenti's *Tropic of Chaos*.[39] But that's only another way of admitting that the society of the future will be the outcome of struggles in the present. So, we will end with Andreas Malm's compelling refusal of fashionable philosophical pessimism about the possibilities of human political action:

> There is that itching feeling that the only meaningful thing to do now is to let go of everything else and physically cut off fossil fuel combustion, deflate the tyres, block the runways, lay siege to the platforms, invade the mines. Indeed, the only salubrious thing about the election of Donald Trump is that it dispels the last lingering illusions that anything else than organised collective militant resistance has at least a fighting chance of pushing the world anywhere else than head first, at maximum speed, into cataclysmic climate change. All has already been said; now is the time for confrontation. This essay presents no arguments for restraining such impulses.[40]

Nor does this book. Expropriate the fossil fuel corporations! Cap the oil wells! Close down the mines! Nationalise the banks to pay for full decarbonisation now! In this century, we face a catastrophic loss of biodiversity on a scale not seen since the end of the cretaceous period more than sixty million years ago. It is simply not true, Malm insists, that all humans have caused this emergency, a sort of undifferentiated *Anthropos* that has brought about the new geological epoch of the *Anthropocene*, though of course it *is* true that all humans have a responsibility for addressing it. Some humans have created the fossil economy, which we have argued is also a colonial economy, and some humans now profit from sustaining it. We refer, of course, to the oligarchs, speculators and hedge-fund managers, the rulers of rentier states in the Middle East and elsewhere, the oil cartel CEOs and the 'populist' politicians who respond to inequality, precarity, climate breakdown and exoduses of impoverished populations with xenophobia and border walls. Only action that rapidly decarbonises the world economy, which will necessitate a rapid transformation of current models of finance, consumption and ownership as well as the overturning of imperialist structures and ideologies, will avert total calamity. So, what can literature do? Or rather, what can postcolonial literature do? Our experience as critics and especially as teachers has taught us that postcolonial literature illuminates imperialism's origins and manifold effects, awakens critical and cosmopolitan sensibilities and furnishes glimpses of 'other forms of human existence'

CONCLUSION

(to use Ghosh's phrase) or 'justice in the world' (to invoke Salih's), new ways of organising production as well as new forms of collective life. Today these are achievements of the utmost importance.

Notes

1. Louis MacNeice, 'Snow', *The Collected Poems*, ed. E.R. Dodds, London: Faber & Faber, 1966, p. 30.
2. Fredric Jameson, *The Political Unconscious: Narrative as a Socially Symbolic Act*, London: Routledge, 1981, p. 17.
3. Sharae Deckard, 'Inherit the World: World-Literature, Rising Asia and the World-Ecology', in Anna Bernard, Zia Elmarsafy and Stuart Murray (eds), *What Postcolonial Theory Doesn't Say*, London: Routledge, 2016, pp. 239–255, p. 239.
4. Giovanni Arrighi, *The Long Twentieth Century: Money, Power, and the Origins of Our Time*, London: Verso, 2010 [1994], p. 34. See also Robert Spencer, 'Political Economy and the Iraq War: Said and Arrighi', in Bashir Abu-Manneh (ed), *After Said: Postcolonial Literary Studies in the Twenty-First Century*, Cambridge: Cambridge University Press, 2019, pp. 190–209.
5. On the 'continuing relevance of postcolonial studies as a body of knowledge and political imperative for justice', see Monika Bhagat-Kennedy, 'Nation After World: Rethinking "The End of the Postcolonial Theory"', *Interventions*, 20:3 (2018), 335–344.
6. Warwick Research Collective, *Combined and Uneven Development*, p. 8.
7. Elleke Boehmer, *Colonial and Postcolonial Literature: Migrant Metaphors*, Second Edition, Oxford: Oxford University Press, 2005, p. 3, emphasis in original.
8. Ngũgĩ wa Thiong'o, *Devil on the Cross*, London: Heinemann, 1982, p. 253.
9. Robert Duggan, *The Grotesque in Contemporary British Fiction*, Manchester: Manchester University Press, 2013, pp. 117–149.
10. Ian McEwan, *Saturday*, London: Vintage, 2006, p. 127.
11. See, for example, Howard J. Booth and Nigel Rigby (eds), *Modernism and Empire*, Manchester: Manchester University Press, 2000; and Mark Wollaeger and Matt Eatough (eds), *The Oxford Handbook of Global Modernisms*, Oxford: Oxford University Press, 2012. A key initial contribution to this debate is Fredric Jameson's 'Modernism and Imperialism', in Fredric Jameson, Terry Eagleton and Edward W. Said, *Nationalism, Colonialism, and Literature*, Minneapolis, MN: University of Minnesota Press, 1990, pp. 43–66. For reasons set out in the Introduction, we don't find Susan Stanford Friedman's approach to 'planetary modernisms' convincing because, in her hands, the term becomes so elastic it ends up being effectively indiscriminate; modernism encompasses everything, in other words. *Planetary Modernisms: Provocations on Modernity Across Time*, New York: Columbia University Press, 2015.
12. Raj Patel and Jason W. Moore, *A History of the World in Seven Cheap Things: A Guide to Capitalism, Nature, and the Future of Our Planet*, London: Verso, 2018, p. 24.
13. Joan Martinez-Alier, '"Environmental Justice" (Local and Global)', *Cultures of Globalization*, in Fredric Jameson and Masao Miyoshi (eds), Durham, NC: Duke University Press, 1998, pp. 312–326.

14 T.S. Eliot, 'Literature, Science, and Dogma', *I.A. Richards: Selected Writings, 1919–1938, vol 10: I.A. Richards and his Critics*, ed. John Constable, London: Routledge, 2001, pp. 74–79, p. 79.
15 Amitav Ghosh, *The Great Derangement: Climate Change and the Unthinkable*, Chicago, IL: The University of Chicago Press, 2016, p. 7. Subsequent references are given after *GD* in the main text.
16 Many of these writers' works are analysed in Graham Huggan and Helen Tiffin's *Postcolonial Ecocriticism: Literature, Animals, Environment*, Second Edition, London: Routledge, 2015. The best materialist analysis of Ghosh's oeuvre is Pablo Mukherjee's, *Postcolonial Environments: Nature, Culture and the Contemporary Indian Novel in English*, Basingstoke: Palgrave, 2010, pp. 108–133. See also Anthony Carrigan's comprehensive essay on 'postcolonial engagement with climate change and contested natures that focuses not just on the depiction of extreme events but also on the long-term processes of environmental exploitation that have led to humanity becoming a geological force', 'Nature, Ecocriticism, and the Postcolonial Novel', *The Cambridge Companion to the Postcolonial Novel*, ed. Ato Quayson, Cambridge: Cambridge University Press, 2016, pp. 81–98, p. 95.
17 See Adam Trexler, *Anthropocene Fictions: The Novel in a Time of Climate Change*, Charlottesville, VA: University of Virginia Press, 2015. For representative anthologies see Sheena Wilson, Adam Carlson and Imre Szeman (eds), *Petrocultures: Oil, Politics, Culture*, Quebec: McGill-Queen's University Press, 2017; and Imre Szeman and Dominic Boyer (eds), *Energy Humanities: An Anthology*, Baltimore, MD: John Hopkins University Press, 2017.
18 Munif's quintet is mentioned a lot in recent studies of 'petrofiction', such as Graeme Macdonald's '"Monstrous transformer": Petrofiction and world literature', *Journal of Postcolonial Writing*, 53:3 (2017), 289–302. By far the most illuminating discussion of *Cities of Salt* available in English and the only one to tackle all five novels (only three of which have so far been translated into English) is Rayah Al-Raddadi's 'Munif's *Cities of Salt* as Counter Narrative: Capitalism, Ideology and Transformation', unpublished PhD Thesis, University of Kent, 2018.
19 Amitav Ghosh, *Gun Island*, London: John Murray, 2019, p. 106.
20 Theodor Adorno, 'Commitment', in Ernst Bloch et al. (eds), *Aesthetics and Politics*, London: Verso, 1977 [1962], pp. 77–116.
21 Andreas Malm, *Fossil Capital: The Rise of Steam Power and the Roots of Global Warming*, London: Verso, 2016, p. 11.
22 Fredric Jameson, *The Geopolitical Aesthetic: Cinema and Space in the World System*, Bloomington, IN: Indiana University Press, 1992, p. 37.
23 WReC, *Combined and Uneven Development*, p. 84.
24 Tayeb Salih, *Season of Migration to the North*, trans. Denys Johnson-Davies, Harmondsworth: Penguin, 2003 [1969], p. 105. Subsequent references are given in brackets after *SOM* in the main text.
25 The science of global warming was unknown in the 1960s, except to the president's Science Advisory Committee report to Lyndon Johnson on 'atmospheric carbon dioxide' in 1965. Exxon and Shell knew all about the catastrophic implications forty years ago but opted for secrecy and denial. As Nathaniel Rich has shown, the tragedy is that the science of climate change was established beyond doubt at the exact historical moment (i.e. neoliberalism: the triumph

CONCLUSION

of capital over socialist and anti-imperialist movements across the globe) when collective political action against ecocidal corporations became impermissible, *Losing Earth: The Decade We Could Have Stopped Climate Change*, London: Picador, 2019.

26 Andreas Malm, '"This Is The Hell That I Have Heard Of": Some Dialectical Images in Fossil Fuel Fiction', *Forum for Modern Language Studies*, 53:2 (2017), 121–141, 135. Bashir Abu-Manneh's matchless account of the Palestinian novel argues that *Men in the Sun* is an enraging and ultimately politically galvanising indictment of Palestinian inertia and desperation in the era of the oil boom. *The Palestinian Novel: From 1948 to the Present*, Cambridge: Cambridge University Press, 2016, pp. 78–86.

27 Herman Melville, *Moby-Dick, or, The Whale*, Harmondsworth: Penguin, 1992 [1851], p. 178.

28 Timothy Mitchell, *Carbon Democracy: Political Power in the Age of Oil*, London: Verso, 2013.

29 Malm, *Fossil Capital*, p. 68.

30 The definitive study of the commodification of third-world agriculture in the late-Victorian period and the forcible incorporation of many millions of men, women and children into the world-economy, a process that actually produced the dependent and 'semi-proletarianized' 'third world', is Mike Davis's *Late Victorian Holocausts: El Niño Famines and the Making of the Third World*, London: Verso, 2001.

31 See Thomas Pakenham, *The Scramble for Africa: 1876–1912*, London: Abacus, 1992, pp. 72–85.

32 See Robert Vitalis, *America's Kingdom: Mythmaking on the Saudi Oil Frontier*, London: Verso, 2009. Another key study is David Wearing's *AngloArabia: Why Gulf Wealth Matters to Britain*, Cambridge: Polity, 2018. Wearing's argument is that Britain and the US do not rely on oil supplies from Saudi Arabia and the Persian Gulf (though many of their allies and competitors, most notably China, do) but their companies, as well as their banks and consumers, currently demand the enormous flow of petrodollars generated by oil sales. In return, these profoundly conservative and autocratic rentier states with their racially segregated migrant workforces receive military supplies and diplomatic cover.

33 Aaron Bastani, *Fully Automated Luxury Communism: A Manifesto*, London: Verso, 2019, p. 222.

34 On the different kinds of 'planetary sovereignty' being forged by global warming, see also Joel Wainwright and Geoff Mann, *Climate Leviathan: A Political Theory of Our Planetary Future*, London: Verso, 2018.

35 We are namechecking Richard H. Grove's indispensable study of how imperialism conceptualised nature and destructively transformed ecosystems, *Green Imperialism: Colonial Expansion, Tropical Island Edens and the Origins of Environmentalism, 1600–1860*, Cambridge: Cambridge University Press, 2010.

36 Stephen Graham, *Cities Under Siege: The New Military Urbanism*, London: Verso, 2010, p. 337.

37 William Davies, 'The New Neoliberalism', *New Left Review*, 101 (2016), 121–134.

38 Peter Fleming, *The Worst is Yet to Come: A Post-Capitalist Survival Guide*, London: Repeater Books, 2018, p. 20.

39 Christian Parenti, *Tropic of Chaos: Climate Change and the New Geography of Violence*, New York: Nation Books, 2011.
40 Andreas Malm, *The Progress of the Storm: Nature and Society in a Warming World*, London: Verso, 2018, p. 16.

Bibliography

Abu-Manneh, B., *The Palestinian Novel: From 1948 to the Present*, Cambridge: Cambridge University Press, 2016.

Adorno, T., 'Commitment', in Ernst Bloch, Theodor Adorno, Georg Lukács, Bertolt Brecht and Fredric Jameson (eds), *Aesthetics and Politics*, London: Verso, 1977 [1962], pp. 77–116.

Al-Raddadi, R., 'Munif's *Cities of Salt* as Counter Narrative: Capitalism, Ideology and Transformation', unpublished PhD. Thesis, University of Kent, 2018.

Arrighi, G., *The Long Twentieth Century: Money, Power, and the Origins of Our Time*, London: Verso, 2010 [1994].

Bastani, A., *Fully Automated Luxury Communism: A Manifesto*, London: Verso, 2019.

Bhagat-Kennedy, M., 'Nation After World: Rethinking "The End of the Postcolonial Theory"', *Interventions*, 20:3 (2018), 335–344.

Boehmer, E., *Colonial and Postcolonial Literature: Migrant Metaphors*, Second Edition, Oxford: Oxford University Press, 2005.

Booth, H.J. and Rigby, N. (eds), *Modernism and Empire*, Manchester: Manchester University Press, 2000.

Carrigan, A., 'Nature, Ecocriticism, and the Postcolonial Novel', *The Cambridge Companion to the Postcolonial Novel*, ed. Ato Quayson, Cambridge: Cambridge University Press, 2016, pp. 81–98.

Davies, W., 'The New Neoliberalism', *New Left Review*, 101 (2016), 121–134.

Davis, M., *Late Victorian Holocausts: El Niño Famines and the Making of the Third World*, London: Verso, 2001.

Deckard, S., 'Inherit the World: World-Literature, Rising Asia and the World-Ecology', in Anna Bernard, Zia Elmarsafy and Stuart Murray (eds), *What Postcolonial Theory Doesn't Say*, London: Routledge, 2016, pp. 239–255.

Duggan, R., *The Grotesque in Contemporary British Fiction*, Manchester: Manchester University Press, 2013.

Eliot, T.S., 'Literature, Science, and Dogma', in John Constable (ed), *I.A. Richards: Selected Writings, 1919–1938, vol 10: I.A. Richards and his Critics*, London: Routledge, 2001, pp. 74–79.

Fleming, P., *The Worst is Yet to Come: A Post-Capitalist Survival Guide*, London: Repeater Books, 2018.

Friedman, S.S., *Planetary Modernisms: Provocations on Modernity Across Time*, New York: Columbia University Press, 2015.

Ghosh, A., *The Great Derangement: Climate Change and the Unthinkable*, Chicago, IL: University of Chicago Press, 2016.

Ghosh, A., *Gun Island*, London: John Murray, 2019.

Graham, S., *Cities Under Siege: The New Military Urbanism*, London: Verso, 2010.

Grove, R.H., *Green Imperialism: Colonial Expansion, Tropical Island Edens and the Origins of Environmentalism, 1600–1860*, Cambridge: Cambridge University Press, 2010.

Huggan. G. and Tiffin, H., *Postcolonial Ecocriticism: Literature, Animals, Environment*, Second Edition, London: Routledge, 2015.

Jameson, F., *The Political Unconscious: Narrative as a Socially Symbolic Act*, London: Routledge, 1981.

Jameson, F., 'Modernism and Imperialism', in Frederic Jameson, Terry Eagleton and Edward Said (eds), *Nationalism, Colonialism, and Literature*, Minneapolis, MN: University of Minnesota Press, 1990, pp. 43–66.

Jameson, F., *The Geopolitical Aesthetic: Cinema and Space in the World System*, Bloomington, IN: Indiana University Press, 1992.

Macdonald, G., '"Monstrous Transformer": Petrofiction and World Literature', *Journal of Postcolonial Writing*, 53:3 (2017), 289–302.

MacNeice, L., 'Snow', *The Collected Poems*, ed. E.R. Dodds, London: Faber & Faber, 1966.

Malm, A., *Fossil Capital: The Rise of Steam Power and the Roots of Global Warming*, London: Verso, 2016.

Malm, A., '"This Is The Hell That I Have Heard Of": Some Dialectical Images in Fossil Fuel Fiction', *Forum for Modern Language Studies*, 53:2 (2017), 121–141.

Malm, A., *The Progress of the Storm: Nature and Society in a Warming World*, London: Verso, 2018.

Martinez-Alier, J., '"Environmental Justice" (Local and Global)', *Cultures of Globalization*, in Fredric Jameson and Masao Miyoshi (eds), Durham, NC: Duke University Press, 1998, pp. 312–326.

McEwan, I., *Saturday*, London: Vintage, 2006.

Melville, H., *Moby-Dick, or, The Whale*, Harmondsworth: Penguin, 1992 [1851].

Mitchell, T., *Carbon Democracy: Political Power in the Age of Oil*, London: Verso, 2013.

Mukherjee, U.P., *Postcolonial Environments: Nature, Culture and the Contemporary Indian Novel in English*, Basingstoke: Palgrave, 2010.

Ngũgĩ wa Thiong'o, *Devil on the Cross*, London: Heinemann, 1982.

Pakenham, T., *The Scramble for Africa: 1876–1912*, London: Abacus, 1992.

Parenti, C., *Tropic of Chaos: Climate Change and the New Geography of Violence*, New York: Nation Books, 2011.

Patel, R. and Moore, J.W., *A History of the World in Seven Cheap Things: A Guide to Capitalism, Nature, and the Future of Our Planet*, London: Verso, 2018.

Rich, N., *Losing Earth: The Decade We Could Have Stopped Climate Change*, London: Picador, 2019.

Salih, T., *Season of Migration to the North*, trans. Denys Johnson-Davies, Harmondsworth: Penguin, 2003 [1969].

Spencer, R., 'Political Economy and the Iraq War: Said and Arrighi', in Bashir Abu-Manneh (ed), *After Said: Postcolonial Literary Studies in the Twenty-First Century*, Cambridge: Cambridge University Press, 2019.

Szeman, I. and Boyer, D. (eds), *Energy Humanities: An Anthology*, Baltimore, MD: John Hopkins University Press, 2017.

Trexler, A., *Anthropocene Fictions: The Novel in a Time of Climate Change*, Charlottesville, VA: University of Virginia Press, 2015.

CONCLUSION

Vitalis, R., *America's Kingdom: Mythmaking on the Saudi Oil Frontier*, London: Verso, 2009.

Wainwright, J. and Mann, G., *Climate Leviathan: A Political Theory of Our Planetary Future*, London: Verso, 2018.

Wearing, D., *AngloArabia: Why Gulf Wealth Matters to Britain*, Cambridge: Polity, 2018.

Wilson, S., Carlson, A. and Szeman, I. (eds), *Petrocultures: Oil, Politics, Culture*, Montreal: McGill-Queen's University Press, 2017.

Wollaeger, M. and Eatough, M., (eds), *The Oxford Handbook of Global Modernisms*, Oxford: Oxford University Press, 2012.

INDEX

Abderrezak, Hakim 94–5, 97–8
Abu-Manneh, Bashir 217n26
Adjepong, Anima 145–6n73
Adorno, Theodor W. 100, 143n60, 206–7
Agier, Michel 98
Alier, Joan-Martínez 203
Anderson, Benedict 70
apartheid 35, 38–9, 82, 84, 91, 98–9, 115–17, 140
Appadurai, Arjun 137
Arendt, Hannah 74, 103n34
Arrighi, Giovanni 60, 101n7, 198
Attenborough, Richard *see Gandhi*
Auden, W.H. 174–5
Avruch, Kevin 112–14

Ball, Anna 93
Banjo 63–4
Barthes, Roland 142–3n58
Bastani, Aaron, 213
Benjamin, Walter 41, 154, 162
Bitter Fruit 115–18, 139–40
Boehmer, Elleke 199
Boland, Eavan 159–69
border regimes 38, 48–50, 59, 60, 75, 78–81, 82, 84, 87–8, 95, 97–100, 104n50, 209, 214
Borges, Jorge Luis 150
Bourdieu, Pierre 81
Brennan, Timothy 10
Brexit 45, 48, 62, 80–1, 104n50
Brink, André 39
Butler, Judith 103n38

capitalism 8–10
Carpentaria 24–5, 27–8
Carrigan, Anthony 178, 216n16

Chalk, Bridget T. 64
Chamayou, Grégoire 72
Chauvel, Charles *see Jedda*
checkpoint 91–4, 96
Chibber, Vivek 9–10
Coetzee, J.M. 3, 36–8, 139, 156–8; *Disgrace* 113–115
Colls, Robert 55n84
Collumpar, Corrin 118–20
Conrad, Joseph 209
Creed, Barbara 21
cricket 123–39

Dabydeen, David 55n90; *see also Disappearance*
Dangor, Achmat *see Bitter Fruit*
David, Bruno 29
Davies, William 213–14
Davis, Mike 217n30
Davis, Therese 187
Dawson, Graham 179–80
decarbonisation 8, 104n50, 213–15
Deckard, Sharae 198
decolonisation 4–8
Delisle, Guy 88
Denning, Michael 63–4, 103n37
Dickinson, Kay 91–2, 93–4
Disappearance 39–50, 202
Divine Intervention 87, 91–4
Djebar, Assia *see Fantasia*
dreamtime 188–9
Duff, Alan *see Once Were Warriors*
Duggan, Robert 201
Dussel, Enrique 170–1

ecocriticism 16–19
Edwards, Brent Hayes 63
Elder, Arlene A. 34

221

INDEX

Eliot, T.S. 3, 203
Ellmann, Richard 7, 14n8
Emery, Mary Lou 64
England and Englishness 39–50
The European Union 45, 66–8, 78–81, 95, 102n24, 104n44
Exit West 65–82

fascism, danger of recrudescence of 66, 73–5, 103n34, 213–14
Fanon, Frantz 5, 80
Fantasia: An Algerian Cavalcade 151–4, 190
Ferroukhi, Ismaël *see Le grande voyage*
Fleming, Peter 214
Four Lions 62–3
Friedman, Susan Stanford 13n6
Frenkel, Ronit 115

Galeano, Eduardo 143n58
Gandhi 183–6
Gerrits, André 97–8
Ghosh, Amitav 203–8, 213, 215
Gibbon, Lewis Grassic 202
Gifted 183–6
Gilroy, Paul 42, 78
global warming 51, 100, 202–15, 216–17n25
Gopal, Priyamvada 189–90
Gordimer, Nadine: *The Conservationist* 35–9; *The Pickup* 82–7; short stories 82–7
Gowan, Peter 60
Graham, Stephen 213
Le grande voyage 94–8
Gready, Paul 113–15, 141n16
The Great Gatsby 100
Greenfield, Adam 71–2
Grenfell Tower 102
Grenville, Kate *see The Secret River*
Griffiths, Gareth 32
Gunesekera, Romesh *see The Match*
Gun Island 205–7

Habermas, Jürgen 162
Haj 95
Hall, Stuart 40
Haltof, Marek 30–1
Hamid, Mohsin *see Exit West*
Hardt, Michael 60
Harvey, David 40
Hatherley, Owen 54n82

Heer, Rolf de *see Ten Canoes*
Hobsbawm, Eric 54n81
Hodge, Bob 25
Home Fire 60–1
'hostile environment' immigration policy 45, 49–50, 73–4
Huggan, Graham 17, 24

Ihimaera, Witi *see The Whale Rider*
Innes, C.L. 50, 55n90

James, C.L.R. 124–9, 135, 137–8, 143n60, 143n62, 143–4n64, 145n72, 145–6n73
James, Erin 19
Jameson, Fredric 6, 13n6, 76, 127–9, 167, 198, 207, 215n11
Jedda 19–21, 23, 34
Jindabyne 21–3, 27–9, 32–3
Jolly, Rosemary 115
Jones, Reece 60

Kanafani, Ghassan *see Men in the Sun*
Kanhai, Rohan 127
Keesey, Douglas 28
Kennedy, Joe 45
Kingsnorth, Paul 45
Kortenaar, Neil Ten 184
Kossew, Sue 26–7
Kouvelakis, Stathis 78–9
Kundera, Milan 159

Lalwani, Nikita *see Gifted*
landscapes and land 16–51
Lapavitsas, Costas 79–80, 104n44
Lawrence, D.H. 202
Lawrence of Arabia 178–83
Lawrence, Ray *see Jindabyne*
Lawrence, T.E. 178–82
Lazarus, Neil 9–10, 14–15n15, 39, 65, 102n24, 138, 148, 151, 154, 158, 191n20
Lean, David *see Lawrence of Arabia*
Loh, Lucienne 41–44

MacNeice, Louis 197
Malm, Andreas 206, 209, 211–12, 214
Marqusee, Mike 126, 134–6, 138, 144n64, 144n65, 145n72
Mason, Paul 66
The Match 124–38, 139
McCredden, Lyn 188

INDEX

McEwan, Ian 199–201
McKay, Claude *see Banjo*
McMullan, Gordon 191n28
memory and the past 148–90
Men in the Sun 209–10
migration *see* mobility
Mishra, Vijay 25
Mitchell, Timothy 211–12
Mo, Timothy *see Pure*
mobility 59–100
Moby Dick 6, 210
modernisms 5–6, 13–14n6, 63–4, 202, 215n11
Moore, Jason W. 101n23
Morgan, Sally *see My Place*
Morris, Christopher *see Four Lions*
Munif, Abdelrahman 204–5
My Place 19, 34–5

native title 31–3; *see also* property rights
Negri, Antonio 60
neoliberalism 10, 14–15n15, 40–2, 54n77, 60, 65–6, 104n50, 137, 198, 208–9, 213–14, 216–17n25
Neruda, Pablo 158–9
Ngugi wa Thiong'o 199–200
Nixon, Rob 44
'Norman yoke' 45

Omar, Dullah 112
Once Were Warriors 118–23

Palestine 87–91
Parenti, Christian 214
Parry, Benita 140, 149, 155
partition of the Indian sub-continent 4, 59, 185–6
Pearse, Patrick 166–7
Picnic at Hanging Rock 24, 26, 28–34
Pilkington, Doris 29–30
Plumwood, Val 23
populism 104n50
postcolonial criticism, definitions of 1–3, 17, 197–202, 215n5
Povinelli, Elizabeth 31, 33, 35
Powell, Enoch 48, 50
Poyner, Jane 113–15
property rights 187
Pure 62–3

Rabbit-Proof Fence 29
Rayner, Jonathan 32
reconciliatory practices 111–40
refugees 38n103, 60, 66–8, 73, 75, 77, 79–80, 82, 88, 100, 205
Rekhari, Suneeti 34
Renes, Cornelis Martin 188
Ranger, Terence 54n81
Renton, Dave 143n62
Roeg, Nicolas *see Walkabout*
Rose, Jacqueline 91, 166–7
Rushdie, Salman 48, 183–4
Russell, James 178

Sacco, Joe *see Palestine*
Said, Edward W. 99
Salih, Tayeb *see Season of Migration to the North*
Season of Migration to the North 207–13
The Secret River 18, 22–3, 25–7, 31, 34
Sellman, Johanna 97–8
Shamsie, Kamila *see Home Fire*
Shaw, Kristian 80–1
Sheller, Mimi 60
Smith, Andrew 59–60, 143n60
Smith, Linda Tuhiwai 187
Smith, Neil 54n77
Smith, Zadie 51
Sobers, Garfield 126–7
Solnit, Rebecca 100
space *see* land and landscapes
spatial turn 16
Spivak, Gayatri Chakravorty 149, 153, 155–7
Steiner, George 59
Suleiman, Elia *see Divine Intervention*

Tadié, Alexis 124
Tait, Theo 70–1
Tamahori, Lee *see Once Were Warriors*
teaching 3–8
Ten Canoes 186–9
Thatcherism 40–2, 47–8; constructions of history 41–2
Thompson, E.P. 7, 144n65
Thörn, Håkan 82–3
Tiffin, Helen 17, 24
Tilley, Elspeth 32
Treagus, Mandy 119, 122
Trotsky, Leon 8, 143n60
Trump, Donald 61, 66, 79, 214
Truth and reconciliation commissions 112, 114–16, 139

INDEX

Ulysses 7
universalism 2, 8, 10

Varoufakis, Yanis 104n44
Vejarano, Beatriz 112–14

Walcott, Derek, 169–78
Walkabout 24–6, 32–4
Wallerstein, Immanuel 77
Warwick Research Collective (WReC) 8–10, 13–14n6, 197–9, 207–8
Wearing, David 217n32
Weir, Peter *see Picnic at Hanging Rock*
Weizman, Eyal 17
The Whale Rider 18

Winder, Robert 78
Williams, Raymond 43, 55n86, 125, 142n56
Wilson, Robert McLiam 123–4
Woolf, Virginia 202
world literature 8–10, 197–202
Wright, Alexis *see Carpentaria*
Wright, Erik Olin 77
Wright, Patrick 41

Yeats, W.B. 159–60, 162–3, 170–1, 173–5, 178

Zola, Émile 204